THE COWBOY:

SIX-SHOOTERS,

SONGS,

AND

SEX

UNIVERSITY OF OKLAHOMA PRESS : NORMAN

THE COWBOY:

SIX-SHOOTERS,

SONGS,

AND

SEX

Edited by Charles W. Harris and Buck Rainey

Library of Congress Cataloging in Publication Data
Main entry under title:

The Cowboy: six shooters, songs, and sex.
　　"First appeared in a special topical issue (spring, 1975) of the Red
River Valley historical review."
　　Includes index.
　　1. Cowboys—The West—Addresses, essays, lectures.
2. The West—Social life and customs—Addresses,
essays, lectures.　I. Harris, Charles W.　II. Rainey, Buck.
F596.C875　　978　　75-40959
ISBN 0-8061-1324-3

Preface

BY CHARLES W. HARRIS

J. Frank Dobie once wrote "A Note on Charlie Siringo, Writer and Man" which was appended to an edition of Siringo's *A Texas Cowboy.* He discussed the unique frankness which characterized Siringo's first work and contrasted it with the subsequent writing of his later years. The comparison reminded Dobie of a descriptive phrase from an old cowboy toast recited to him by an old traildriver in San Antonio on October 19, 1928—ironically, the day Siringo died in Hollywood. Custom required that "The toast must be recited with eyes fixed on a glass of red likker held out in the right hand:

> Here's to the vinagaroon that jumped on the
>   centipede's back,
> He looked at him with a glow and a glee,
> And he said, 'You poisonous son-of-a-bitch,
> If I don't get you, you'll get me.' "

Dobie found the true cowboy "glow and glee" in Siringo's early writing. It was honesty. "His style, especially his early style, cannot be called dignified, but it is informed with the innate dignity of honesty." "Degrees of honesty," Dobie thought, "are observable in all human expression, but nowhere more patent than in autobiographical writing." And he mused "Well, God save us all from ever becoming wholly discreet."[1]

What Dobie feared has happened in much subsequent historical writing about the cowboy. Enthusiasts have had to choose between fictive accounts so romanticized or so adventure oriented that they in no way bring the historical character to the reader, or historical narratives so "wholly discreet" that they, too, fail to convey a sense of reality. Only occasionally have brilliantly-done biographies brought the general type closer by focusing on a microcosm of the whole. And while no single volume should pretend to present a comprehensive portrait of the cowboy, it is our hope that this book will bring us closer than before to an appreciation of this unique historical character. We have tried to avoid the pitfall of "becoming wholly discreet," and tried to tell it like it was. The material herein first appeared in a special topical issue (Spring, 1975) of the *Red River Valley Historical Review*. We hope you find it informative and entertaining.

Finally, special credit should be given Dr. Clifford Westermeier, because it was the paper on cowboy sexuality which he read before the Western History Association convention at Fort Worth in 1973 that inspired this project. Dr. Bill G. Rainey not only contributed his article on the movie cowboys, but did the lion's share of the work by corresponding with the contributing authors and bringing the materials together. And of course we must tip our Stetsons to the University of Oklahoma Press staff, for their invaluable assistance.

Contents

Preface   *page* v
By Charles W. Harris

Introduction   1
By Buck Rainey

The Cowboy: from Black Hat to White   5
By Don Russell

The "Reel" Cowboy   17
By Buck Rainey

The Pistol Packin' Cowboy   57
By Philip D. Jordan

The Cowboy and Sex   85
By Clifford P. Westermeier

The Cowboy and the Dude   107
By Lawrence R. Borne

The Cowboy's Bawdy Music   127
By Guy Logsdon

The Cowboy in Indian Territory   139
By Arrell M. Gibson

The Cowboy Myth   154
  By William W. Savage, Jr.

About the Authors   164

Index   165

Introduction

BY BUCK RAINEY

IT IS PERHAPS EASIER MERELY TO SHRUG one's shoulders and verbalize a cliche, "Beauty is in the eye of the beholder," than it is to try seriously to define "The Cowboy." For at the mention of "cowboy" a hundred different images are fashioned in the minds of as many different people. Some will think of the heroes of wild west stories or rodeo performers or movie actors; others, the guitar pickin' yodelers of radio, television, and stage, or the dude ranch wrangler, or the wild west show performer; still others, more realistically, the *vaquero* of Texas, the wild roughrider of the plains, or the present-day rancher of the Great Southwest. For the cowboy has become part of a make-believe world in which each of us has fashioned him in the image that suits our own requirements.

There's an old saying that a cowboy is "a man with guts and a hoss." Probably that is a good beginning in describing the typical cowboy of 1860–1910 or thereabouts. Perhaps it is, after all, as definitive and brief a definition of the cowboy as we can attain. But where do we go from there? Fiction has created a myth, and the myth has fashioned The Cowboy into the most romantic occupant of the West, consistently gunning down bad-men and saving virgins from "a fate worse than death." Yet, if the truth be known, there were neither enough badmen nor virgins available in the Old West for the involvement of any sizable number of cowboys in either of the activities. And besides, that was the job of the sheriff.

No, the real cowboy's life was anything but romantic or exciting. There was little romance "in gettin' up at four o'clock in the mornin', eatin' dust behind a trail herd, swimmin' muddy and turbulent rivers, nor in doctorin' screw worms, pullin' stupid cows from bog holes, sweatin' in the heat of summer and freezin' in the cold of winter."[1]

[1] Ramon F. Adams, *The Old-Time Cowhand* (New York, 1961), p. 5.

1

The cowboy no doubt can be regarded as a proud rider, skilled, observant, alert, resourceful, unyielding, daring, punctilious in a code peculiar to his occupation, and faithful to his trust. His individualism was so marked that he molded in his own image, as it were, all aspirants to his occupation. True, there were some who were mean, vicious, vulgar, dishonest, and cheap—even ignorant—but they did not fit in.[2]

The Cowboy captured the imagination of the world, and few groups have been commercialized as intensively as the poor cow tender. Thousands of books have been written about him, thousands of films made about him, and millions of dollars lavished on cowboy toys, regalia, and paraphernalia. Yet the public, with an insatiable appetite, has continued to devour every morsel of "cowboydom" put on the market. As one of America's truly unique contributions to culture, The Cowboy seems destined to live on forever in that favored corner of our hearts reserved for vicarious thoughts about experiences which—because of a combination of circumstance, era, and cowardice—we shall never have.

Ramon F. Adams in his excellent work on The Cowboy has said:

> . . . No class of men were ever so unfaithfully represented, and in consequence so misunderstood and unfairly judged by people generally, as the old-time cowboy has been. He suffered severely from the bad publicity of ill-informed writers who had no real conception of his life and work. They pictured the rough, crude, brutal aspects of the cattle country; the reckless, happy-go-lucky visits to town, the careless use of the six-shooter, the drinkin', the fightin', practical jokes that were rough, the gamblin', and the profanity. All them things were subjects for the writer who painted, in the most lurid colors, slanderous accounts for eager Eastern readers. . . . but still, in spite of all that's been wrote 'bout 'im, them who knowed 'im best and lived with 'im found 'im to be good-natured and a rollickin' whole-souled feller, quick to do a kindness, and as quick to resent an insult.[3]

In this volume we have attempted to differentiate between myth and reality regarding certain aspects of The Cowboy. The historian will appreciate the research that has gone into the effort and the factual information provided; the casual reader will find the articles not only informative but also very readable and interesting from the purely entertainment point of view. No single volume can do justice to all the facets of cowboy life. We have made no attempt in this one to concentrate on a single topic, time period, or predetermined set of cowboy characteristics, or in any way to construct a smooth-flowing history of The Cowboy. Each author has worked independently, following one simple request: "Write an article pertaining to The Cowboy and in line with your own interests and field of

---

[2] J. Frank Dobie, *A Vaquero of the Brush Country* (Dallas, 1929), p. xii.
[3] Adams, *The Old-Time Cowhand*, pp. 3–4.

expertise." The authors responded admirably, and you have before you a compilation of articles about The Cowboy that we think you will thoroughly enjoy. Perhaps there is not something for everybody, but there is at least something for widely divergent interests in "cowboy readin'."

So saddle up now, won't you, and ride with us along uncovered trails into the semi-mythical world of THE COWBOY.

Illustration of lobby card courtesy of Buck Rainey.

Illustration of lobby card courtesy of Buck Rainey.

The Cowboy: from Black Hat to White

BY DON RUSSELL

THE COWBOY HAS BEEN CALLED AMERICA'S folk hero. This is odd, because the cowboy is peculiarly anonymous. Thomas Carlyle, a century and a third ago, opined that "Worship of a Hero is transcendant admiration of a Great Man."[1] No one seriously considers the cowboy hero to be a Great Man, although as Clifford P. Westermeier puts it, "The cowboy's character is best revealed by his courage, independence, cheerfulness, and ready acceptance of danger and hardship."[2] Philip Ashton Rollins agrees that "Universality of courage was an earmark of the cowboys' trade. Bravery was a prerequisite . . ."[3] Ramon F. Adams tones it down a bit, but not much, in his *Western Words* definition of cowboy: "The West, who knows him best, knows that he has always been 'just a plain, everyday, bow-legged human,' carefree and courageous, fun-loving and loyal, uncomplaining and doing his best to live up to a tradition of which he is proud."[4]

As we read this, and much more to the same effect, we are apt to forget that we are talking about an occupation followed by thousands of diverse men, of a "hired man on horseback" ruefully celebrated by Eugene Manlove Rhodes.[5] Clichés based on hasty generalization abound in the mythology of the West. All soldiers were brave and noble; all sheriffs and marshals were honest and incorruptible; all Indian agents were corruptible; all Indians "lived at one with nature." Yet the entire theme of Westward

---

[1] Thomas Carlyle, *On Heroes, Hero-Worship, and the Heroic in History* (1841). I have used the Everyman's Library edition, p. 248.

[2] Clifford P. Westermier, compiler and editor, *Trailing the Cowboy, His Life and Lore as Told by Frontier Journalists* (Caldwell, Idaho, 1935), p. 18.

[3] Philip Ashton Rollins, *The Cowboy: His Characteristics, His Equipment, and His Part in the Development of the West* (New York, 1922), p. 65.

[4] Ramon F. Adams, *Western Words: A Dictionary of the American West* (Norman, 1968), p. 78.

[5] May Davison Rhodes, *The Hired Man on Horseback: My Story of Eugene Manlove Rhodes* (Boston, 1938).

expansion was individual initiative. But who can name an individual cowboy?

Those who succeeded at the occupation became cowmen or cattle barons, such as Charles Goodnight or Shanghai Pierce, and ceased to be cowboys. We remember a few cowboys who wrote about being cowboys, such as Andy Adams, Teddy Blue Abbott, and Rhodes. Even more familiar are the names of those who acted the role of cowboy: Bronco Billy Anderson, William S. Hart, Tom Mix, Hoot Gibson, Gene Autry, Roy Rogers. And peculiarly long-lived is the name of one who lived the legend, Will Rogers. But of Adams's "plain, everyday, bow-legged" cowboy, no specimen attained legendary immortality.

It may be offered that the cowboy hero was created in fiction. Curiously, the hero of the prototype Western, *The Virginian*, is anonymous. Nowhere in anything Owen Wister wrote about him does he have a name; he is just "the Virginian." Marshall W. Fishwick has noted that "few readers remember the names" of Zane Grey's heroes.[6] A doubtful exception to cowboy hero anonymity is Clarence E. Mulford's Hopalong Cassidy. He attained wide, but perhaps temporary, recognition by mere repetition through monopolizing television in that medium's infancy with William Boyd's fifty-four B-movies.[7] Even here, the Hopalong of Boyd's movies little resembled the character created in Mulford's novels.

According to Joe B. Frantz and Julian Ernest Choate, Jr., the cowboy exists on three levels, the historical, the fictional, and "the folklore level, on which the cowboy sits as an idealized creation of the American folk mind."[8] Folklore, myth, and legend generally connote antiquity and the prehistoric, except perhaps in America, where we hold meetings to create instant traditions, or manufacture folklore—more accurately "fakelore," according to Professor Richard M. Dorson—for purpose of commercial exploitation or profit.[9]

Folklore or fakelore, the cowboy hero can be traced to his beginnings without the aid of stratigraphy, dendrochronology, or carbon-14 dating. In fact, a lineage so brief would be scorned by Burke's Peerage. Unfortunately, birth certificates were not universally required until well into the twentieth century, a fact of considerable annoyance to the Social Security bureaucracy, so we depend on scattered records of christenings. These records show that the historical cowboy of Frantz and Choate is 108 years

[6] Marshall W. Fishwick, *American Heroes: Myth and Reality* (Washington, 1954), p. 212.

[7] *Ibid.*, p. 217–19.

[8] Joe B. Frantz and Julian Ernest Choate, Jr., *The American Cowboy: The Myth and the Reality* (Norman, 1955), p. 15.

[9] Richard M. Dorson, *American Folklore and the Historian* (Chicago, 1971).

old, the fictional cowboy, 72, preceded by the 87-year-old dime novel cowboy, and the folklore cowboy is only a year over the alloted three score years and ten. It makes one almost believe the extravagance of virtues ascribed to the perennially youthful cowboy.

Yet, less than a century ago, the very word cowboy was derogatory, disreputable, opprobrious, even infamous. Earliest notable use of "Cowboys" in American annals was to denote bands of irregulars, *banditti*, or outlaws operating in the Neutral Ground between the British forces occupying New York City during the American Revolution and the American forces hovering about the upper Hudson in ineffective but persistent siege. "The Cowboys received their name from the fact that, among their many dastardly deeds, they seized the cattle on the farms near the camps and sold their stolen possessions to the redcoats."[10] They were Tories in addition to being guerrillas—an opprobrious designation that came into use during the Napoleonic adventures in Spain; the guerrillas of the American Civil War added further infamy. The New York guerrillas professing Patriot attachment were called Skinners, also a reference to cattle stealing. Perhaps they were interested in hides to be made into leather shoes for Washington's barefoot soldiers at Valley Forge, but that speculation stretches their patriotic motivation well toward its limit. However, three soldiers, John Paulding, Isaac Van Wert, and David Williams, attained Patriot Hero status by their capture of Major John André. They were highway robbers; they violated his civil rights by a search without a warrant; but they refused to be bribed; and they turned up the treason of Benedict Arnold. They were enrolled in the pantheon of Revolutionary heroes in school textbooks,[11] and cities were named for them (Paulding and Van Wert, Ohio). A little more, and "Skinner" might have become the folk hero.

The bushwhacker Tories got "Cowboys" off to a bad start. Apparently no one admitted to being a cowboy until there appeared, according to Ramon Adams, "a bunch of wild-riding, reckless Texans under the leadership of Ewen Cameron, who spent their time chasing longhorns and Mexicans soon after Texas became a republic."[12] Cameron's following added

[10] Everett T. Tomlinson, *Days and Deeds of '76* (New York, 1927), p. 139. Tomlinson, popular writer of juvenile historical fiction (*Three Young Continentals, With Flintlock and Fife*, etc.) collected much lore and trivia on the Revolution, embodied in this book, including a chapter on "Cowboys and Skinners" detailing some of their atrocities. *See also* Wilber C. Abbott, *New York in the American Revolution* (New York, 1929), pp. 244, 249.

[11] *A Brief History of the United States*, Barnes' Historical Series (New York, 1871–85), p. 136, where the three are identified as "incorruptible patriots." A later edition (American Book Company, 1900) on the same page gives the authorship as Joel Dorman Steele and Ester Baker Steele.

[12] Adams, *Western Words*, p. 78.

little to the folk hero idea, especially among Mexicans. Of course there had been cattle roundups and cattle drives since 1655, when John Pynchon brought a herd from Springfield, Massachusetts, to Boston, and although the personnel were more commonly called drovers or cowherds, it is quite possible that the word cowboy was used on occasion.[13] It is generally conceded that the cowboy of history got his start in 1867. During the Civil War, neglected longhorns ran wild over southern Texas, were hunted occasionally for their hides, but were of little other commercial value. Joseph G. McCoy perceived that if they could be brought to the railheads of the rapidly expanding railroads, they could supply cheap beef for Easterners. He set up business in Abilene, Kansas, and the ensuing trail drives were spectacular, romantic, and adventurous. Yet the cattle drives contributed little to the image of the cowboy aside from Chisholm Trail balladry and two notable novels, both belated, Andy Adams's *Log of a Cowboy* in 1903 and Emerson Hough's *North of '36* in 1924.

As late as 1881 a Western newspaper could say, "It is possible that there is not a wilder or more lawless set of men in any country that pretends to be civilized than the gangs of nomads that live in some of our frontier states and territories and are referred to in our dispatches as 'the cow boys.' . . . most of them merit the gallows."[14] In that same year, President Chester A. Arthur, in his annual message to Congress, denounced a band of "armed desperadoes known as 'Cowboys' " as a menace to the peace of Arizona Territory. An Eastern visitor reported in 1886, "Our cowboy is shockingly cruel, hasty in temper, and unbridled in tongue. In the branding pen and with a half-broken tired or unwilling horse, he is a perfect fiend; his contempt for life often leads to needless bloodshed . . . ."[15]

Of course there were contemporary defenders of the cowboy, but as long as he needed defenders he was in no way a candidate to become a folk-lore hero. Just how the cowboy reputation became completely reversed within a couple of decades cannot be explained completely, for no one can forecast or analyze the popularity of an idea. If anyone could, it would be a great boon to advertisers. A number of promising trails converge on William F. Cody of Buffalo Bill's Wild West.

When Cody staged an "Old Glory Blow Out" for the Fourth of July, 1882, in his home town, North Platte, Nebraska, he was astounded at getting a thousand entrants for a series of contests we would now call a rodeo.

---

[13] Robert West Howard, "America's First Commercial Cattle Drive," *The Westerners Brand Book*, Vol. XII, No. 1 (March, 1955), pp. 1–3, 6–8.

[14] *Las Vegas Daily Optic*, June 28, 1881, quoted in Westermeier, *Trailing the Cowboy*, pp. 47–48.

[15] John Bauman, "Experiences of a Cow-Boy," *Lippincott's Magazine* (September, 1886), quoted in Westermeier, *Trailing the Cowboy*, pp. 43–44.

However, Cody did not invent rodeo; such contests had been held on ranches, at roundups, and in Fourth of July and other civic celebrations for a generation or so. But he was inspired to take his show on the road as an exhibition that became Buffalo Bill's Wild West, first and greatest of the Wild West shows that contributed largely to the glamorization and romanticization of the American West, not only in America, but in Europe.[16]

Cody had been an outstanding scout for the army in Indian campaigns; he had been Pony Express rider, professional buffalo hunter and guide, teamster, stagecoach driver, and rancher—but not a cowboy. Edward Zane Carroll Judson, writing as Ned Buntline, glamorized some of this in three dime novels and persuaded Buffalo Bill to play himself on the stage in Chicago, opening December 18, 1872. Cody brought along a fellow scout, John Burwell Omohundro, Jr., known as Texas Jack.

Texas Jack also had a flair for publicity. He had served in the Confederate Cavalry and was cast as a master spy by Joel Chandler Harris of "Uncle Remus" fame in a series of stories called *On the Wing of Occasions.* Texas Jack did some writing on his own account, and his article on "The Cow-Boy" appeared in *Wilkes' Spirit of the Times* of March 24, 1877. Cody and Omohundro parted after four seasons together on the stage, each thereafter heading his own theatrical combination, but apparently their parting was amicable, since Omohundro's piece appeared in whole or in part in many annual issues of the *Programme and Historical Review* of Buffalo Bill's Wild West.

"The cow-boy!" ejaculated Texas Jack, and note that "cow-boy" was then hyphenated, . . .

> How often spoken of, how falsely imagined, how greatly despised (where he is not known), how little understood! I've been there considerable. How sneeringly referred to, and how little appreciated, although his title has been gained by the possession of many of the noblest qualities that form the romantic hero of the poet, novelist, and historian; the plainsman and the scout.[17]

It is interesting that Texas Jack mourns the passing of the long drive—it was just ending—and recites the classic perils of bucking horses, cattle stampedes, milling cattle at river crossings, and the "absolutely necessary" singing on night herd, even to quoting a verse of a cow-boy's own composition:

> Lay nicely, now, cattle, don't heed any rattle,
> But quietly rest until morn;

16 Don Russell, *The Lives and Legends of Buffalo Bill* (Norman, 1960), pp. 290–91.
17 *Wilkes' Spirit of the Times*, March 24, 1877.

For if you skedaddle, we'll jump in the saddle,
And head you as sure as you're born.[18]

The cow-boy was on his way up. The purpose was to introduce the cowboys of the Wild West show, "lassoing and riding the wild Texas steers," riding the bucking ponies, and in numerous races. Johnnie Baker, a protege of Cody, was featured as "The Cow-boy Kid" in feats of marksmanship. But the star of this part of the show was billed as " 'Buck' Taylor, King of the Cowboys." William Levi Taylor was born in Fredericksburg, Texas; his father was killed in an early skirmish of Texas cavalry in the Civil War; his mother died two years later; and Buck was raised on an uncle's ranch. He was employed on the Dismal River ranch of Cody and Major Frank North when the Old Glory Blowout was staged, and he was an original member of the Wild West troupe. Six feet, three and a half inches tall, he was credited with "easily throwing a steer by the horns or tail, lassoing and tying single-handed," and "his mastery of wild horses," and he was "amiable as a child."[19]

Contributing to the success of Buffalo Bill in show business were the dime novels about Buffalo Bill totaling some 557 original stories, which with reprints came to seventeen hundred issues published over a period of 63 years, much of the time weekly. Some twenty authors contributed, starting with Ned Buntline in 1869, but he wrote only three or four more. The largest producer was Colonel Prentiss Ingraham, who wrote a stage play for Cody in 1879 and followed with at least 121 original stories and was still writing them when he died in 1904. He was the son of the Reverend J. H. Ingraham, author of *The Prince of the House of David*, which his son irreverently called a dime novel about the Bible, but it was tremendously popular in its day. Prentiss Ingraham is credited with writing a thousand adventure yarns and living some of them. His autobiography, perhaps no more authentic than some of the dime novel biographies he wrote, credits him with fighting with the Confederates at Port Hudson, with Juárez in Mexico, in the Battle of Sadowa in Austria, and as filibuster colonel of Cuban rebels.[20]

Ingraham introduced the first cowboy hero of fiction in *Beadle's Half-Dime Library*, February 1, 1887, with *Buck Taylor, King of the Cowboys; or, The Raiders and the Rangers, A Story of the Wild and Thrilling Life of*

---

[18] *Buffalo Bill's Wild West Programme*, 1885, also 1889, 1893, 1894, 1897, and other years. Also quoted in Herschel C. Logan, *Buckskin and Satin: The Life of Texas Jack and His Wife, Mlle. Morlacci* (Harrisburg, 1954).

[19] *Buffalo Bill's Wild West Programme*, 1885 and 1888.

[20] Russell, *Buffalo Bill*, pp. 263–64, 386–415, *passim*.

William L. Taylor. Henry Nash Smith in *Virgin Land* finds this as "probably the earliest use of a cowboy hero in the Beadle novels."[21]

Buck Taylor's bibliography is as brief as the titles are long—there are only six more stories—and because the long-winded titles are almost a synopsis of the action, they are given in full. Buck's second appearance was in *The Banner Weekly*, in a serial story July 6 to September 28, 1889, *The Wild Steer Riders; or, The Red Revolver Rangers, A Story of Lawless Lives, Love, and Adventure in the Lone Star State.* When reissued in *Beadle's Dime Library* in 1894, the title was changed to *The Wild Steer Riders; or Texas Jack's Terrors.* Apparently Buck was not the star of this production, although he had a bit part.

The *Dime Library,* however, starred Buck Taylor in a series of three: *Buck Taylor, the Saddle King; or, The Lasso Rangers' League, A Romance of Heroes in Buckskin,* April 21, 1891; *The Cowboy Clan; or, The Tigers of Texas,* April 29, 1891; and *A Romance of Buck Taylor and His Boys in Buckskin,* June 3, 1891. Back at the *Beadle's Half-Dime Library,* two more titles finish out the year: *Buck Taylor, the Comanche Captive; or, Buckskin Sam to the Rescue, A Romance of Lone Star Heroes,* September 8, 1891; and *Buck Taylor's Boys; or, The Red Riders of the Rio Grande, A Romance of Life among the Rangers and the Raiders of the Southwest Border,* October 20, 1891.[22] Buckskin Sam was Major Sam S. Hall of the Texas Rangers, who was a writer of dime novels as well as the actual hero of some of them.

The literary career of Buck Taylor was brief, and the titles suggest that the newly discovered cowboy hero had as little to do with cows as did most of his successors. However, Ingraham's Buck Taylor came to the rescue of Texas Jack in defending the good name of the cowboys, "noble in their treatment of a friend or a fallen foe."[23] It might be argued that Texas Jack was the first cowboy hero, since dime novels about him were written by Ned Buntline in 1873, by Prentiss Ingraham in 1882, and even by Buffalo Bill in 1883. But Texas Jack was presented as scout and frontiersman, more akin to Fenimore Cooper's Leatherstocking than to Wister's Virginian.

Buck Taylor's impact on the cowboy legend may seem slight, but it is to be remembered that lurid dime novel covers were seen by a great many more people than read their insides—they were widely distributed as paper-

[21] Henry Nash Smith, *Virgin Land: The American West as Symbol and Myth* (Cambridge, Mass., 1950), pp. 110–11.

[22] Albert Johannsen, *The House of Beadle and Adams and Its Dime and Nickel Novels,* Vol. I (Cambridge, 1950), pp. 232, 240, 287, 456.

[23] Smith, *Virgin Land,* p. 111.

backs are today—and "King of the Cowboys" and "The Cowboy Clan" got attention, especially when backed by show publicity. Buck Taylor left Buffalo Bill's Wild West and received little further exploitation. He superintended Denver's Cowboy Tournament and Wild West in 1890 and tried his own Buck Taylor's Wild West briefly in 1894, then retired to a Wyoming Ranch. He died in 1924.[24]

Also, Buck Taylor's impact came at a time when interest in the West was on the upsurge. Buffalo Bill's Wild West introduced the cowboy to England during Queen Victoria's Jubilee in 1887 and repeated the triumph in tours of Paris and the continent, 1889–92 and, again, 1902–1906. Such success provoked imitation, and there were at least 242 Wild West shows at one time or another, with the smaller ones that could not afford gauchos, Cossacks and other Rough Riders, herds of buffalo, or even tribes of Indians, putting the emphasis on the Wild West feature "cowboy fun" that eventually became rodeo. Cheyenne Frontier Days, the oldest extant, dates from 1897, the Pendleton Round-Up from 1910, and the Calgary Stampede from 1919. The word rodeo was not commonly used until after World War I.

If you could not see the Wild West in show or rodeo, you could read about it, and there was much reading for pleasure in those days before movies, radio, or television. Mary Hallock Foote's *The Led-Horse Claim*, 1882, and Captain Charles King's *The Colonel's Daughter*, 1883, were early novels exploiting the Far West, and a few more appeared from time to time. It was a period when there was a great interest in regional literature, and the West was a legitimate region. In 1893 Buffalo Bill's Wild West had its most successful season at the Chicago world's fair. At that same world's fair, Frederick Jackson Turner addressed a meeting of the American Historical Association on "The Significance of the Frontier in American History," turning the attention of historians to the West, and they are still debating the significance. Also in 1893, Frederic Remington met Owen Wister.[25]

Remington certainly takes a large place in the glorification of the cowboy—in fact, his first published picture, in *Harper's Weekly* in 1882, was captioned "Cow Boys of Arizona." He had illustrated Theodore Roosevelt's *Ranch Life and the Hunting Trail*; he had ridden with the black Tenth Cavalry in Arizona, and with General Miles in the last campaign against the Sioux. He was perhaps at his best in depicting the frontier

---

[24] Don Russell, *The Wild West: Or, A History of the Wild West Shows* (Fort Worth, 1970), pp. 57, 59, 100.

[25] Ben Merchant Vorpahl, *My Dear Wister—The Frederick Remington–Owen Wister Letters* (Palo Alto, 1972), pp. 1–2, 20–21.

soldier. He had just returned from a tour of Europe's armies with Poultney Bigelow and was eager to find a collaborator who would write about the West. Wister went West from Philadelphia, in 1885, for his health and eventually began to write about what he had seen. His long articles for *Harper's* were regional sketches rather than short stories, and these Remington was to illustrate. A group of them was assembled in a book as *Red Men and White* in 1895, and a second group as *Lin McLean* in 1897. *Lin McLean* was a cowboy, a predecessor of *The Virginian*; in fact "the Virginian" was a secondary character in some of the stories. Meanwhile, Remington had inveigled Wister into writing a piece on "The Evolution of the Cow-Puncher," published in *Harper's Monthly* in 1895. Both of them looked upon the cowboy as a passing institution to be captured before he vanished.

Remington and Wister had gone their separate ways by the time *The Virginian* was put together in 1902. It is generally conceded to be the prototype Western and to have invented the formula that made the cowboy hero perennial. Wister, with a push from Remington, had builded better than he knew. *The Virginian* halted the evolution they had chronicled. For half a century and more the cowboy hero isolated himself on the ranch of 1902, and those who wrote about him ignored such improvements as the automobile, tractor, telephone, advances in animal husbandry, and other appurtenances of the twentieth century. The cowboy shoot-'em-up was written as contemporary, and accepted by the reader as a part of the formula and the code that built up a folk hero in a never-never land only vaguely associated with the cowboy of history.

While the cowboy hero ignored inventive technology, inventive technology by no means ignored the cowboy. The first motion picture to tell a story was *The Great Train Robbery* of 1903; the story was Western and immensely successful. It played for years in tent shows, as an adjunct to vaudeville bills, and on its own account in rented store-room theaters. Gilbert M. Anderson, who had a small part in it, teamed up with George K. Spoor in 1907 to form the Essanay Film Company of Chicago. Essanay meant "S" for Spoor and "A" for Anderson. Anderson took a company on location in Wyoming and became Broncho Billy Anderson, the first of Western film stars. A few years later Essanay made a series of historical films starring Buffalo Bill. William S. Hart and Tom Mix dominated the silent film, followed by many others—Hoot Gibson, Ken Maynard, Colonel Tim McCoy. The talking film produced the singing cowboy, Gene Autry and Roy Rogers, and such perennial cowboy heroes as Gary Cooper and John Wayne. William Boyd carried Hopalong Cassidy into television, and not to be overlooked is radio's contribution, *The Lone Ranger*. A couple of

Illustration of lobby card courtesy of Buck Rainey.

decades ago Marshall Fishwick said, "The cowboy movie is the only American art form in which the notion of honor retains its full strength."[26] Nothing has happened since to change that finding.

Wister rode the crest of a wave, and not all after him was imitation. Alfred Henry Lewis assembled *Wolfville* in 1897, and followed it with several others. Andy Adams's *Log of a Cowboy* was published in 1903. B. M. Bower's *Chip of the Flying U* was a sensation in 1906 and had the added punch of being illustrated by Charles M. Russell, who excelled Remington in painting the cowboy. Bertha Bower was a ranch woman, but retreated to initials in those pre-woman's lib days when it was assumed male readers of *Popular Magazine* would not read a cowboy yarn written by a woman. Oddly enough, she later added a parenthetical "B.M. Sinclair" in deference to a marriage that proved short-lived. Eugene Manlove Rhodes was a working cowboy, and his stories were rated a cut above his contemporaries, and O. Henry wrote some classic tales, some of which were assembled in *Heart of the West*. But topping them all in popularity was Zane Grey, whose writing was atrocious and whose characters were as wooden as a cigar-store Indian, but who somehow had a gift for story-telling. It was Zane Grey who made "Western" a generic term.

The output has never faltered—William MacLeod Raine, Max Brand, Luke Short, Ernest Haycox, Noel M. Loomis, Bill Gulick, Jack Schaefer, on

[26] Fishwick, *American Heroes*, p. 215.

down to Louis L'Amour, who has outsold them all, including Zane Grey. Their work converts to movies directly, with sometimes astronomical profit. A television series, however, is apt to be ephemeral and evanescent. In 1958, TV discovered the "modern Western" and the "adult Western," and eight of the ten top ratings went to Westerns, but it didn't last except for *Gunsmoke* and the indestructible Matt Dillon.

There are still working cowboys in Marlboro Country,[27] but most of the rodeo performers do little else, and none of them bear much relationship to the folk hero of television and paperbacks. It is quite probable that all the cowboys that ever were are outnumbered by their fictional counterparts. Counting all the novels and short stories, movies, radio programs, and television series, how many cowboy stories have been promulgated to the public? The number of course is incalculable. Each of them presumably has some claim to authenticity. The historian can perhaps find an instance or two resembling the quick-draw shootout as in *High Noon*, a gangster sheriff such as Henry Plummer, the much-debated OK Corral fight, Wyoming's Johnson County War, or the Graham-Tewksbury Feud. Each of these, and a few more, have been multiplied infinitely in the cowboy saga.[28]

It has been said that what is commonly believed by the populace is quite as influential as what actually happened. It may not always be as socially desirable. The notion of honor in the cowboy film may be salutary, but a few years ago, in our days of violence of the late 1960's, it was commonly pointed out that America was traditionally a violent country, with the lawless West as prime example. Statistical research shows that violent crime in the Frontier West was actually no greater than in the rest of the country. Both the virtues and vices of our folk hero are grossly exaggerated, but presumably nothing will shake his hold on our imagination.

[27] Don Johnston, "This Is Marlboro Country!" *The Westerners Brand Book*, Vol. XXX, No. 4 (June, 1973), pp. 25–27.

[28] A summary of all this that should not be overlooked, written by an English enthusiast, is Escott North, *The Saga of the Cowboy* (London, n.d., *circa* 1942).

BUCK JONES
A Personal Hero to Millions

Generally conceded to be the greatest of all movie cowboys. Jones's films were a compromise between the stark realism of William S. Hart and Harry Carey Westerns and the flamboyant showmanship of Tom Mix and Ken Maynard Westerns. Photograph from the collection of Buck Rainey.

The "Reel" Cowboy

BY BUCK RAINEY

No DISCUSSION OF "THE COWBOY" WOULD BE complete without some attention to the "Reel" cowboy, for it is he, the cinema cowboy of yesteryear, along with the cowboy of literary fiction, that has provided the basis for the popular misconception of the Wild West of the 1800's and early 1900's. To the chagrin, perhaps, of historians whose scholarly reposits of factual information barely reap enough in sales to pay publication costs, the world has turned to writers such as Zane Grey, Peter Field, Louis L'Amour, Luke Short, Jackson Gregory, William Colt MacDonald, and E. C. Mann to formulate its impression of the West, receiving for the billions of dollars spent on Western fiction a sensationalized, glorified, romanticized, distorted, imaginative, and downright inaccurate impression of the American cowboy that has given body and form to the legend that now exists about the cowboy and his era. But, worse still, millions have in part formulated their image of the West and of the cowboy from reading pulp magazines authored by nameless numbers of writers depending mainly on their own imagination to paint in words a commercially marketable cowboy.

The pulps had many predecessors in the low-priced heroics field of the dime novel and story paper serials. Ned Buntline, the pen name of a long-time hack named Edward Z. C. Judson, made a fortune in fictionalizing the exploits of an obscure William F. Cody. The first of these stories, "Buffalo Bill, the King of the Border Men," began running in Street & Smith's *New York Weekly* in 1869.[1] Other wild west heroes followed, most notable being Deadwood Dick and Kit Carson. Completely fictional heroes such as The Rio Kid, Jim Hatfield, and Zorro were also created.

In 1919 *Western Story Magazine* made its appearance, and within a year had a circulation of three hundred thousand per issue.[2] Other pulps

[1] Ron Goulart, *Cheap Thrills* (New Rochelle, 1972), p. 23.
[2] *Ibid.*, p. 135.

followed—magazines such as *Triple-X Western, Dime Western, Ace Western, New Western, West, Western Adventures, Golden West, North-West, Six-Gun, Spicy Western, Crack Shot, Double Action, Ranch Romances, Wild West Weekly, Thrilling Ranch Stories, Texas Rangers, The Rio Kid, Popular Western, Far West, Ace High*, ad infinitum. Thus were added more mythical interpretations of the West and the cowboy by hundreds of gregarious writers, most of whom knew little about the West, seeking to make their fortunes catering to the insatiable appetites of Americans for cheap, vicarious thrills. And, to put it kindly, the average American, reading four or five pulps a week, preferred western realism in heavily diluted doses.

Many famous western writers got their start in the pulps before graduating to the slicks and the hardcover books—Zane Grey, William MacLeod Raine, Walt Coburn, James B. Hyndrix, W. C. Tuttle, Max Brand, Clarence E. Mulford, and Ernest Haycox, to name a few. It was Frederick Faust (Max Brand) who stated the guiding formula for most pulp stories *and* B-western movies when he said:

> Action, action, action is the thing. So long as you keep your hero jumping through fiery hoops on every page you're all right. The basic formula I use is simple: good man turns bad, bad man turns good. Naturally, there is considerable variation on the theme. . . . There has to be a woman, but not much of a one. A good horse is much more important.[3]

That the cowboy is one of the most romantic figures in American history is uncontested. Few other characters have received more attention in the pages of books and magazines, or have had more film footage devoted to them than has this almost legendary vestige of the West. Yet the true cowboy has seldom been discovered by either authors or directors. The image which the world has of the cowboy is one of three types—depending mainly on one's age—the one of the silent, strong, bashful, and virginal deliverer of damsels popular with the generations before 1935; or the gaudy, guitar-strumming, croonin' mutations of the late 30's and 40's; or the virile, violent types which appeared in the 60's and 70's.

The movies have perpetuated, perfected, and extended the myth to such a degree that the average person cannot easily differentiate reality from myth when thinking about the cowboy. More likely than not, "cowboy" conjures up memories of Saturday afternoons at the Ritz, or Erie, or Bijou—whatever your hometown theater might have been called—and Buck Jones, Jack Perrin, Pete Morrison, Rex Bell, or Buddy Roosevelt dashing across the prairie to save the heroine from "a fate worse than death." As a cynical adult, after reading Professor Westermeier's scholarly

---

[3] *Ibid.*, p. 134.

article in this issue, one might wonder if perhaps a real cowboy might not have been dashing to carry through the vile deed rather than save the pretty maiden. But the old memories and the movies and personalities that gave life to them constitute a bit of nostalgic history that is pleasant to remember, to savor, to cherish, and to perpetuate. And so this article recalls the "reel" cowboys of yesteryear who starred in series westerns commonly referred to as B-Westerns. To most Western aficionados, the occasional Westerns (generally called "A," "Big," "Major," or "super") made by "dudes" (non-series stars) are repugnant and undeserving of acknowledgment in a tribute to the memory of revered cowboy stalwarts of Western filmdom. For, strangely, "major" western films, although touted by historians and Hollywood publicity departments, have, relatively speaking, had an insignificant influence in shaping the image of the cowboy. Perhaps it is because there have been so few of them in comparison to the output of B-Westerns, which number in the thousands. Seeing an occasional film such as *Stagecoach*, *The Virginian*, *The Covered Wagon*, *Shane*, *The Iron Horse*, *The Searchers*, or *Red River* could hardly have the lasting effect that the film output of Leo Maloney, Tom Mix, Bob Steele, Harry Carey and confreres had from week to week, month to month, and year to year. Millions of boys and girls grew to adulthood during fifty years of B-Westerns from 1903 to 1954, thoroughly enmeshed in the continuing heroics of these bigger-than-life performers who were always "cowboys," not something different each time they were seen.

When I was a kid growing up in the Age of Innocence—the 20's and 30's—my best and closest friends were "reel" cowboys. I knew and loved them all—Buck Jones, Ken Maynard, Hoot Gibson, George O'Brien, Rex Lease, Bill Cody, and Tim McCoy were intimate acquaintances. I shared their adventures, and it was when Buck Jones kissed Loretta Sayers in *The Fighting Sheriff* (Columbia, 1931) that I knew the first terrible pangs of unrequited love. It mattered not that the B-Westerns of yesteryear were devoid of much substance, we ("we" being literally millions of people) loved them then and remember them now as the greatest movies ever made and the finest aggregation of stars ever to inhabit Hollywood. For the uninitiated, the allegiance that untold numbers of people have for the B-Western is hardly understandable. They find it strange that a Western fan will cherish and remember forever Ken Maynard leaping along rooftops, Buck Jones being nudged by Silver into the arms of the heroine, Bob Steele outslugging an opponent three times as large as himself, Hoot Gibson's clowning, and Tom Mix's foolhardy stunts, while at the same time rejecting altogether the super-Westerns of the big studios, films starring big name actors like Peck, Fonda, McCrea, Ladd, Taylor, Hudson, Brando, Newman, etc. Only John Wayne, who came up through the ranks of B-Westerns and serials, and Randolph Scott, who voluntarily shifted almost entirely to Westerns, among the "outsiders" (non-series Western stars) have been accepted by Western devotees. All others who were not exclusively Western stars have been contemptuously labeled "frauds" and rejected. Thus, few "A" Westerns have been taken seriously by those who are identified as "oater," "horse-opera," "sagebrusher," "shoot-em-up," "formula Western," or "programmer Western" fans. While a Western fan might travel a long distance to catch an old Charles Starrett or Reb Russell oater (Western film festivals held in Dallas and Memphis in the summer of 1974 drew people from throughout the United States and England), they just as likely would not step across the street to see a Western starring the likes of Clint Eastwood or James Stewart—not unless one of the "accepted" cowboys had a supporting role in it. John Ford films have drawn respect from Western enthusiasts, but primarily because Ford worked mostly with stars such as Hoot Gibson, Harry Carey, Buck Jones, Tom Mix, John Wayne, and George O'Brien. This being the case, he could be forgiven an occasional transgression when he made a Western without any "sure-nuff" cowboy stars in it.

To the present generation, the thrill of attending a weekend matinee at a local theater to see a new Western along with a two-reeler comedy and the latest episode of an exciting cliffhanger is something unexperienced. Perhaps in this age of sophistication, anti-heroes, and declining moral standards, the young person cannot be expected to understand the thrill of ecstasy reverberating through one's body at the sight of Tim McCoy icily "staring down" an opponent; Buck Jones in white hat astride his white horse Silver riding in pursuit of that ace villain Charlie King with his black hat and riding a black horse; Yakima Canutt dashing across the prairie on his steed at top speed, standing erect with the reins in his teeth and pumping lead with both hands; or Tom Tyler knocking badmen in all directions in a saloon free-for-all. One must have lived it to fully appreciate it. Today's goosepimples acquired at viewing one of the old shoot-em-ups were earned twenty to forty years ago, in the era of heroes, by youngsters clutching their dimes and fighting for a place in line at the popcorn counter.

McClure and Jones, in one of the many books on the Western film, said:

> The popularity of the "B" Western was an extension of the cowboy myth in American life. Historian Carl Becker noted that Americans are prone to cling to what he called "useful myths." The Western film hero received an adoration and continuing loyalty of amazing proportions. Villains were hissed with equal fervor. Westerns moved audiences emotionally as no other type

of film. The emotional conditioning provided by these films, and the durability of that conditioning should never be underestimated by historians of American life. Some historians have dismissed the "B" western as simply a novelty or tasteless fad with no real substance or significance. However, it is entirely possible that in the midst of the confusion and uncertainty created by the Depression and World War II audiences sustained many of their "faiths" by identifying with such admirable and powerful symbols of straightforward righteousness as seen in the "B" westerns.[4]

They go on to say that the "B" Westerns were "fascinating historical examples of the romantic flavor of a haunting nostalgia for a more individualistic and flamboyant past," and that "the B-Western was very much a part of the evasion of reality in a mundane world."[5]

By 1900, Edison's Kinetoscope—"moving pictures"—was well established. Motion pictures were being accepted by the public. Films were short—less than one reel—and were merely incidents caught at random or staged by enterprising photographers representing the emerging companies that would give birth to a full-fledged industry. Films were—if it can be imagined—worse efforts than the most offensive home movies made by doting parents at their children's birthday parties. There were no stories, no plots, no acting as such, no direction, nothing. Nothing, that is, but exposed film of moving trains, the seashore, prizefights, circus acts, etc. No theaters existed for the exclusive showing of film. Rather, the innumerable one-reelers were shown as intermission quieters in vaudeville houses, kinetoscope parlors, and in penny arcades and museums across the country.[6]

Changes were coming about rapidly after the turn of the century, though. In spite of the crudeness of the moving pictures of that day, they were catching on. One must remember that they were not being watched by the cynical, sophisticated audiences of seventy years later, but by people caught up with the novelty of seeing pictures actually move. Nickelodeon theaters were growing in number, and moving picture companies were being formed to exploit the medium. Anything that moved would draw an audience in the beginning, but the novelty began to wear thin, and so producers were of necessity becoming more innovative. The public liked movies that told a story of sorts.

Edwin S. Porter, employed by the Edison Company, was quick to catch

[4] Arthur F. McClure and Ken D. Jones, *Heroes, Heavies and Sagebrush* (Cranbury, New Jersey, 1972), p. 11.

[5] *Ibid.*

[6] Bill G. (Buck) Rainey, "A Nostalgic and Capsule Review of 'Hoss Opera' Stars 1900–73," *Wild West Stars*, Vol. 4, No. 14, p. 2.

the mood of the public and hastened to put together a film concerning a Western railroad robbery (although filmed in New Jersey), 1903's *The Great Train Robbery*. The rest is motion picture history. This 740-foot, 9-minute film was the first serious attempt at a story film. In addition, it had a Western plot and introduced many principles of motion picture production followed by later film makers—the close-up, the chase, changing locales, cutting from one scene to another, a climax, specially designed props, the escape, cliffhanger action, stop motion, and even a musical interlude (long before Ken Maynard or Gene Autry). And it introduced the first Western star, G. M. "Broncho Billy" Anderson, playing three parts. Scheduled for a fourth part, that of a posse member, he fell off his horse and thus was not seen in this capacity.[7] Hardly an auspicious beginning for the screen's first cowboy actor.

The Western genre's beginning pre-dated *The Great Train Robbery* by about five years, although it was a very inauspicious and shaky one. The Edison Company had committed to film a number of one-and two-minute vignettes of cowboys, Indians, buffalo, Indians scalping cowboys, cattle roundups, and such, and even William F. (Buffalo Bill) Cody had been filmed during his Wild West act. And so it was that the company in 1898 filmed a short tableau entitled *Cripple Creek Bar-room*, devoid of a moving story and only a few minutes in length. Nevertheless, it did contain a "cast" who were coached in what they were to do, and it did attempt to realistically depict life in a Cripple Creek saloon. The seed was planted.

Subsequent to Porter's *The Great Train Robbery*, other films such as his own *Rescued from an Eagle's Nest* (1907); D. W. Griffith's *The Massacre* (1912), *Fighting Blood* (1911) and *The Last Drop of Water* (1911); Selig's *Boots and Saddles* (1909); and Thomas Ince's *War of the Plains* (1911) contributed bits and pieces to what would become the tried-and-true, bread-and-butter formula for countless sagebrush heroes over a period of sixty years.[8]

These early Western opuses appealed to the multitudes, and picture makers hastened to appease their seemingly insatiable thirst for action film entertainment. The Western story remained most popular with movie audiences, particularly when coupled with a new screen innovation, romance.

G. M. Anderson remained in the film business, first going to work for Vitagraph, then, in partnership with George K. Spoor, organizing Essanay

[7] *Ibid.*
[8] Bill G. (Buck) Rainey, "A Nostalgic and Capsule Review of 'Hos Opera' Stars 1900–73," *Wild West Stars*, Vol. 5, No. 15, p. 4.

Film Manufacturing Company. It prospered, and Anderson eventually established a West coast studio at Niles, California. It was here that he was to produce, direct, and star in the highly successful "Broncho Billy" Westerns that would cause an industry to be formed within an industry—the cowboy movie. Because he was unable to find an actor to play in the Westerns he wanted to make, Anderson became a "Cowboy" and made close to five hundred one- and two-reelers before his career ground to a halt about 1920. His first one-reeler, *Broncho Billy and the Baby*, was made in 1908 and established the basic good-badman character of Broncho Billy. "The public lapped up Anderson's heroic characterization of a good-badman who aids a stricken child and is reformed by love, and so both the name and the characterization (with many variations) stuck. The Billy character had genuine charm, was basically realistic, and could supply sentimentality and action in equal doses."[9] However, Anderson is not usually thought of as a realist.

"Realism" is a rather nebulous quality, one hard to pin down and describe appropriately. Most B-Westerns had within them elements of both reality and myth, for if the cowboy had been depicted solely as he actually was—a mostly drab, hard working, hard drinking, illiterate, shabbily dressed, over-sexed, and unambitious drifter—there would have been little audience for such movies. No, there had to be a bigger-than-life hero. But ingredients of most westerns from the mid-twenties on, which we, as kids, accepted without thought included:

Clean, unlingering, unsuffering deaths. Did you ever stop to wonder why everyone died so conveniently quick, sparing our hero the frustration and responsibility associated with caring for a villain he has shot out on the range somewhere?

Cowless cowboys. Where did all the cows go? And why did we call them cowboys when, in fact, most of the time they were marshals or Texas Rangers or just drifters? Only in a minority of Westerns was the cowboy star ever depicted as a working cowboy.

Well-lodged hats. Yes, neither gravity, force, or "all hell turned loose" seemed to be able to separate a cowboy's fancy Stetson from his head. It was an interesting phenomenon when you stop to think about it.

Unerring accuracy. In spite of the poor weapons of the late nineteenth century, our nonchalant heroes seemed always able to shoot the gun out of a man's hand at fifty yards, without aiming and without hitting the antagonist's hand.

Perpetual summers. I wonder why there was never winter in the West? Like the bears, the cowboy seemed to hibernate in the winter, and our only glimpse of him or of the West was invariably in a summer setting.

[9] Michael Parkinson and Clyde Jeavons, *A Pictorial History of Westerns* (London, 1972), p. 94.

Corpses galore! As Duncan Renaldo (of Cisco Kid fame) once said, "There have been more people killed in Westerns than ever populated the West!" Killing seemed to be taken nonchalantly in many Westerns, as if it were an everyday occurrence. And hardly ever was there an inquest or legal red tape for our hero, who might have finished off six or seven men in as many minutes—nor did such killings ever seem to rest heavily on his mind.

Biological freaks. Most of the heroines in Westerns had but a single parent, nearly always a father. Less than one percent of them ever had a living mother in the film.

Perpetual-firing six-shooters. The "six-shooters" that fired fifteen times without reloading would certainly be collector's items today if we could get our hands on them. I wonder where The Durango Kid got that pistol anyway?

Sarsaparilla drinking, girl-shy heroes. It was always strange that the cowboys thought asexual thoughts only—must have been all that sarsaprilla!

"Fists only" heroes. A guy, cowboy hero or not, had to be a little stupid not to pick up a chair, break a whisky bottle, run, or pull a gun in the face of a dozen hoodlums out to kill him.

Full musical orchestrations. I never could figure out where all the music was coming from out there on the desert when Gene Autry or Roy Rogers was riding along singing to his horse. I could have sworn that either the whole Lawrence Welk Orchestra or Bob Wills and his Texas Playboys were hidden behind a boulder somewhere.

Superior social graces. Where did the cowboy heroes obtain the culture they displayed—speech, etiquette, education? Certainly not out in the barn, or behind it in the haystack with the neighbor girl, or closely trailing the south end of a herd of cattle headed north along The Chisholm Trail.

Ambiguous film titles. A title such as "Outlaws of Cherokee Pass" for some reason seemed odd at times when there was neither a town nor a "pass" by that name in the movie. And downright misleading were such titles as "Conquest of Cheyenne" when the heroine, it turns out, is named "Cheyenne" and is the subject of the conquest rather than a booming, lawless frontier town.

Instantaneous recovery. After a bruising battle with several badmen weighing no less than two hundred pounds each, the hero would come up with all his teeth intact, bloodless, his clothes immaculately clean, and with a smile on his face. It was especially unbelievable when the hero was non-athletic John King, Eddie Dean, Jimmy Wakely, or Lash LaRue.

Ridiculous wearing apparel. Can you believe a cowboy in the 1870's wearing a costume like that of Gene Autry, Tom Mix, Roy Rogers, or William Boyd? Well, really! Not if he wanted to live long.

Bullet-proof horses. I wonder why, with all the bullets flying around, the horses never got hit, but only the humans? Those horses sure knew how to duck!

Happy endings only. You could always count on the fact that the hero would be vindicated, win the girl, and bring about the downfall of the lawless element. The hero's luck in this respect seldom wavered.

Physical Adonises. Why was the hero nearly always six feet tall, muscular, clean shaven, handsome? Anyway, was it necessary for him, at the conclusion of a knock-down-and-drag-out encounter with two dozen villains in a Western drinking hell, to appear in his close-ups as though he had just left the beauty shop?

Unencumbered heroes. Very seldom was the hero of a B-Western laden with the responsibilities that beset the ordinary man. He seldom was married, seldom presented as a widower with children, and almost never had a mother or father or maiden aunt to see after.

Simple plot structures. A dusty one-street town; one young, beautiful woman; one outlaw gang headed by the town's leading citizen, one saloon serving as the social gathering place; and one hero. Very seldom was there a deviation from this basic structure—yet Western towns came in all sizes; some of them had several beautiful women worth fighting for or rescuing; some had more than one outlaw gang; and, upon occasion, a town might even have several heroes capable of thwarting the nefarious plans of the villain and of vying for the affections of the girl(s).

We could go on and on, but the point has been made, I think, that few Western movies were ever completely realistic. However, for our purposes, we can define realism as believability—with regard to plots, characterizations, action, dress, authenticity, sets and locales, dialogue, and quality of acting.

But back to Broncho Billy. For a man who knew nothing about the West, he produced horse operas with a surprising ring of authenticity to them. The customs were sometimes a little strange, and the dialogue subtitles were often overdone, in the manner of Western pulp fiction. But the stories were strong, and the films themselves were nicely directed, photographed, and edited.[10] They were often surprisingly strong and vigorous in their action content, with elaborately constructed and absolutely convincing Western town sets. A trifle dour in the later Hart tradition, Anderson presented a reasonably realistic and not too glamourized portrait of the frontier's manhood.[11] Truly, Anderson made the first "series" Westerns and was the first cowboy "star" of the movies, and his films established Westerns as a genre, one in which erstwhile cowboys such as Mix, Jones, Maynard, Autry, and Boyd would excel in the basic formula laid down by the dude cowboy from New Jersey.

Much of the credit for Western realism in the early years of silent film production goes to Thomas H. Ince and D. W. Griffith, both of whom produced superb little Westerns having characteristics similar to both the "A" and "B" Westerns of later years. Griffith's *The Battle of Elderbush Gulch* and *The Massacre* both vividly depict the rawness of the West, spar-

[10] Joe Franklin, *Classics of the Silent Screen* (New York, 1959), p. 120.
[11] George N. Fenin and William K. Everson, *The Western from Silents to Cinerama*, Rev. edition (New York, 1973), p. 54.

ing none of its savagery, while Ince's *The Indian Massacre* was one of the first films ever to present the Indian in a sympathetic light.

Griffith and Ince each made a number of one- and two-reel* Westerns in the pre-1920's, all of them fairly realistic regarding stories, scenery, costume, and action. Griffith's output included remarkably realistic little gems such as *The Stage Rustler, The Redman and the Child, The Goddess of Sagebrush Gulch, The Last Drop of Water, The Gold Seekers, The Twisted Trail, The Wanderer, The Sheriff's Baby, A Pueblo Legend*, and *Two Men of the Desert*. Being a master technician who possessed considerable finesse both as a director and film editor, Griffith developed to a fine art the use of panoramic shots and running inserts, both techniques adding a sense of reality to his films. Not interested in complicated plots per se, he leaned toward presenting "situations" and then directing his actors and actresses to the hilt, sapping every bit of talent they might muster. Significantly, he did not create a "cowboy star," as did Anderson, nor did he produce series Westerns. What he did accomplish was to partially create the mold out of which came the realistic Westerns of series cowboys Carey, Hart, Holt, Scott, Wayne, and confreres.

Thomas Ince, remembered today as the man who brought William S. Hart to the screen, turned out a great many Westerns and had a preference for strong plots and action scenes, as well as for telling the story of the Indian. *Across the Plains, The Heart of an Indian, The Raiders, The Lieutenant's Last Fight*, and *Custer's Last Fight* were illustrative of his films, which became guidelines for later practitioners of the art of serious Western film production.

Many pre-1920 Western films stressed realism—in fact, most. There were no cowboy heroes in white hats and gaudy clothes twirling pearl-handled six-shooters as they casually, almost contempuously, faced half a dozen degenerates "collected by the broom which swept hell." Broncho Billy Anderson, from 1908 to 1913, made the films which most closely resembled the B-Westerns of the 20's, 30's, and 40's; but even his series, as already noted, attempted to project Western realism as Anderson envisioned it to be from reading the pulp Western magazines and dime novels of the day.

Realism reigned supreme until the early 20's, when Tom Mix and cohorts caused a shift in popularity to the non-realistic, streamlined Westerns which were to predominate until the end of the genre in 1954. Dustin Farnum's *The Squaw Man* (Lasky, 1913), William Farnum's *The Spoilers* (Selig, 1914) and *Last of the Duanes* (Fox, 1918), William Duncan's *The*

---

* The term one-reel or two-reel refers to time. A reel could vary from ten to fourteen minutes; hence, a two-reeler usually ran about twenty-five minutes.

WILLIAM S. HART
Photograph from the collection of Buck Rainey.

Range Law (Selig, 1913), J. Warren Kerrigan's *The Covered Wagon* (Lasky, 1923), and George O'Brien's *The Iron Horse* (Fox, 1924), and others too numerous to mention kept stark realism in the forefront, with solid acting, good locations, strong stories, appropriate costuming, great camera work, and logical action. The cowboy was not glorified—his weaknesses many times were emphasized. He could drink, smoke, desire a woman, be a sloppy dresser and slow on the draw, ride a cayuse that was a reject from the glue factory, and he could even wind up quite dead in the final reel—something that never happened to Gene Autry, Rex Bell, or Bob Steele in all their years as cowboy heroes.

The pre-1920 years were indeed formative years. The Western movie, as a distinct form of motion picture entertainment, was born before hardly anyone knew the industry was pregnant with child. And like other infants, the Western genre struggled to survive its own blunders and oppression from outside forces. But the "hoss opera" mastered life, grew rapidly, and prospered; by 1920 it was an industry within an industry, with its own horde of stars and technicians especially trained for bringing the wild west to life on the screen each week. As the nation entered upon the peaceful decade of the 20's, Westerns—good, bad, mediocre—were rushing in to fill the need for film of the rapidly growing number of small-town theaters, much as a thundering herd of buffalo in the real wild west of yesteryear might converge upon a valley of lush green grass and plentiful water.[12]

But it is the series Western stars who are so fondly remembered by millions today and who created the image of the cowboy held by those same millions, and we will concentrate on their careers and influence in the remainder of this article. The star system developed gradually, and during the period 1915–54 a herd of "reel" cowboys rode the silver screen into the hearts of the world.

When realism in the Western "B" movie is discussed, the two names invariably mentioned are Harry Carey and William S. Hart. Carey actually pre-dated Hart by about five years, since he entered movies about 1908. However, it was not until about 1915 that he became almost exclusively a Western star. Hart entered movies as a Western star in 1914 for Triangle Studios, later moved to Artclass, and remained a Western star until his retirement in 1925 as a result of his refusal to streamline his films. Both Hart and Carey were Easterners; yet, ironically, they made more authentic cowboy movies than did their contemporaries with true Western backgrounds.

Hart brought authenticity and a kind of poetry to the Western.[13] And, although he arrived on the film scene after Anderson and Mix, and retired while Mix was still in his prime, his contributions to Westerns were original, and their influence was of greater importance than those of Anderson and Mix. As a youth, Hart had spent some time in the Dakota Territory, but his adult years had been spent as a stage actor in the East. Brought to California by his friend Thomas Ince in 1914, Hart was cast as the villain

[12] Rainey, "A Nostalgic and Capsule Review of 'Hoss Opera' Stars 1900–73," *Wild West Stars*, Vol. 4, p. 13.

[13] Joe Franklin, *Classics of the Silent Screen*, p. 203.

Tom Mix
Photograph from the collection of Buck Rainey.

29

in a couple of two-reel Westerns starring Tom Chatterton, and then was starred in *The Bargain* and *On the Night Stage*. To the surprise of everyone, including Hart, his two features proved highly popular, and he was placed under contract as star and director of his own films. The Hart era was underway. Hart is credited with being the epitome of Western film realism, and he developed to a fine art the good badman motif. His costume was an unforgettable trademark—a flat-brimmed Stetson with four dents, boots rising above the knee, and a flowing neckerchief—and most of all a strong, silent expression that indicated a man of granite will.[14]

Hart loved the West and was determined to put the truth, the poetry, and the history of the West on film. His films were raw, unglamorous, and gutsy, the costumes and livery trappings accurate, the ramshackle Western towns and their inhabitants like untouched Matthew Brady photographs, the sense of dry heat ever-present, and the clouds of dust everywhere.[15]

Hart was the embodiment of the strong, silent hero of the saddle, respectful of all womanhood and kind to children, and he loved his horse. He brought sentimentality into his films while avoiding the romanticism common to most other Westerns. Yet the drab and stark existence he brought forth in his pictures soon became a negative image of the very stereotype he had sought to destroy. Its validity was as questionable as that which it replaced.[16]

Hell's Hinges (1916) is a classic Hart Western, one of his very best. The story concerns the seduction of a minister by a local prostitute, a good badman (Hart) who falls in love with the minister's sister after being hired to run him out of town, and the destruction of the town by burning, as of Sodom of old. It was a masterpiece of realism, and as different from the formula Westerns of Roy Rogers or Reb Russell as night from day. But by 1925 the public had tired of Hart's stern-faced, uncompromising Westerns, which had become formalized in their own unique way. Rather than change his style and cater more to the public's interest in slick, fresh, escapist Westerns, Hart chose retirement after the release of his finest Western of all —*Tumbleweeds* (United Artist, 1925).

In commenting on Hart's contributions to realism and his stressing of the morality inherent in the West's history, Fenin and Everson note that:

> Life in the old West was certainly a lawless one in many communities, but the generalized concept of the shooting down of endless villains and ranchers without so much as a second glance at the corpses is very much at

[14] Ray Stuart, *Immortals of the Screen* (New York, 1965), p. 146.

[15] William K. Everson, *A Pictorial History of the Western Film* (New York, 1969), p. 40.

[16] Kalton C. Lahue, *Winners of the West: The Sagebrush Heroes of the Silent Screen* (New York, 1970), p. 148.

odds with fact. A killing was as serious a matter in the West as it was in the East, although admittedly the justice meted out was a less standardized one. . . . The Westerns of William S. Hart recognized this principle; there was no casual extermination of badmen in the Hart-Ince Pictures . . . .[17]

Hart's films made one feel as if he were actually living a part of the West's history, not merely being entertained—and his films accomplished this without resort to quasi-documentary presentation.

Harry Carey was second only to Hart as an exponent of realism, his brand being more palatable to the masses in the long run than Hart's. Like many of the early favorites who epitomized the Western hero on the screen, he was born in the East and knew nothing about "cowboying" when he made his first Western, *Bill Sharkey's Last Game*, on Staten Island in 1908 for D. W. Griffith. He became a Griffith regular and moved with him to California in 1913, when Griffith decided he would seek his fame and fortune in the film colony springing up there. Harry alternated between Westerns and straight drama.

A Griffith one-reeler produced about 1911 for busy nickelodean trade was *The Sheriff's Dilemma*, a film in which Harry plays what would be called today an anti-hero. He is an on-again, off-again sheriff who also happens to be a bit of a tippler. And one of his earliest Western successes was *The Wanderer* (1912); as a drifter, Harry saves two settlers and goes on his way, leaving them to a happy future with no knowledge of his having saved them. He was to play the part of a lovable drifter often, just as Hart many times duplicated his good badman theme.[18]

George N. Fenin and William K. Everson, in their excellent history of the Western movies, state with regard to the Westerns of the twenties:

> Only two Western stars remained in any way in the Hart tradition: Harry Carey and Buck Jones. In actual fact, Carey's taciturn characterization predates Hart's in that he was active in early Biograph Westerns for Griffith. Perhaps partly because his leathery and nonyouthful appearance so dictated, Carey avoided the "streamlined" Westerns that Maynard, Gibson, and Fred Thomson made so popular. His were always Westerns of the old school, sometimes a little slow on action, but always strong on plot, with a definite sign of Hart's influence. Carey's *Satan Town*, for example, was a very creditable lesser *Hell's Hinges*. Respect for womanhood was a staple ingredient with Carey, and in *The Prairie Pirate*, a good Carey film for Hunt Stromberg in 1925, this extended to another typical Hart plot motivation— the death of the hero's sister (she commits suicide when threatened with rape by the villain) and the tracking down of the man responsible.[19]

[17] Fenin and Everson, *The Western*, p. 10.
[18] Buck Rainey, "Reminiscences of Harry Carey," *Remember When*, No. 14 (1974), pages unnumbered.
[19] Fenin and Everson, *The Western*, p. 150.

31

HARRY CAREY
Photograph from the collection of Buck Rainey.

The authors are correct in their comparison of the films of Carey and Hart. Both played up strong, often sentimental, stories, always insisting upon realism. The moral rectitude of Carey's films was no less than that shown in those of Hart, yet he continued as a popular star, making films in the Hart mold, so to speak, long after the public had tired of Hart's screen characterizations. The difference seemed to lie in the two stars' personalities. Often likened to Will Rogers, Carey could empathize with his audience more successfully than Hart. His personal charm somehow struck a responsive chord in his audience, and people warmed to him. That wrinkled face, those kindly eyes, and the boyishly innocent smile got to people. Too, his characters were always a little more human, more flexible, than those of Hart. And by no means least, Harry Carey was a better actor than Hart. He just sort of grew on you and became a part of you, without your conscious realization of it. Other heroes came and went—Hart, Hoxie, Stewart, Acord, Maloney, Duncan, Thomson—but Carey was always there. Like mother and dad and the old home town with its familiar haunts, Carey was there to return to when the glamorous heroes had shot their wad and ridden into the sunset for the last time.

Jon Tuska, noted film historian and publisher of *Views and Reviews*, a quarterly magazine of the reproduced arts, has said:

> Harry Carey as a screen cowboy was quite dissimilar to William S. Hart. His personality was engaging with a comfortable self-sufficiency. He was incapable of Hart's moral intensity and lacked utterly Hart's penchant for sustained melodrama. Carey's natural humor and charm resulted in a characterization that, in some ways, anticipated Will Rogers.[20]

Carey left Biograph in 1915 to join Universal, where he teamed with director John Ford in a long series of "Cheyenne Harry" movies, first two-reelers and then feature Westerns. Carey was Ford's first big star, and the famed director has said "He was a great actor, and we didn't doll him up— made him sort of a bum, a saddle tramp, in a dirty blue shirt, and old vest and patched overalls . . . ."[21]

Glenn Shirley, commenting on *Straight Shooting* (1917), the first Carey-Ford full-length feature (which also featured Hoot Gibson, another Ford favorite), states:

> The William S. Hart influence is apparent, both in austerity of production and the intermingling of good and bad in both the good guys and bad guys.
>
> In these early pictures, Hart's "good badman" style even overlapped Carey's role as "Cheyenne Harry." Generally there was showmanship and polish, a more epic and grander view of man and the land, and a deliberate striving for realism and detail typical of Ford in later years.[22]

By 1919 Carey was one of Universal's hottest properties, and his salary

---

[20] Jon Tuska, "From 100 Finest Westerns: 'Straight Shooting,'" *Views and Reviews*, Vol. 4, No. 3 (Spring, 1973), p. 55.

[21] Glenn Shirley, "Harry Carey, Western Natural," *True West*, Vol. 21, No. 5 (May–June, 1974), p. 7.

[22] *Ibid.*, p. 9.

jumped to $1,250 a week. He and Ford continued as a team for another three years, with the plots continuing strong and unusual, always uncomplicated. *Marked Men* was an early version of Peter B. Kynes' "The Three Godfathers" and a Ford favorite. Carey, after 1922, worked for R-C Pictures, Steller, PDC, and Pathe, continuing to grind out exceptionally well-scripted realistic filmfare such as *The Prairie Pirate, The Man from Red Gulch, Satan Town, Silent Sanderson,* and *The Seventh Bandit.* And although his fame never matched that of Hart or the streamlined cowboys to be discussed below, his films probably presented the West and the Cowboy in a truer light than did even those of Hart.

The third major cowboy star to maintain some roots in Western realism was Charles (Buck) Jones, generally conceded to be the most popular and most beloved of all motion picture cowboys. He was the only major Western star other than Harry Carey and Randolph Scott (and maybe Bill Elliott in his later years of "semi-A" Westerns) to retain much of Hart's approach to the making of Westerns. Featuring a laconic personality, with a true love of the West and its lore, Buck's Westerns were in the middle between the extreme and gaudy showmanship of Tom Mix, Fred Thomson, Yakima Canutt, and Ken Maynard, on the one hand, and the austere, heavy plots of William S. Hart and Harry Carey on the other. His westerns—nearly all of which were superior in production values to the majority of programmer Westerns of the time—were a happy blend of action, humor, good stories, and restrained realism.

Jones was among the first to break away from the grim, poker-faced heroes continuously portrayed by Hart, and the fact that he once received more fan mail than matinee idol Clark Gable is a proper example of the wide popularity he enjoyed.[23] Jones could not bring himself to dress in tawdry uniforms or perform in a flamboyant manner, and the action scenes in his films were usually justified by the story development far more than those of Mix, which were quite often included merely to give Tom a chance to show off his fancy riding ability. But Buck could ride and fight with the best of them (a real Oklahoma cowboy, he had worked for the 101 Ranch Wild West Show and later was with the Ringling Brothers Circus as a rider), and he rarely used a double. And he could also act, a feat beyond the reach of many celluloid cowboys. Consequently, he was quite often given first-rate actresses as feminine leads and stories which had adult appeal as well as the necessary ingredients to appease the action appetite of youngsters.

Jones made about sixty Westerns for Fox studios during the 20's, after

<hr>

23 Ernest N. Corneau, *The Hall of Fame of Western Film Stars* (North Quincy, Massachusetts, 1969), p. 71.

starting his career in 1917 as a Universal stuntman and graduating to small parts in Franklyn Farnum, William Farnum, and Tom Mix Westerns in 1918 and 1919. His first starring film was *The Last Straw* in early 1920, and he worked for Fox until 1928, finally overtaking Tom Mix in popularity in the latter part of the decade. Although there was light-heartedness in the Jones films, and plenty of excitement as Buck and Silver swung into action, there was also romance and solid stories that were believable.

Buck seemed to be the epitome of masculinity, magnanimity, courageousness, and virtuousness, and he rode into the hearts of millions on his equally popular white horse "Silver," carving himself a permanent niche not only in the hearts of those who loved him but in the pages of movie history as well. The Buck Jones Rangers, a youth fan organization, alone numbered nearly five million boys at one time, and it is probably safe to say that Jones, through his exemplary life, clean films, and unusual dedication to the welfare of impressionable youth, probably did more to shape the moral fibre of adolescents than did a hundred ministers combined. It was an age of heroes, and Buck Jones came along to fulfill his destiny as truly a "heroes' hero." He made adult Westerns before there was such a differentiation in films, yet they were also "kiddie" Westerns. No other cowboy star was as successful as Buck in attracting a general audience.[24]

Movie historian Jon Tuska has said:

> The image that Buck projected on the screen for most of his career was that of the athletic, rugged, sincere, and capable all-American male. There was horse-play and honesty in his characterizations. While no drinker, he occasionally smoked. He was not restricted by the conventions of glamour which, to an extent, prompted Ken Maynard and Tom Mix to be almost incredibly clean-cut. Buck was a friendly, a warm, genuine personality, the kind of person one would immediately choose for a pal. This image was carefully constructed and went over well with audiences.[25]

For twenty years kids throughout America clip-clopped along neighborhood streets slapping their thighs while playing at being Buck astride Silver. In the sweltering heat of summer and the icy gusts of winter, loyal young fans (and older ones too) would brave the elements trudging to theaters showing the "new Buck Jones movie," never for one moment considering letting an ice storm or a heat wave deter them, even when—as was usually the case in the 20's and 30's—there was no automobile transportation. And the fondest memories of childhood for tens of thousands of de-

---

[24] Buck Rainey, *The Saga of Buck Jones* (publication pending by Western Film Collectors Association).

[25] Jon Tuska, "From the 100 Finest Westerns: Men Without Law," *Views and Reviews*, Vol. 3, No. 1 (Summer, 1971), p. 31.

pression era kids include backyard shootouts in which Buck and confreres such as Ken Maynard and Tim McCoy bested the dastardly villains who dared to usurp the forces of righteousness. Simply to say that Buck Jones was a strong moral force is an understatement of his charisma and influence.[26]

Stone of Silver Creek (Universal, 1935) is illustrative of the difference between a Jones film and a routine B-Western of the time. There was little shooting, riding, or fisticuffs until the final reel, and it was very much like Carey's *Satan Town* or Hart's *Hell's Hinges* in its austerity and evangelistic fervor. In the story, Jones is "T. William Stone," a saloon owner, who gets a half-interest in a mine when he busts two gamblers who cheated one of his saloon customers in a card game. Stone's new partner has a daughter who induces Stone to go to church. He swells the congregation by offering free drinks for church attendance. The new minister is—to quote the Film Daily Review—a regular guy, and he and Stone are rivals for the girl. The gamblers come back to Buck's saloon for a bit of revenge, and in the following fight the minister is wounded. The preacher gets the girl; Buck gets religion and one of his old girl friends who has come back to the saloon to work for him. Buck warn't no prude!

Jones became King of the Cowboys in the early 30's and remained the most popular movie cowboy until finally overtaken by the cowboy mutation, Gene Autry. At Buck's death, in 1942, he had just completed a series of "Rough Riders" films with Tim McCoy and Raymond Hatton for Monogram, a series that was both realistic and popular.

Among the other cowboys of the time, there were a few whose films stressed realism to a great extent. Jack Holt, who starred in a Zane Grey series for Paramount in the 20's, was one of the greatest Western heroes of the period, playing pretty much a no-nonsense type hero in well-budgeted films which paid close attention to Western realism. Jack's Paramount films far exceeded the attempts of other studios to film the old West as Grey dreamed it and wrote it. The emphasis in these films was on story and production values. Curiously enough, virile, steely-jawed Jack was the only cowboy hero who got by with wearing a mustache. This was a period when the mustache was symbolic of evil. Jack's career continued throughout the 30's and 40's; however, his last important Western was Columbia's *The End of the Trail* (1936), adapted from a Zane Grey story entitled "Outlaws of Palouse." Beautiful in its pathos and simplicity, and excellently directed, acted, and photographed, the film presents Holt at his dramatic best. No true Western buff could forget Jack as "Dale Brittenham," ex-Rough

[26] *Ibid.*

Rider, walking to the gallows leaving behind both the girl he loves and his best friend, who was forced to bring him to justice.[27]

Holt was one of the first to make adult Westerns. Oddly, he has been practically ignored by Western film historians, even though he was almost exclusively a Western star for a decade. But, in his day, he romped through wild western adventures and achieved greater fame and fortune than his son Tim was ever able to accomplish, even though Tim is justly hailed as one of the better actors who made Westerns. (Tim was nominated for an academy award for *The Treasure of Sierra Madre* in '48.)[28]

Minor stars Roy Stewart and Art Acord made fairly realistic Westerns, as a whole. Acord achieved considerable popularity as a Universal star in the late teens and throughout the 20's. A real, rugged Oklahoma cowboy, he preferred just the simple essentials in cowhands' duds and usually projected a rather realistic view of the cowpoke.

Roy Stewart had taken Williams S. Hart's place at Triangle in 1917 and for a decade was a cowboy star for various studios. His best and most realistic series was for Sunset Productions in the mid-20's, in a group of historical Westerns—*Buffalo Bill on the U.P. Trail, With General Custer at the Little Big Horn, With Kit Carson over the Great Divide*. His *Daniel Boone Through the Wilderness* remained quite faithful to the popular conception of the backwoods hero. Only George O'Brien in his 1936 *Daniel Boone* brought more realism to the portrayal of Boone.[29]

During the 30's, Fox and RKO Radio each produced a fine series with George O'Brien, extrovert without equal, who was for a decade one of the top luminaries in the Western film World. He brought to the genre a quality of acting and action seldom seen. At Fox, in the 20's, he had been John Ford's favorite star and had the male lead in the academy-award-winning *Sunrise* (a non-Ford film). His Fox Westerns, in particular, based mostly on Zane Grey stories, were well-made and certainly believable, even though O'Brien sometimes came on like Tom Mix or Ken Maynard in the action sequences. In keeping with his popularity, his Westerns were budgeted at around $300,000 each, as compared with $15,000 to $60,000 normally expended on B-Westerns. *Robber's Roost, The Last Trail, Thunder Mountain, Riders of the Purple Sage*, and *Last of the Duanes* certainly stand up well with the best of Hart and Carey in overall realism. But his RKO series in the late 30's consisted of the super-streamlined Westerns of the type turned out by Maynard, Steele, McCoy, Boyd, and Brown, although

[27] Bill Rainey, "The Holts," *Views and Reviews*, Vol. 5, No. 4 (Summer, 1974), p. 15.
[28] Buck Rainey, "Reminiscences of Jack Holt," *Remember When*, No. 16 (1974), pages unnumbered.
[29] Kalton Lahue, *Winners of the West*, pp. 288–89.

O'Brien's films were more polished and realistic in the sense that they were well scripted, filmed on location, well cast, and competently edited.[30]

Buster Crabbe and Randolph Scott each made some fine Westerns at Paramount in the 30's that, first of all, established them as Western stars of some importance and, secondly, were very realistic, adult Westerns, not dissimilar to those of Hart and Carey. Again, many of them were based on Zane Grey stories. Both men became major Western stars in the 40's and Scott continued making realistic Westerns right on up to the 60's. Scott was very similar to Hart, not only in looks but in mannerisms as well. His Westerns, John Wayne notwithstanding, were the most realistic Westerns produced during the 50's and he had a tremendous adult following. But his films were too adult, too realistic for the young fans, and he was not looked upon and remembered as a Saturday matinee hero in the same way as one fondly remembered the screen adventures of Wild Bill Elliott, Charles Starrett, or Allan (Rocky) Lane.

Tom Keene in the early 30's was a popular RKO Western star in a slick series of polished little B-gems. But in 1936–37 he made eight historical Westerns for Crescent that reeked with realism and were made on a larger scale than regular Western programmers. But they failed to win over the juvenile audiences, who preferred the hell-for-leather, thrill-a-second action that was provided by Maynard, Steele, Bell, Perrin, Lease, and countless others who made escapist Westerns.[31]

In the late 40's and early 50's William Elliott, formerly known as "Wild Bill," made first-class Westerns in the Hart tradition. Everson states:

> Unquestionably the most interesting aspect of this series was the realistic quality of the hero's personal conduct. While Elliott remained essentially a man of integrity, at the same time he upset many of the Boy Scout behavior codes by which most of the cowboy heroes had abided since Tom Mix's day. Foremost among these of course was a taboo on alcoholic drinking . . . Elliott drank the hard stuff whenever it seemed logical for him to do so—and in fairness to him he frequented restaurants too, something that other cowboy heroes rarely seemed to find necessary! When he played an outlaw, or a reformed outlaw, he was just that—not a lawman posing as a bad guy. . . . he could also be ruthless, selfish, and even unsportsmanlike, sufficiently sensible not to mind holding a gun on an unarmed opponent and beating the truth out of him if the circumstances warranted.[32]

---

[30] Buck Rainey, "Down Nostalgia Trails with George O'Brien," *Western Film Collector*, Vol. 2, No. 1 (March–May, 1974), *passim.*

[31] Buck Rainey, "Film Career of Tom Keene," *Western Film Collector*, Vol. 1, No. 6 (January, 1974), p. 25.

[32] Everson, *A Pictorial History of the Western*, p. 212.

Left: Hoot Gibson. Photograph from the collection of Buck Rainey.

Right: Jack Hoxie. Photograph from the collection of Buck Rainey.

Left: Fred Thomson. Photograph from the collection of Buck Rainey.

Right: Bob Steele. Photograph from the collection of Buck Rainey.

Significant, however, is the fact that in attaining his adult audience Elliott lost his juvenile one. Few cowboy stars could hold both—Jones did and, for awhile, Autry, Mix, and O'Brien did. But it was the rare star who could play to the general audience and keep them coming back for more.

If we can conveniently categorize movie cowboys into three groups—realists, semi-realists, mythics—by far the larger number would have to be classified as semi-realists. This group became dominant about 1920 and remained so until the demise of the genre in 1954, although in the last decade the mythics numbered almost as many. As the term implies, semi-realist Westerns had both elements of realism and escapism in them, with the escapist elements dominant.

Without question, the greatest of all semi-realists, and many believe the greatest of all Western stars ever, was Tom Mix—the embodiment of the world's yearning for a bigger-than-life hero. Tom was for real, in spite of exaggerated studio ballyhoo as to his exploits. He was a real cowpoke and lawman in Oklahoma in the early 1900's (although he was born in Pennsylvania in 1880), bartender in Oklahoma City, a rider for the Miller Brothers 101 Wild West Show, the Wildman Wild West Show, and the Will Dickey Circle D Wild West Show, and a genuine soldier of fortune.

Tom's first big break came in 1909, when, hired by the Selig Company as a supporting actor, he was featured in a "broncho busting" sequence in *Ranch Life in the Great Southwest*. The one-reeler was advertised as "The greatest western picture ever put before the public." It was probably one of the first filmed sequences of rodeo events, and was filmed near Dewey, Oklahoma. Tom first was featured as a regular in a two-reeler entitled *The Range Rider*, filmed in Missouri. After that, about half a dozen Selig shorts followed, including *An Indian Wife's Devotion*, *Up San Juan Hill*, and *The Millionaire Cowboy*.[33]

Tom became a popular star at Selig, performing feats that not even stuntmen like Dave Sharpe would perform today without considerable thought and planning. Sometimes things happened that were not in the scripts, such as the time in 1910, while filming a jungle thriller titled *Back to the Primitive*, that Tom barehandedly wrestled a leopard that had attacked the heroine Kathlyn Williams.

By 1916 Mix had become Selig's top western star, and his brand of Westerns was catching on, although he was still several years away from overtaking Hart in popularity. Tom was still making only one- and two-reelers. Author Paul Mix states:

> Tom's screen personality was well established by this time and he defi-

[33] Paul E. Mix, *The Life and Legend of Tom Mix* (New York, 1972), pp. 76–78.

nitely wanted his pictures to be accepted as a form of proper family entertainment. He was proud that any mother could take her child to see a Tom
Mix movie. He boasted that he never drank or smoked while on the screen.
Tom was always the good guy—never the neurotic anti-hero torn between
good and evil. Tom usually helped a girl in distress and won her heart in the
end. Tom didn't really prefer to kiss the horse instead of the girl! Occasionally, the movie ended with Tom kissing the girl, but more often, they merely
held hands and smiled affectionately at each other. Tom was rough on villains,
although he seldom killed one in a movie. He roped plenty of them and
defeated many in a good old-fashioned fist fight. He would of course use his
gun to blast the villain's gun out of his hands.[34]

Mix established a formula for the sexless Western that lasted into the
1950's when the new realism returned it a little in films like *High Noon* and
Shane. Cowboys from Hoot Gibson and Ken Maynard to Roy Rogers and
Gene Autry were all heir to the Mix flirt-and-run legacy, and these Mixian
heroes, to the glee of youngsters who bought comic books and cap guns
embossed with their names, were more infatuated with horses and pearl-
handled revolvers than with their leading ladies.[35]

In 1917 Tom was induced by William Fox to come to work for him,
and it was at Fox that Tom made his greatest Westerns. By 1920 he had
overtaken Hart in popularity, and he remained the most popular screen
cowboy until the advent of sound.

Tom was not a Western "purist." He did on the screen what he knew
best how to do. He rode hard, performing daredevil stunts calculated to
keep the audience on the edge of their seats.[36]

Gradually a deliberate kind of "circus" format was created for the Mix
films. They were full of fights and chases, essentially realistic in such details
as costuming and locations, but emphatically escapist in dramatic terms.
No serious issues were ever raised by the Mix plots, and nobody was expected to take them too seriously. As their popularity increased, their story-
lines tended to become even less realistic.[37]

Mix was everything Hart was not. He wore a frilly cowboy suit and
flamboyant ten-gallon hat which made Hart's simple leather trousers seem
ragged in comparison. Hart would cinematically shoot to kill, as it was
really done in the West, but Mix only grazed the bad guys, nicked the
tops of their heads so they "fainted" long enough to bring them in for a fair
trial.[38] Mix being a tough-as-nails westerner himself, his performance nat-

---

[34] *Ibid.*, pp. 87–88.

[35] David Carroll, *The Matinee Idols* (New York, 1972), p. 113.

[36] Mix, *The Life and Legend of Tom Mix*, p. 94.

[37] Everson, *A Pictorial History of the Western Film*, p. 66.

[38] Carroll, *The Matinee Idols*, p. 110.

urally carried authority, but otherwise his films were breezy, cheerful, streamlined, aimed at a wide audience, careful not to contain elements that might disturb children, and free of serious romantic entanglements.[39]

When a director would set up a scene, Tom would often joke about his own acting ability asking the director, "Do you want expression number one, two, or three?" Tom created the character of the fun-loving loner who was always a clear-minded and right-livin' cow puncher, always tryin' to do the right thing because it was the right thing to do.[40]

Above all, Tom Mix and Tony represented the finest in vicarious thrills and escapist entertainment. The cowboy, in his broadbrimmed white Stetson hat, and the well-groomed, white-stockinged chestnut horse rode together to fame and fortune. The fancy duds and hand-carved boots were never intended to represent the working clothes of the average cowboy—neither were the intricate stunts intended to represent the everyday happenings in the life of a cowboy. The costume and stunts exaggerated the adventure and romance of the "Old West" and the audience loved every minute of it.[41]

After Hart and Ford, Tom Mix unquestionably was the greatest single influence on the Western in its formative years. "Where Hart had instilled realism in the Western and John Ford was to provide its poetry, Mix's greatest contribution to the genre was showmanship. He turned the Western into an entertainment industry, created many of the traditions of the action western, and achieved a popularity and box-office value equaled by no other star."[42] Most important of all, he gave the Western to the kids and the young at heart.

Ken Maynard, too, was one of the greatest movie cowboys ever to sit in a saddle. And, like his friend Tom, Ken was something of a ladies' man, heavy drinker, and hell raiser off the screen. He had traveled with a number of wild west shows and with Ringling Brothers before entering movies in the mid-20's. He was also, at one time, the world's champion trick rider. He tended to go overboard on trick riding and elaborate stunting, and rooftop chases were his specialty. Millions thrilled at the exploits of Ken and his horse Tarzan in both silent and sound features, and he earned and squandered several million dollars during his 20-year career as a horse opera star.

Red Raiders (First National, 1927) is a particularly illuminating

[39] Franklin, *Classics of the Silent Screen*, p. 204.

[40] Stewart Roberts, "Tom Mix, The Tinsel Cowboy," *Westerner*, Vol. 4, No. 4 (July–August, 1972), p. 12.

[41] Mix, *The Life and Legend of Tom Mix*, pp. 92, 98.

[42] Jeavons and Parkinson, *A Pictorial History of Westerns*, p. 97.

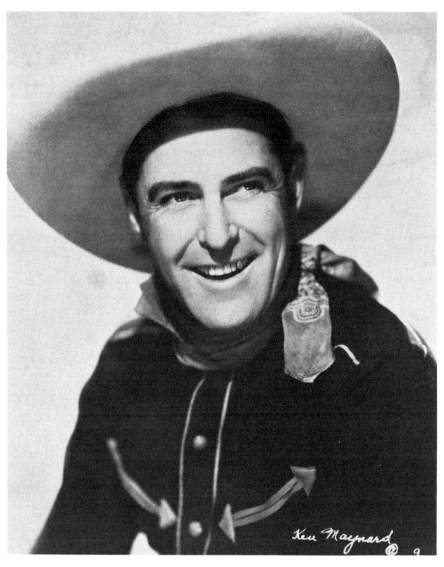

KEN MAYNARD
Photograph from the collection of Buck Rainey.

example of the really slick and well-made Westerns of the 20's. Aside from consideration of the stars involved, it is quite as big a picture as *Stagecoach* and other epics. The action is staged on a massive scale, and the entire picture seems dedicated to the proposition that action matters far more than plot.[43] Another film, *Senior Daredevil* (First National, 1926), had for its

[43] Fenin and Everson, *The Western from Silents to Cinerama*, p. 155.

climax a spectacular sequence of Maynard racing a convoy of wagons loaded with food to a town starved and besieged by villains. Several critics compared this sequence with the chariot race in *Ben Hur* for the excitement it generated.[44]

In *Fiddlin' Buckaroo* and *Strawberry Roan* (both Universal, 1933) Ken introduced musical instruments and complexly staged musical numbers. This, the musical Western, was perhaps an inevitable development following the introduction of sound and dialogue. It helped renew the popularity of the Western, and, in Ken's pictures at least, was never allowed to interfere with the action.[45] However, the day came when Ken made the mistake of allowing a young dude by the name of Gene Autry to sing a couple of numbers in his *In Old Santa Fe* (Mascot, 1934). The Western was never the same again.

Ken had charm and a personality that endeared him to millions of people of all ages and classes. His horse Tarzan was a sensitive, highly intelligent creature, whose own personality complemented that of Ken. Together, Ken and Tarzan "allowed theatre-goers to pretend, to take part in a fantasy far-removed from the bleak realities of the Depression and the frightful rejection of the faith of the frontier which the circumstances of the modern world imposed upon them."[46]

A name synonymous with cowboy movies is that of Hoot Gibson, clown prince of horse operas for twenty-five years. Hoot dared to be human—and discovered a great secret. Audiences like human beings. They could be thrilled to death when Bill Hart blew into a saloon full of bad men and shot out all the lights. Just the same, they knew that when the lights went on again, steel-eyed Hart would be standing there with his pistols smoking and the floor would need a dozen janitors to sweep out the corpses. With Hoot you never could tell. He might well be the one on the floor, and audiences worried about him. His horse could throw him twenty feet. His gun would jam. His pack mule paid him "no never'mine," and even the heroine blackened his eye.[47]

Hoot had won the all-around cowboy championship at age seventeen at Pendleton, Oregon, and was appearing in Universal two-reelers in 1917. By 1920 he was ready for stardom and was given the lead in *Action*, directed by his buddy John Ford. The public liked him. The action in his films was

[44] *Ibid.*

[45] Jon Tuska, "In Retrospect: Ken Maynard," *Views and Reviews*, Vol. 1, No. 1 (Summer, 1969), p. 17.

[46] Jon Tuska, "In Retrospect: Ken Maynard," Part 3, *Views and Reviews*, Vol. 1, No. 3 (Winter, 1970), p. 39.

[47] Joel McCrea, "Hoot Gibson, Even the Heroine Blackened his Eye," *Western Stars*, Vol. 1, No. 5 (Spring, 1950), p. 75.

usually at a frenzied pace, the comedy refreshing. Strangely, Hoot's films appealed as much to mommy and daddy as to junior. Probably more. By 1925 Hoot was earning $14,000 a week, just $3,000 less than the salary commanded by Mix. Hoot remained a top star throughout the 20's, playing usually a clowning, fumbling, all-thumbs hero, but during the 30's his popularity fell off considerably, and he was relegated to minor star status.[48]

Fred Thomson's popularity transcended a following by Western fans alone. Next to Mix he was the most successful cowboy star of the 20's, earning nearly $2.5 million in a career that lasted but six years. His films were very much in the mold of Mix and Maynard as far as flamboyant action, and he probably was a better athlete than either.[49]

Thomson's movies were streamlined and showy, specialized in action for its own sake, and presented a customary superficial and glamorized picture of the West. His clothing had a dude-like appearance too, much as Mix's did. But Thomson himself was far from a phony; he had a pleasant personality and was a fine athlete. Most of the trick stunts in his films he performed without a double. And his effortless acrobatics were often introduced in the interests of comedy.[50] Thomson had been a minister; and therefore he stressed strong moral values, avoided sex and undue violence, intended his films to be a good influence on youth as well as entertaining them, and often included subplots that he felt would be meaningful to youngsters.[51] In 1928 it seemed that Thomson and his handsome white horse Silver King might ride on forever, conquering everything in their paths, but he was taken ill and died on Christmas day.[52]

Bob Steele has to be rated as one of the top cowboy stars of all time, including both the silent and sound era. Few Westerns stars have had careers as long as that of the "little giant of Westerns," whose activities have encompassed silents, sound, and television. It would take several pages just to list the titles of Steele's many films during the past fifty years. His first starring Western was *The Mojave Kid* (FBO, 1927), but he had been in movies for five years then. Although rather short in height for a cowboy star, he proved that he could handle all the action the role called for, whether it was stunt riding or the fist fights for which he became so well

[48] Rainey, "A Nostalgic and Capsule Review of 'Hoss Opera' Stars, 1900–73," Part II, *Wild West Stars*, pp. 12–13.

[49] Buck Rainey, "Fred Thomson, Great But Forgotten Hero," *Western Film Collector*, Vol. 1, No. 3 (July, 1973), pp. 5–6.

[50] Franklin, *Classics of the Silent Screen*, p. 232.

[51] Everson, *A Pictorial History of the Western*, p. 81.

[52] Rainey, "Fred Thomson, Great But Forgotten Hero," *Western Film Collector*, Vol. 1, No. 3 (July, 1973), p. 13.

known.[53] Bob's Westerns were mostly straightforward, assembly-line affairs, but they were always entertaining, and Steele was a fine, believable actor. As did most of the other "slick" stars, Bob sometimes made surprisingly realistic films, e.g., *Drifting Sands* (1928), *Near the Trail's End* (1930), *The Land of Missing Men* (1930), *The Man from Hell's Edges* (1932), *Smoky Smith* (1934), and *Wildfire* (1945). Bob shared "most handsome" honors with Rex Bell, Tim Holt, and Charles Starrett, and romance was usually included in his roles. However, it was never allowed to mire the action.

Tim McCoy was one of the most authentic cowboys ever to appear in Westerns. As a boy he worked on cattle ranches in Wyoming and became an authority on Indian sign language. After serving in World War I, he became an aid to General Scott, Indian fighter of the late nineteenth century and later army chief of staff. He was ranked by General Scott as one of the best Indian sign talkers in the United States Army.[54]

McCoy presented a strong, handsome figure, with virile qualities that made him an appealing star. His first series, at MGM in 1927–28, was a very realistic, high-budgeted group of historical Westerns featuring authentic Indians and locales. And Tim dressed in what he felt was the proper attire of the period.[55] The films played the MGM circuit of plush theaters, but, because the action content was sometimes slow-paced, the juvenile audience did not take to him as they did to Mix, Jones, and Maynard.

There was really no other cowboy star like McCoy in personality and manner. Throughout his long, illustrious career he maintained a military aloofness that set him apart from his contemporaries. Wisps of the same personality were to be found in Bill Cody and William Boyd, yet they did not command the awed respect that McCoy invariably did. Only Jack Holt came close to demonstrating the same qualities that set McCoy apart, and an icy stare from either man was apt to melt even the most courageous soul.[56]

McCoy, whether or not you realized it as a popcorn-munching kid, was different. You really did not expect, if you will but think back, to see him crawl up on a bucking bronc "a la Gibson or Mix" to engage in fantastic riding stunts such as those performed by Kermit or Ken Maynard or Yakima Canutt, or to give-and-take in a face-to-face slugfest with half a

[53] Powell Craig, "We Ride the Range with Daredevil Bob Steele," *Wild West Stars*, Vol. 2, No. 6, p. 2.

[54] McClure and Jones, *Heroes, Heavies and Sagebrush*, p. 69.

[55] Glenn Shirley, "Colonel Tim McCoy—Army Man, Movie Star," *Golden West*, Vol. 10, No. 9 (August, 1974), p. 44.

[56] Buck Rainey, "Reminiscences of Tim McCoy," *Remember When*, No. 15 (1974), pages unnumbered.

dozen villains in every picture. Somehow it wasn't expected of this straight-backed, coldly reserved, glove-wearing hero with the distinguishing black suit and wide-brimmed white stetson. It was expected, rather, that he would draw his pearl-handled pistol with the speed of greased lightning (Tim was acknowledged as the fastest draw of the movie cowboys), foil the attempts of all who would despoil and bring dishonor to the range, win the hand of the heroine if he so pleased, and bring a quality of acting and charm to the screen not usually seen in Westerns of the "B" category. And this he did with gusto in a starring career that lasted sixteen years.[57]

Johnny Mack Brown, ex-football great from Alabama, began his screen career in 1928 at MGM and played opposite such lovelies as Greta Garbo, Norma Shearer, and Joan Crawford before being co-starred along with Wallace Beery in the super production of *Billy the Kid*. After many dramatic roles, Johnny eventually drifted into Westerns in the early 30's and remained in the genre for twenty years. He was a very believable Western ace, possessing all the attributes necessary for success as a cowboy (riding ability, physique, good looks, athletic prowess) and with the added asset of being an exceptionally good actor. He was a fixture at Universal and Monogram from 1939 to 1953 and consistently made fine, compact little formula Westerns that never failed to entertain. "Always the good guy or an undercover agent from start to finish, there was little chance of casting this Southern gentleman as anything else. Johnny just exuded those wholesome qualities that make a family hero, which worked to his advantage by attracting not only the kids as fans, but many of their parents as well."[58]

Charles Starrett and John Wayne, too, came to the screen via their football heroics. Starrett, from 1935 to 1952, had the longest reign for any cowboy star at a single studio. Although he is best remembered today for the sixty-five mythic Durango Kid films he starred in, his best films were the ones made from 1937 to 1945. Starrett was extremely handsome, well built, a good actor, and highly personable.[59] Wayne, still active today, starred in a 1932 series of B-Westerns for Warner Brothers after spending several years as a supporting actor. In 1933 he went to work for Lonestar Pictures, later working for Monogram, Mascot, and Republic, where he eventually became a member of the highly popular Three Mesquiteer trio, along with Ray Corrigan and Max Terhune. Wayne was a believable cowboy and handled action very well. In fact, he and Yakima Canutt developed

---

[57] *Ibid.*

[58] Kalton C. Lahue, *Riders of the Range* (New York, 1973), p. 67.

[59] John Stoginski, "Charles Starrett, the Gallant Defender," *Western Film Collector*, Vol. 1, No. 2 (May, 1973), p. 23.

the science of screen fighting while working together in early sound features. After *Stagecoach* (1939) and the completion of his Three Mesquiteer contract, Wayne graduated to "A" films and has continued to turn out first-class Westerns. Some of them, like *The Man Who Shot Liberty Valance*, are reminiscent of his great Westerns at Lonestar.

Many outstanding athletes, whether or not they knew one end of a cow from the other, have parlayed athletic prowess into cowboy stardom in the flickers. For example, forty years ago a handsome young athlete could be seen charging onto the screen as a rip-snortin', hell-bent-for leather cowboy in the tradition laid down by Tom Mix. The picture was *Border Warfare*, and the star was Reb Russell, an All-American from Kansas that Knute Rockne called "the greatest fullback I ever saw." Reb was a great athlete and looked like a million dollars on his white gelding "Rebel" in action sequences. But in dialogue or romantic interludes, he sounded and looked like twenty-five cents. As Reb laughingly says, "I needed two expressions as a cowboy hero—constipation and relief." But his films, like other independent Westerns of that era, made money. Whereas Paramount might take more of the proceeds of, say, a Mae West film as rental, a theater manager could book Reb Russell Westerns for a weekend, pay a flat rental of $25, pack his theater, and pocket nearly all the proceeds.[60]

About the time Russell was making his series, another athlete, Kermit Maynard (brother of Ken), was signed by Ambassador pictures to star in a series of outdoor action films. Kermit had won world championships for both trick and fancy riding and had starred earlier in a silent series (1927) after coming to Hollywood as a football hero.[61]

One of the greatest athletes to grace a saddle was Buster Crabbe, the swimming ace from Hawaii, who, before the end of 1933, had won a gold medal for the 400-meter free-style event in the 1932 Olympic meet and set a dozen world records in swimming. Forty years later he was still setting world records in the "senior citizen" competition. During the 30's he starred in some very realistic Zane Grey Westerns, but he is primarily remembered for his cheapie Westerns (in many of them playing a white-washed "Billy the Kid turned hero") with Al St. John from 1941 through 1946 at PRC Studios and as the King of the Sound Serials (*Flash Gordon, Tarzan the Fearless, Buck Rogers, Red Barry, Flash Gordon Conquers the Universe, King of the Congo*, etc.). As the last of the great serial stars and

[60] Buck Rainey, "Reb Russell, His Interlude as Western Star," *Filmograph*, Vol. 3, No. 3, p. 36.

[61] Nick Williams, "Kermit Maynard as Western Star and Stunt Man," *Filmograph*, Vol. 2, No. 1, pp. 25–26.

one of few remaining B-Western stars of the Golden Age of the Movies, he is once again a popular figure at Western and serial film festivals.[62]

Yakima Canutt, a star in the 20's and later a character actor, stuntman, and second unit director, was probably the greatest athlete of all. Before entering movies he was a champion of many events in the rodeo world, and some of his wild Westerns (e.g., *The Devil Horse*, 1926) even put Tom Mix to shame. Art Acord and Jack Hoxie, two of Universal's top cowboys in the silent period, were also rodeo champs. Acord was an authentic Oklahoma cowboy and rodeo performer who entered movies about 1909 and became extremely popular as a Western lead. His drinking caused Universal to fire him a number of times—popularity caused the studio to rehire him, but he could never kick the drinking habit. Hoxie was a big, amiable oaf, whose large frame made him seem clumsy afoot and whose expression suggested that his mind was a complete blank except when the director told him to pantomime a specific emotion. But on a horse, he was something else again, an expert rider and stunter.[63]

Tom Tyler, in 1928, established a new world's weight lifting record in the Senior Heavyweight class by lifting a total of 760 pounds. This record would remain unbroken for nearly fourteen years.[64]

George O'Brien was light-heavyweight boxing champion of the Pacific Fleet during World War I. Bob Steele, William Russell, and William Duncan were also noted as boxers. Many of the early Western stars were authentic rodeo and wild west show performers, for example, Buck Jones, Ken and Kermit Maynard, Fred Burns, Bud Osborne, Neal Hart, Bill Cody, Buffalo Bill, Jr., Pee Wee Holmes, Fred Humes, Don Coleman, Bob Custer, Ted Wells, Sunset Carson, Bill Patton, and Buddy Roosevelt. Their natural ruggedness, aided by scriptwriters, directors, and cameramen, created in the minds of millions the mythic cowboy who was virtuous to a fault, physically perfect, handsome, and a super athlete. Although not necessarily rodeo or wild west performers, other real cowboys became screen cowboys too—Wally Wales, Pete Morrison, Edmund Cobb, William Fairbanks, and Al Hoxie.

Other semi-realist cinematic cowboys in the 20's and early 30's, although not real life cowboys or professional athletes, were Jack Perrin, Leo Maloney, William Desmond, Rex Bell, Rex Lease, Lane Chandler, Franklyn Farnum, Wallace MacDonald, and Guinn (Big Boy) Williams,

---

[62] Buck Rainey, "The Film Career of Buster Crabbe," *Western Film Collector*, Vol. 2, No. 3 (July, 1974), *passim*.

[63] Everson, *A Pictorial History of the Western*, p. 83.

[64] Glenn Shirley, "Cowboy Strongman—Tom Tyler," *Old West*, Vol. II, No. 2 (Winter, 1974), p. 12.

each attaining a sizeable following of fans. In the late 30's came Tim Holt, whose Western series at RKO held to high standards until the very end of B-Western production in 1954. Tim projected the nice, clean-cut, handsome young cowboy that most of us like to think existed. He was the epitome of what Western movie fans wanted their heroes to be. He was real. When a drunken Gene Autry fell off his horse at the Fort Worth Colliseum Rodeo, landing on his guitar and smashing it to bits, Tim, appearing in the same show, looked on sadly. He was sorry for the embarrassed actor, but even sadder to see the hurt look on all the young faces in the bleachers. Tim Holt never disappointed his fans.[65]

Don (Red) Barry was another popular cowboy who combined dramatic roles with Westerns and whose career has lasted to the present. Coming to the screen as "Red Ryder" in Republic's 1940 serial *The Adventures of Red Ryder*, Barry's Westerns were mostly tautly-wrought little gems that often stressed the dramatic rather than physical conflicts in the stories.[66] His husky voice set him apart from other Western stars, as did his stature; but what he lacked in size was more than compensated by his intestinal fortitude. Like Bob Steele, Don "Red" Barry was one of the best scrappers to appear in the B-Westerns.[67]

One cowboy star who simply can't be passed over without comment is William Boyd, the non-athletic, dramatic actor who was a Cecil B. deMille protégé for years before being launched into the Hopalong Cassidy Westerns in 1935. A quite distinguished figure, usually dressed in black and riding a snow-white horse called Topper, Boyd projected as soft-spoken and retiring, presenting more the father figure than the hard-hitting, rough-fighting stereotype Western hero—on some occasions he even came across as a genuine gentleman.[68] You might say he was the "Ben Cartwright" of the pre-television era. His portrayal won instant approval from audiences and launched Boyd on a series that was to span thirteen years and produce sixty-six titles. Boyd's distinct screen personality was one of the most pleasing ever presented to viewers, and a single flash of his smile and a quick burst of his hearty laughter alone were worth the price of admission to one of his films. The Cassidy films were usually filmed on location in more picturesque areas than the minor studios used, primarily because a good deal more money and time were spent on their production; they had well-written scripts and relatively long running times.[69]

---

[65] Bill Rainey, "The Holts," *Views and Reviews*, Vol. 5, No. 4 (Summer, 1974), p. 18.
[66] Alan G. Barbour, *A Thousand and One Delights* (New York, 1971), p. 121.
[67] Lahue, *Riders of the Range*, p. 51.
[68] *Ibid.*, p. 59.
[69] Alan G. Barbour, *The Thrill of it All* (New York, 1971), p. 47.

Robert Livingston, Rod Cameron, Dave O'Brien, Russell Hayden, Bill Elliott, Ray Corrigan, and Allan (Rocky) Lane all made Westerns that were predictable, and the heroes they played were above reproach. You could always count on their keeping the cowboy's reputation untarnished, as clean as the driven snow. And speaking of snow, although there was no basis for it in the real West, the color white played an important part in the Westerns of the 30's and early 40's. The trend to white hats was led by such stars as Starrett, Wayne, Livingston, Maynard, Jones, McCoy, Bob Allen, Tex Ritter, and Bob Baker. White horses were introduced by Jones (Silver), Maynard (Tarzan), Boyd (Topper), Ballew (Sheik), Starrett (Raider), Russell (Rebel), Perrin (Starlight), Scott (White Dust), Ritter (White Flash), and Thomson (Silver King). Pearl-handled guns were used by a number of stars. The traditional symbol of purity in the Western film had completed the flow from Stetson and revolver handle to "old faithful." Not until milkiness had been overdone could an off-white charger again achieve status.[70]

The 30's, especially, were a veritable heaven for those millions who loved the escapist adventures of innumerable sagebrush cavaliers who galloped inexorably through film after film filled with exploding six-shooters, bone-crunching fist fights, and unbelievable stuntwork, but which were inefficaciously realistic.

Mythicism, of course, made its way into the Western film from the very beginning. Hart, Carey, Anderson, Jack Holt, and a few others fought it hard, while Jones, O'Brien, and Roy Stewart, among others, tolerated it in reasonable doses only. Tom Mix, Maynard, McCoy, Gibson, and other "streamlined" cowboys took larger doses, while keeping their feet in the stirrups of semi-realism.

But sound brought music to the Western genre, and with the introduction of the singing cowboy the essence of reality (and any pretense of such) disappeared from the screen.[71]

Gene Autry was a singer of country music on a Chicago radio station in 1933 when Nat Levine of Mascot Pictures met him. Although Autry was not much to look at physically, Levine detected an elusive quality about him that he thought might be worth an investment. Ken Maynard was "acting up," Westerns were in a slump, and Nat was looking for something "fresh." Thus Gene Autry entered the Hollywood scene. It took a year of tutoring in acting and horsemanship (Reb Russell helped him learn to ride and found a gentle horse for him in the form of "Champion") before the

[70] Raymond Stedman, *The Serials* (Norman, 1971), p. 115.
[71] Lahue, *Riders of the Range*, p. 9.

studio dared turn him loose on the screen in a cliffhanger entitled *Phantom Empire*, a bizarre science-fiction Western. The rest is screen history.[72]

The remarkable thing about the Autry Westerns is how quickly they, and Autry, improved and acquired a definite style of their own. Autry never aspired to the acting standards of a Buck Jones, but, on the other hand, his scripts seldom required it. Warmth and geniality were enough. His films were given modern trappings (cars, airplanes, radio stations) and plots quite often touched on contemporary politics, big business, and social problems.[73] The sandy-haired, blue-eyed, gum-chewing vocalist soon became the top box office star of his field. Personal appearances in rodeos and a string of hit records broadened his national following. With his ever-increasing income, he built a vast financial empire that ranged from oil wells to radio stations to a major-league baseball team. By 1950 his holdings were estimated at $4–7 million. By 1970 his worth was figured at over $100 million.[74]

While it's true that Gene left much to be desired as an actor, was only a marginal action-adventure performer, and but a fair musician, he managed to combine these qualities in a unique package that spelled cash and plenty of it wherever he appeared.[75] He adopted what he called his cowboy's code. In ninety-three movies, from 1934 to 1953, he never shot first, hit first, hit a smaller man, took a drink, or smoked. He never took unfair advantage of anyone, never broke his word, rarely kissed a leading lady.[76] And most other cowboys followed his code, too.

Although Autry's films were entertaining and immensely popular, the mythic content completely obliterated realism. For example, *Strawberry Roan* (Columbia, 1948) opens with the Autry singers and stooges performing the theme song, with full orchestral accompaniment, while stringing a fence. And in *Mexicali Rose* (Republic, 1939), when villain Noah Beery's recording of the title song is broken, Autry takes over and continues the song, a full orchestra accompanying him right out there on the prairie with the banditos forming a male chorus![77]

Gene's success brought forth many imitators, and the musical range was soon grazed to capacity. No one matched Gene's success, although Roy Rogers came close and, like Gene, became a millionaire many times over. Rogers had a likable personality, but could not match the charisma of

[72] Gene Fernett, *Next Time Drive off the Cliff*, Collector's Edition (Cocoa, Florida, 1968), pp. 80–82.

[73] Everson, *A Pictorial History of the Western*, p. 147.

[74] David Zinman, *Saturday Afternoon at the Bijou* (New York, 1973), p. 108.

[75] Lahue, *Riders of the Range*, p. 31.

[76] Zinman, *Saturday Afternoon at the Bijou*, p. 111.

[77] Jon Tuska, "The Vanishing Legion, Continued," *Views and Reviews*, Vol. 4, Issue 2 (Winter, 1972), p. 43.

Autry. Rogers did not star in his first Western, *Under Western Stars*, until 1938, four years after Autry's initial starring vehicle, *Tumbling Tumbleweeds*, shook the Western film world. The first Autry imitators were Dick Foran, Tex Ritter, and Smith Ballew. Ritter was the most successful singing cowboy after Autry and Rogers and was an authentic Texan, although without any cowboy background. Ballew had the best voice of them all and was also a Texan. His background was in music, and during the late 20's and early 30's he was a very popular band leader and vocalist. Foran was probably the most competent actor-singer and went on to become a very successful dramatic actor after his stint as a singing cowboy. Fred Scott, George Houston, James Newill, Jimmy Wakely, Ray Whitley, Eddie Dean, John King, Bill (Cowboy Rambler) Boyd, Art Davis, Art Jarrett, Monte Hale, Kirby Grant, and Jack Randall all found a measure of fame and fortune in musical Westerns. Only two singing cowboys were anything near to being real cowboys before strapping on a guitar and riding Hollywood's cinematic trails—Bob Baker and Rex Allen. Both hailed from Arizona and Baker, particularly, had been a working cowboy and rodeo performer. Allen had grown up on a ranch and so knew something about cowboy life. Baker's career was short, although he was handsome, had a better voice than Rogers or Autry, was rugged, and turned out a series of well-made Westerns. Bad handling by his studio, Universal, was the primary cause. Allen, who got into films only five years before the termination of series Westerns, is still active today as an entertainer on television, on the rodeo and state fair circuit, as a recording artist, and in Walt Disney nature films.

Any concern for realism was thrown out the window with the coming of the crooners and pluckers, but the musical Western was not the only bastardization of the West. In the late 40's production standards slipped, as costs rose and the market for B-Westerns shrank. Charles Starrett, a good actor who deserved better, was foisted on audiences as "The Durango Kid," a masked fighter for justice, in a series of cheaply made pictures. But the kids ate it up, and the series continued profitably for nearly ten years. Even earlier, in 1938, "The Lone Ranger" had made his appearance. "The Cisco Kid" dated back to the 20's, and in the 40's was portrayed by Cesar Romero, Duncan Renaldo, and Gilbert Roland. Renaldo—a former member of the Three Mesquiteers—was most successful in the role, especially on television. Zorro, too, had a long screen history. "The Avenger," "The Eagle," and other masked hero mutations appeared, and the heroines even got in the act as super women behind masks. Then came the whip crackers—Whip Wilson and Lash LaRue. It was more than the genre could stand. And so the B-Western died in 1954, after putting up a heroic struggle against the onslaught of television and the closing of small theaters across the country.

In its final years, 1946–54, the quality of the average B-Western reflected the illness that had beset the industry. The genre died a peaceful death with the conclusion of a short-lived series starring Wayne Morris (previously unassociated with Westerns), for Allied Artists, and the completion of the last serial ever made, Columbia's *Perils of the Wilderness* (1956), starring Dennis Moore, long a member of the B-Western fraternity of featured players. Of course B-Westerns have continued to be made on a non-series basis (some of them starring or featuring reel/real cowboys such as Buster Crabbe, Bob Steele, and Donald Barry), but the old fashioned shoot-em-ups that provided yesteryear's thrills and generated a mythical conception of the cowboy shared by millions throughout the world are gone, evidently forever.

I wonder how many a graying man today sits with pipe and newspaper in a lounging chair before a television set watching mediocre fare and longing to see once again the cinematic cowboy heroes of yesterday's Saturdays dashing across the prairie on our favorite steeds in pursuit of arch villains such as Stanford Jolley, George Chesebro, or Charles King? I suspect that large numbers would pay handsomely for the privilege, even though they can catch a different type of mythic Western drama on the tube. The reel cowboys of B-films left a great legacy to millions upon millions of young boys. They left us a dream—a dream that we could conveniently tuck away in our minds and enjoy whenever we wished. And in the dead of winter, as I sit comfortably gazing into the burning logs of a fireplace, with the howling wind outside providing an eerie, chilling tune as snow is driven relentlessly against the windows, I dream my dreams—for a few minutes freed from the frustrations and worries of a job, children, the world.

I help my hero to escape death at the hands of assorted villains, dash furiously down mountain trails with him in a hundred thrill-packed adventures, empathize with him as he romances his way through never-to-be-forgotten features. I envy him in those oft-recalled love scenes with heroines who captured my heart forty years ago, and I inwardly chuckle at the antics of my hero and his horse when they decide to clown around.

After tamping fresh tobacco into my pipe, I reach for the coffee pot to refill a now empty cup, light the pipe, and gaze at the dying flame of the match against a backdrop of pine logs sputtering and flickering in the fireplace. Then I drift again into dreams of long-past Saturdays from the Age of Innocence.

And so the dreams continue, year after year, decade after decade . . . . The logs burn low, the flames flicker into an abyss of darkness, the chill creeps in, and, suddenly, reality in all its harshness is thrust upon me—and I worry about the kids, the job, the economy, my health. But the dreams will return—dreams of things that can never be again—and how wonderful it is to have a brief respite from the real world and to have had a boyhood filled with heroes such as Buck Jones, Bob Steele, and Hoot Gibson. They "done themselves proud," providing the best entertainment ever given a youngster and teaching simple moral lessons that would sustain a world. So what if the image projected was somewhat different from that of the typical real-life cowboy? Deep down we knew it was fantasy, even as kids.

THE VIRGINIAN
by
Charles M. Russell
Photograph courtesy of the Amon Carter Museum of Western Art, Fort Worth, Texas.

The Pistol Packin' Cowboy

BY PHILIP D. JORDAN

How WELL A COWBOY COULD SHOOT is a matter of conjecture. If he aimed and killed, he was considered a good shot. If he wounded his victim, he was right handy. If he missed and was seared by return fire, he was put down as less than tolerable. If he was slain, he was dead, and there was not much use wasting time talking about his lightning draw. The best way to send an ugly, no-account enemy cantering to hell was to dry-gulch him from a safe distance with a Winchester, or slip up close and pistol him through the eye of his belly button. A heavy slug might then continue through the body to shatter the spine. In such a case, there was little need for a doctor, whether Doc John Henry Holliday (who was a dentist) or some available veterinarian.[1]

The average wrangler, busy with range chores, round-ups, and the rigors of the long drive, was no professional gunslinger, although a few, to their chagrin, believed they were. Cowboy marksmanship with a handgun was about on a par with the shooting skill of most town marshals, county sheriffs, United States marshals, and yokels generally. A puncher who carried a gun for show or because it was a custom was a fool, yet among them were those who "could not hit the side of a barn with all day to aim in."[2]

---

[1] Although no monograph treats the cowboy and his gun as the topic is handled in this article, the following selected titles may be of background value: Nyle H. Miller and Joseph W. Snell, *Great Gunfighters of the Kansas Cowtowns, 1867–1886* (Lincoln, 1963); Dale T. Schoenberger, *The Gunfighters* (Caldwell, Idaho, 1971); Philip D. Jordan, *Frontier Law and Order: Ten Essays* (Lincoln, 1970); Editors of Time-Life Books With Text by William H. Forbis, *The Cowboys* (New York, 1973); Joseph G. McCoy, *Historic Sketches of the Cattle Trade of the West and Southwest* (Kansas City, 1874); W. Eugene Hollon, *Frontier Violence Another Look* (New York, 1974); Richard Slotkin, *Regeneration Through Violence, The Mythology of the American Frontier, 1600–1860* (Middletown, Connecticut, 1974); W. Eugene Hollon, "Frontier Violence: Another Look" and Philip D. Jordan, "The Town Marshal and the Police" in Ray Allen Billington, ed., *People of the Plains and Mountains, Essays in the History of the West Dedicated to Everett Dick* (Westport, Connecticut, 1973), pp. 86–100, 101–119; and Joseph G. Rosa, *The Gunfighter: Man or Myth?* (Norman, 1969).

[2] J. Frank Dobie, *A Vaquero of the Brush Country* (Dallas, 1929), p. 265. Another common expression was "He could not hit the side of a barn if he was in one."

William Perlstrom, who in his youth rode shotgun on stages, soberly affirmed that a cowboy was a jackass on horseback. He further stated that there was a difference between firing a revolver and shooting one. It was his opinion that the majority of cowboys shot pool better than pistols. "They jerked the trigger," he lamented, "even though I warned them to hold steady and never fart when squeezin' off."[3]

Expertise with a handgun is not a God-given, natural talent. Bullets do not fall upon a victim like a gentle rain from heaven. Proficiency is a learned technique, demanding self-control and hours of practice. Excellent marksmanship, in short, is a hard-earned art. Any competent shooter will testify that riders of the range were no better or worse with a gun than innate aptitude and the extent of target practice warranted.[4]

Much of the nonsense written about cowboy gun magic—hammer fanning, finger twirling, six shots which sound as one—is set down by those who never have handled weapons consistently or been tutored in their use. It is one thing to get off a few rounds with a modern, automatic spraying weapon and quite another to fire those nineteenth-century pieces which "bathed the frontier in fire," leaving a bullet-riddled corpse behind every tumbleweed.

Yet myth and legend, despite evidence to the contrary, persist. A cowboy—any cowboy—could shoot the head off a rattlesnake, lift a lizard a foot in the air, knock a predetermined feather from a road runner, and snip the tail from a jumping rabbit. He wasn't worth his beans and bacon if he couldn't. Yet a rabbit-hunting wrangler using a heavy pistol wished he owned a light rifle, for he was "kind of scared of the heavy six-shooter so close to my nose and my aim wasn't so good."[5]

A rider would bounce his butt in a saddle all day and at night was sufficiently spry to drill center holes in silver dollars two hundred yards away. Even the chuckwagon cook, in flour-sack apron, flipped flapjacks with one hand while sharpshooting coyotes with the other. When in town, punchers habitually shattered bottles on back-bars, knocked out street lamps, and forced tenderfeet to dance to the music of thudding bullets. Such exaggerated misrepresentations were recognized for what they were during the time they circulated. George W. Peck, the humorist, lampooned the knocking out of street lights.

"Someone must have been trying to deceive you," Peck wrote, "when they told you out west, every night, the town was raken by cow-boys who shot out the lights, hung the marshal, and scared the timid people into

[3] Interview with author, Minneapolis, Minnesota, January 14, 1951.

[4] Philip A. Rollins, *The Cowboy, An Unconventional History of Civilization on the Old-Time Cattle Range* (New York, 1936), p. 49.

[5] Will James, *Lone Cowboy, My Life Story* (New York, 1930), p. 147.

DANCE! YOU SHORT-HORN DANCE! By Charles M. Russell. Photograph courtesy of Amon Carter Museum of Western Art, Fort Worth, Texas.

cat-fits." He continued, "Now I think cow-boys are pretty nice fellows, and I am their firm friend, and I think it only justice to them to say they do not shoot out the lights every night." Finally, Peck sunk the barb. "Why, I have known a whole week to pass when every light in town was left luming."[6] Another writer commented that pistols were used so infrequently to make strangers dance or to extinguish lamps that the practices amounted to little more than laying foundations for amusing legends.[7]

Who but a wide-eyed dude or innocent traveler could believe a tourist who set down as sober fact this absurd account of cowboy marksmanship?

> They will make him stand still and hold out his hand, and then try to shoot between his fingers, or shoot a hole through his ears, or see how closely they can shoot to the top of his head by shooting through his hat. . . . There is not much danger until they get pretty full and want to take *too fine* a shot, such as shooting between the flesh and the skin, and then the thing is too fine to be pleasant.[8]

Various observers, of course, interpreted cowboys differently, so that the term seldom meant the same to all. It is generally accepted that cowboys were laborers, frequently mounted, who nursed cattle, and an old saying has it that a cowboy without a horse is a man without legs. This is good enough to start with, but it is only a beginning. E. Douglas Branch, who

[6] *Peck's Sun* (Milwaukee, Wisconsin), October 1, 1887.
[7] Rollins, *The Cowboy*, p. 44.
[8] George W. Romspert, *The Western Echo: A Description of the Western States and Territories of the United States as Gathered in a Tour by Wagon*, quoted in Louis Pelzer, *The Cattlemen's Frontier* (Glendale, California, 1936), p. 245.

concocted a master's essay while smoking black cigars during the long nightmare hours, characterized the Texas cowboy as a "fearless rider, a workman of sublime self-confidence, unequalled in the technique and the tricks of 'cowpunching,' the most accurate on the trigger, and the last to leave untasted the glass which the bartender silently refilled."[9]

Branch, during his romantic graduate school sojourn, also put down as history that a cowboy generally wore a revolver on each side of his person, which he used "with as little hesitation on a man as on a wild animal." About a decade later, when Branch had learned a little more, he contented himself by saying that one revolver was carried. He never was able to admit that frequently punchers wore no guns at all.[10] A cowman's wife published an entire volume devoted to the vagaries of living with a cowpuncher and mentioned guns and shooting only when her husband took off after horse thieves. When the rightful owner came upon the Mexican miscreants, he said, "We must shoot high, for the horses are mine." His wife's comment provides the anti-climax. "They did not shoot, however, high or low, and the long night dragged through uneventfully."[11]

At times, a bluff was better than a gun, but not always. During the 1860's, for example, an Iowan journeyed to Texas to purchase cattle, hire wranglers, and drive his herd from the Lone Star State, through Indian Territory, Kansas, and Nebraska back to Iowa. George Duffields entered an episode of the drive in his diary after the party met up with Indians: "15 Indians came to Herd & tried to take some Beeves. Would not let them. Hada big muss. One drew his Knife & I my Revolver. Made them leave." That bluff worked.[12] So did another. A novelist, writing of two groups of antagonistic cowboys facing one another, said that eyes watched hands and that revolvers lay itching with corded nerves tight above them. But nothing happened.[13] Andy Adams, however, liberally shatters the pages of his classic with bluffs that failed,[14] helping to sustain the judgment of an historian of the cow country who maintained that more men were killed on account of bluffing with their guns than ever were slain because they carried guns.[15]

What type of men were doing all the boasting, bluffing, and shooting attributed to them? As early as the 1850's, the designation "cowboys" was a name applied to men who were outlaws. During the Cowboy War in

[9] *The Cowboy and His Interpreters* (New York, 1926), p. 16.

[10] *Ibid.*, pp. 11–12; Branch, *Westward* (New York, 1938), p. 571.

[11] Mary Kidder Rak, *A Cowman's Wife* (Boston, 1934), p. 125.

[12] "Driving Cattle from Texas to Iowa, 1866," *Annals of Iowa*, 3d ser., Vol. 14, No. 4 (April 1924), p. 254.

[13] Emerson Hough, *North of 36* (New York, 1929), p. 67.

[14] *The Log of a Cowboy* (Boston, 1903), *passim*.

[15] Dobie, *Vaquero of the Brush Country*, p. 265.

Arizona in 1881, F. B. Pomroy, United State attorney, attempted to explain to the Attorney General of the United States just what a cowboy was. "Cowboys," Pomroy wrote, "is a generic designation, originally applied to cow drivers, and herders in Western Texas, but that name has been corrupted in the Territories of New Mexico and Arizona, and in the local significance includes the lawless element that exists upon the border, who subsist by rapine, plunder and highway robbery, and whose amusements are drinking orgies and murder."[16]

Pomroy was correct enough in what he wrote his superior in the nation's capital, but he did not say as much as he should have. Texans themselves added some helpful information when they spoke of being divided into two groups—Old Texans and the "late burn." Late Burns was a term indiscriminately given to emigrants from east of the Mississippi River who had come in since the Civil War. Old Texans subdivided themselves into an agricultural and settled class of landowners, and, as did Pomroy, into cowboys, including roving desperadoes and horse thieves.[17]

A lot of sour hay has been pitchforked from loft to ground and back to barn attempting to explain what a cowboy really was. The work which all did was about the same, but each man was an individual with his own personality and behavior pattern. No two were alike. Any gazabo from the Yazoo River in Mississippi en route to the waters of the Trinity in Texas or the Verde in Arizona could, if determined, become, not a rascal, but an honest range hand astride a pony. A lad young enough to shave with a saucer of cream and a cat, if he rode a horse and swung a lariat without strangling himself or his mount, could with experience become fully the equal of veterans who knew the rigors of the Osage Trace, the Chisholm Trail, or the Goodnight-Loving Trail from the Texas Panhandle into Colorado.

Or, if he wished, he could follow the trail to hell. Eugene Catchings, a mulatto from Mississippi, began breaking horses for R. H. Hale, Rockwood County, Texas, in 1873. Three years later, at age twenty, he was hanged for murder. Jessie W. Jones tried his hand at punching and then turned to robbing stages. When arrested, fully armed, in October, 1885, he

[16] E. B. Pomroy to Wayne MacVeigh, June 23, 1881, National Archives, Legislative, Judicial, and Diplomatic Division, Records of the Department of Justice Concerning Wyatt Earp, 1881–1882. Record Group 60, microcopy 701, roll 6.

[17] The emphasis upon the cowboy as an undesirable person is frequently commented upon. See, for example, Walker D. Wyman, *Nothing But Prairie and Sky* (Norman, 1954), p. 101: "All in all, most of the old-time cowhands were a scrubby bunch. Only a few good ones got into the cow business and made good." For the psychology of violent men, see National Commission on the Causes and Prevention of Violence, *Crimes of Violence: A Staff Report Submitted to the National Commission on the Causes & Prevention of Violence*, Vol. 12, Chapters 8, 9 (Washington, December, 1969).

explained that he was given to reading the adventures of Jesse James and similar books, which so affected him that he ran away from home and turned stage-robber. Others turned from bawling calves to painted bawds. Two of the six men legally hanged in the Territory of Wyoming were cowboys.[18]

Battle-hardened Billy Yanks and Johnny Rebs, who suffered with Grant or Lee and who knew horseflesh and the tribulations of long marches and the barren bivouac, found a new life as cowboys after the war. They were accustomed to handling weapons, were seared with the branding iron of conflict, and were willing to face the labor and perils of cattle ranges. Cowboys were of all breeds, types, races, nationalities, and trades and professions. There were Mexican, Negro, and foreign-born cowboys; there were cowboys who never left their native state, and some who drifted all over hell and gone; and there were cowboy medicine men and preachers. Each, in his way, was an individualist, and no reliable or authentic stereotype is possible.[19]

Perhaps it is easier to say what the cowboy was not. He was not a colonizer, not a farmer, not a cotton planter, not a town founder, not a merchant, not a railroad builder, not a cattle king, not a stockyard capitalist. Only rarely was he a cold-blooded murderer, a horse thief, a rustler, a counterfeiter, a robber of stages, a looter of the overland mail, or a crack shot.

The puncher was a hired hand, a working man who had to perform or be fired. He worked from "can't see" until "can't see," and sometimes after that. He possessed certain traits and well-defined skills, but being a gunman was not among them. His abilities were not primarily the result of the impact of the land upon him—soil, grasses, length of seasons. He was motivated and molded both by geographic factors and by his own personality traits, his previous life experiences, his origin and economic status, his religion or lack of it, his political creed, his social outlook, and by Lady Luck, although he would not have understood all this.

The American people themselves, including those well-versed in the cattle trade of both Mexico and the United States, were confused about both the character of the man who tended livestock and about what to call him. Apparently, the term "cowhand" was used as early as 1847, and apparently the word "cowboy" meant a herdsman when it appeared in *Wilkes'*

[18] *Dallas* (Texas) *Weekly Herald*, November 11, 1876; *Bismarck* (North Dakota) *Daily Tribune*, October 10, 1885; Harry Sinclair Drago, *Great American Cattle Trails* (New York, 1965), p. 108; T. A. Larson, *History of Wyoming* (Lincoln, 1965), 231.

[19] For details of "slaves on horseback," see Philip Durham and Everett L. Jones, *The Negro Cowboys* (New York, 1965).

Spirit of the Times of April 21, 1866, although this may not have been the first time it was printed with such a connotation. But it certainly seems correct to say that "cowboy" was not generally in vogue, either orally or in print, throughout the United States until about 1880.

Prior to that time, a cattle driver was referred to as a herder, ranchero, *vaquero*, herdsman, or drover. Of these, drover appears to have been the most popular. Men in Abilene and Junction City, Kansas, spoke of drovers in 1869 and 1870. When Colonel T. G. Williams, of San Antonio, Texas, attended the American Institute Farmers' Club in New York City during December, 1872, he referred to the ranchero or herdsman. A year later, the general agent of the Kansas and Pacific Railway advertised in newspapers that citizens of Ellsworth, Texas, had appointed a committee to aid the interests of arriving drovers and would give drovers the benefit of all available water and also good locations for their herds. This does not mean that the term cowboy was never used prior to 1880, but only that it was not generally in the vocabulary as was drover.[20]

Gradually, but surely, the term drover gave way to cowboy. A dispatch, for example, from Fort Griffin, situated on the Clear Fork of the Brazos River, in January, 1877, stated that "Two cowboys, full of old rye and the devil," fired several shots from their Colts and broke up a saloon dance. The appeal of the word was great. Editors preferred it to drover, and authors of dime novels seized upon it, and almost before anyone realized it, the cowboy was a quick-tempered, gun-slinging, no-account character. He lent color, romance, and falsehood to tales such as Prentiss Ingraham's, *Lone Star, the Cowboy Captain; or, The Mysterious Ranchero, A Romance of Wild Life in Texas*, published in 1882, and in subsequent yarns such as Joseph E. Badger's, *The Cowboy Chief's Sure-Shot; or, Hard Knox the Rogue Rancher*, and *A Romance of Wyoming Range Rustlers*, which appeared in 1895. The Wild West Show, beginning in North Platte, Nebraska, July 4, 1882, emphasized, as did the dime novel, the cowboy's skills and reckless nature.[21]

In real life, as in novels, the crimson of personal danger threatened, if it did not touch, the professional and personal lives of punchers. Falls from high-spirited mustangs, stampedes, quicksands, Indians, feuds, rattle-

[20] *Dallas Herald*, January 16, 1869; March 10, April 30, 1870; January 20, June 29, December 7, 1872; April 12, 1873.

[21] Mitford M. Mathews, editor, *A Dictionary of Americanisms on Historical Principles*, 2 vols. (Chicago, 1951), I: p. 423; H. L. Mencken, *The American Language* (New York, 1957), p. 152; Albert Johannsen, *The House of Beadle and Adams and Its Dime and Nickel Novels: The Story of a Vanished Literature*, 2 vols. (Norman, 1950), I:p. 245; Don Russell, *The Wild West, or A History of the Wild West Shows* (Fort Worth, 1970), p. 2; *Bismarck Tribune, Dallas Herald, Cheyenne* (Wyoming) *State Leader*, and the *Nebraska State Journal* illustrate the use of driver and cowboy.

snakes and other varmints—all these and more were hazards. Ill-tempered psychopaths and deviates rode side by side with calm, normal men. The dangers of ranch, range, and trail—and of companions—made pistols and rifles as much occupational tools as hats of various design, chaps of wool, gloves of superior buckskin, and the Texas, Denver, or California saddle. The holster fitted the Colt, and the butt fitted the hand. The scabbard held the Winchester, tied snugly to saddle.

The wearing of weapons, openly or concealed, was proscribed by law in territories, states, counties, villages, and cities. Yet some laws are made to be observed, others to be flouted. Legislatures throughout the cattle country passed statutes which permitted weapon-toting individuals to observe the letter of the law and rape the intent of it. The "intent" clause was the escape mechanism. Two examples must suffice.

Nebraska stipulated in the code of 1867 that "if any person shall have upon him any pistol, gun, knife, dirk, bludgeon, or other offensive weapon with intent to assault any person," an offender, if convicted, was subject to a fine not exceeding a hundred dollars and imprisonment not exceeding three months. In 1880, the statutes of New Mexico plainly stated that it was unlawful for any persons to carry deadly weapons, concealed or otherwise, "within any of the settlements" of the territory, "except it be in the lawful defense of themselves, their families, or their property." Notice the implied intent as well as the fact that this section of the statute applied only to the carrying of weapons within settlements. The act did not prevent persons traveling from one place to another within the territory from bearing arms. This section was the wild, one-eyed jack in the legal deck.[22]

Municipal fathers quickly followed suit, and in so doing paved the way for many a good fight. In Texas, a Dallas ordinance, passed in July, 1871, prohibited the wearing of concealed weapons by persons holding the intent and avowed purpose of harming their fellow men. Note that the ordinance proscribed only concealed weapons. A Chetopa, Kansas, ordinance of April, 1879, forbade persons from carrying deadly weapons "for the purpose of personal attack or defense" without first securing written permission from the mayor. Such grants were issued generously. There was scarcely a constable or marshal who could not, if he desired, enforce ordinances or rules against the carrying of weapons. The marshal of Wichita erected two signs warning against the wearing of firearms. Tollkeepers at the privately operated Chisholm Trail bridge, appointed as special policemen without pay, exchanged metal tokens for weapons when cowboys cantered into

---

22 E. Estabrook, comp., *Statutes of Nebraska* (Chicago, 1867), p. 624; L. Bradford Price, comp., *General Laws of New Mexico* (Albany, 1880), pp. 312–15.

64

IN WITHOUT KNOCKING. By Charles M. Russell. Photograph courtesy of Amon Carter Museum of Western Art, Fort Worth, Texas.

town. Other marshals took it upon themselves to insist that cowboys check handguns at saloon doors, dance halls, and, upon occasion, at churches.[23]

Such statutes and ordinances, it must be emphasized, did not originally stem from a blazing cattlemen's frontier, nor were they designed primarily to curb the wild use of pistols by cowboys. The nation had been committed to the carrying and wearing and using of weapons since its infancy. Travelers, both native and foreign, commented upon the practice. "The Law is tolerably strong relative to carrying dirks, pistols or other weapons of assault," wrote a New Orleans editor in 1835. "Why is it not enforced?" James Logan, during a sojourn in the United States, noted numerous New Orleans stalls selling pocket pistols and knives. In 1857, another traveler commented that Americans slept with revolvers at their sides.[24]

The cowboy was no more or less addicted to carrying weapons than

[23] *Dallas Herald*, July 1, 1871; on September 2, 1871, the *Herald* reported that the Dallas County Democratic Committee resolved that "Every person shall have the right to bear arms, in the lawful defense of himself or the State, under such regulations as the Legislature may prescribe." See also the Chetopa, Kansas, Ordinance Book, 1879–1881, Ordinance 7, April 9, 1879, microfilm, Kansas State Historical Society; Robert R. Dystra, *The Cattle Towns* (New York, 1958), p. 121.

[24] *New Orleans Bee*, August 10, 1835; James Logan, *Notes of a Journey Through Canada, the United States of America, and the West Indies* (Edinburgh, 1838), p. 178; T. H. Gladstone, *The Englishman in Kansas* (New York, 1857), p. 128.

was the population generally. But for some curious reason, he has been singled out as both the outstanding wearer of shooting irons and the most skilled in their use. Steamboat captains carried weapons almost to a man; miners wore and used guns upon one another; lawyers and judges attended court with pistols behind their coattails; emigrants, crossing the plains, were armed to the teeth; traveling salesmen habitually tucked a gun in valises; and railroad brakemen and conductors kept weapons handy.[25] It was said, although this may be folklore, that a cattle auctioneer without a pistol on him could not sell a pot of cow pee.

Handguns, rifles, and shotguns always had been easy enough to come by. It was an unusual community which did not support a gunsmith or an emporium which stocked weapons. Cowboys, during the 1870's, patronized J. W. Johnson's shop in Tebuscara, Texas, where a sixteen-gauge scatter-gun sold for fifty dollars and a twelve-gauge for from seventy-five to a hundred. W. H. Watkins, at Waco, kept a complete stock of pistols, Spencer and Henry rifles, and cartridges of all descriptions. Dallas boasted of a few fine shops during the next decade. Wasseman and Sasse's Sportsmen Warehouse, in Lincoln, Nebraska, was known throughout the cattle country. D. A. Tyler, Bismarck, North Dakota, purveyor of rifles, shotguns, revolvers, and ammunition opened in 1886 an establishment opposite the Custer House. At the century's turn, when the boom times were almost over, Tyler was advertising secondhand guns at half prices. Used Colts, depending upon model and condition, ranged upwards from twelve dollars. Punchers swapped and traded for hog legs, and, if stories can be believed, won weapons at gaming tables. Mysterious Joe Fately, it is alleged, won six new six-shooters, two Winchesters, and nearly three hundred dollars in a monte game.[26]

Cowboys, wishing elaborately ornamental pistols for show or plain guns for work, had a wide variety from which to select. Whether they shot at wolf or rabbit or man depended in large degree upon a gun's accuracy and dependability. It simply is not enough to say, when discussing the buckaroo as a marksman, that he used a revolver. The aim depended upon the quality of gun, just as the gun responded to the aim. Many weavers of western fiction never realize this. A handgun, suitable for one purpose, could be entirely unsuitable for another, although a weapon of almost any

---

[25] Charles A. Siringo, *Riata and Spurs* (Boston, 1927), p. 195: "With a lantern in one hand and a double-barreled shot-gun in the other Conductor Harrington jumped to the ground from the step of the front coach."

[26] *Dallas Herald*, September 24, October 22, November 12, 1870; Lincoln (Nebraska) *Daily State Journal*, January 26, July 1, 24, 1870; *Bismarck Daily Tribune*, January 1, 1886, January 2, 1890; J. W. McCauley, *A Stove-Up Cowboy's Story* (Austin, 1943), p. 51. The latter smells more of the tall tale than of the trail.

caliber, large or small, was capable of wounding and even killing if held close enough and if it struck a vital, vulnerable area.

Dance hall girls, who doubled in brass beds as boudoir contortionists, at times concealed a derringer in their bodices. To the trade, these were known as boob guns. More elegant nightingales, working in plush establishments, wished to avoid the appearance of what was called the boob gun's three-tit front. As a substitute, some girls fastened high on the inside of the leg, close to the thigh, the Ladies' Friend. First manufactured by Frank Wesson in 1868, it was modified to include a dirk attached to the barrel. A two-shot weapon, it came in three calibers—.22, .32, and .44. Its octagon barrel measured a little over two inches in length. Many a cowboy, after negotiation with a floosy with not enough clothes on to flag a handcar, was horrified that the last item she removed and laid cautiously on the bureau was a Ladies' Friend. The playboy might be burned before the evening was over, but he did not hanker to be shot or dirked when stark naked.[27] Not after he had spent two bucks.

Cowboys knew guns. Many were brought up with them. To assume they were naïve is about as ridiculous as creating the impression, as some authors do, that all towns supported sporting houses, that the inmates of these houses were beautiful, and that all cowboys frequented the joints. Believe it or not, there were towns visited by riders which provided no such entertainment; there were girls whose photographs reveal them as less than attractive; and there were cowboys who never saw the inside of such a place.[28]

Scores of others, however, took advantage of whatever was offered in every area of entertainment and left town broke, as they said, as the Ten Commandments. Owen Wister, visiting Coulee City, Washington, during the autumn of 1892, wrote that there was only one professional woman in the whole town, "and from what I heard the men say, she is a forlorn old wreck, so unsightly that even her monopoly brings no profit."[29]

All in all, however, the supply of guns was larger than that of whores. Pistols were said to be as thick as blackberries in Wichita; in Lincoln, teachers were admonished to report all boys carrying firearms; and, also in Lincoln, when "some young roosters" bored a hole through the Opera House dressing room of Mlle. Jarbeau, the star pulled a small revolver from

[27] Perlstrom interview with author, Minneapolis, January 18, 1951; Charles Edward Chapel, *Guns of the Old West* (New York, 1961), p. 144.

[28] Although ladies of the evening did not generally sit for photographs, a few did, and some pictures of them are scattered through the pages of Fred and Jo Mazzula's *Brass Checks and Red Lights* (Denver, 1966).

[29] Fanny Kemble Wister, editor, *Owen Wister Out West His Journals and Letters* (Chicago, 1958), p. 136.

her pocket and told the rascals to "git." Earlier a traveler learned that small-bore weapons were inferior to those of heavier caliber because, "Suppose you hit your man mortally? He may still run in upon you and rip you up with a bowie knife before he falls dead." If, however, he is struck by a good, heavy bullet, "he gets faintish and drops at once."[30]

Cowboys, who debated their guns' striking power, agreed. Small-bores were no good. Their revolvers must be of sufficiently heavy caliber so that they could handle a variety of situations, both expected and unexpected. Wranglers used guns for offense and defense against personal enemies. They needed them in hostile Mexican areas or in areas where Indians were a menace. They wore them while riding ranges, for there they might meet unfriendly trespassers, or be forced to eliminate dangerous cattle, injured or diseased stock, or animals unfit for breeding purposes. They strapped on guns when visiting other ranches, when going to town, or when paying a formal call upon a girl.

No puncher in his right mind would attempt to control a stampede of snorting longhorns with gunfire, although such is standard procedure in western fiction. Eyewitnesses to stampedes testify over and again that gunfire was not used against frightened cattle. Passengers on a train passing through the Badlands in July, 1885, witnessed a stampede of a thousand Texas steers. They watched "fearless cowboys" whip their "sinewy bronchos up the steep and dizzy heights in hot pursuit," but they saw no shots fired. No guns went off during a stampede near the Pecos River in New Mexico in 1890. Only when a stampede had to be stopped—then and there—and not controlled were guns fired, and they were aimed at cattle, not into the air.[31]

When cowboys fought Mexicans and Indians, their proficiency was little better or worse than the marksmanship demonstrated by home-steaders defending their property, by emigrants protecting covered wagons, or by elements of the army. Four cowboys, with reinforcements, killed a band of twenty Indian horse thieves near Billings, Montana, in August, 1885. In June, 1890, a posse of cowboys left Rosebud, vowing they would drive tribes back to their reservation without any assistance from troops. They failed. Twenty or thirty Indians hit a camp of cowboys near Lords-duro, New Mexico, in June, 1890, and killed all but one. Such examples are

[30] *Plattsmouth* (Nebraska) *Daily State Journal*, February 1, May 7, 1881; William H. Russell, *My Diary North and South*, 2 vols. (London, 1863), 2: 9–10.

[31] *Bismarck Daily Tribune*, July 10, 1885; October 11, 1890; J. Frank Dobie, *The Longhorns* (New York, 1941), pp. 87–106; Walter Prescott Webb, *The Great Plains* (New York, 1931), pp. 264–67. Webb, on p. 267, quotes Andy Adams: "We threw our ropes in their faces [cattle] and when this failed we resorted to shooting."

only illustrative and prove nothing about the marksmanship of either cowboys or Indians. There is insufficient evidence to make a case either way.[32]

Indeed, controlling stampedes and knocking off Mexicans and Indians were exceptional episodes in the lives of cowboys. They looked after their weapons as a matter of habit, although some neglected to keep them oiled and in good repair. At times riders wrangled over the merits and makes and styles of handguns and rifles. Many were disinterested in the lightning draw, with oiling a holster so as to unshuck its pistol faster than a snake strikes, or with wasting costly cartridges shooting at rows of bottles or tin cans, in order to develop the deadly skill of slaying some mean-eyed sonofabitch who someday might insult them in a squalid cantina. A good many, having no constant need for a handgun while at work, kept weapons safely tied in blanket rolls or left them behind in bunkhouses. It is incorrect to state that punchers always wore weapons. It was the badman, not the cowboy—as an editor made clear—who was armed to the teeth with a double-barreled shotgun, two six-shooters, and a derringer.[33] There was another difference. The professional gunman wore his weapons low on the leg. The cowboy wore his pistol about his waist. Had he carried it low, it would have fallen out of its holster when he straddled a saddle.

Among the most popular revolvers was the Colt Model 1872 Single Action Army revolver, a .45 caliber, six-shot weapon weighing a little more than two pounds. First produced in 1873, it came in three barrel lengths, each with its own designation: seven and a half inches was the "Cavalry" model; five and a half inches the "Artillery" model; and four and three-quarters inches the "Civilian" model. In 1878 the company sold a version in .44–40 caliber which they called the "Frontier Six-Shooter." This version was popular with frontiersmen because its ammunition was the same as that used in the equally favored Winchester rifle, Model of 1873. Cowboys also found the single action Smith and Wesson Model 1869, a .44 caliber weapon, and the .45 Model 1875 Schofield-Smith and Wesson single action revolvers handy and accurate for range use. A Colt with a seven-and-a-half-inch barrel was preferred by some punchers to one with a five-and-a-half-inch barrel, but no hard-and-fast generalization can be made. Riders wore what best suited their tastes, ranging from horse pistols to English-made pistols.

Molded from soft lead, they were measured in grains, not in ounces; but

---

[32] *Bismarck Daily Tribune*, August 15, 1885; *Dallas Weekly Times-Herald*, June 14, 21, 1890; J. Evetts Haley, *The XIT Ranch of Texas and the Early Days of the Llano Estacado* (Norman, 1967), pp. 38–39 for Indians and Mexicans; for cowboy-Mexican relationships, see Walter Prescott Webb, *The Texas Rangers* (Austin, 1965), pp. 321–22; George Durham As Told to Clyde Wantland, *Taming the Nueces Strip* (Austin, 1962), *passim*.

[33] *Dallas Weekly Herald*, June 30, 1877.

laymen, concerning themselves with cowboy shooting, have difficulty visualizing a slug, say a Colt .32 caliber, weighing ninety grains, or a Winchester Model 1886 with a projectile weighing from 405 to 500 grains. If it is remembered that 437.5 lead grains equals an ounce, the task is easier. A Sharps .45 used a bullet of 550 grains, which was considerably more than an ounce. Such knowledge should prevent those who write about cowboy shooting from stating that some poor fellow got a five-ounce bullet in the brisket. If he did, he was struck by a cannon, not a handgun! A bullet from a Gatling gun weighed only 575 grains, and that is less than two ounces.

Actually, although this perhaps is hearsay, the workin' range hand frequently was more concerned with the type of rifle he carried in saddle scabbard than with the revolver sagging at hip. About the most reliable and generally approved, although tastes differed in long guns as in short ones, was the Winchester. Model 1873 was chambered for a .44-40 cartridge and was accurate up to about a hundred yards. Model 1886 was a sturdy and serviceable weapon, as was Model 1876. In 1880 such guns ranged in manufacturer's price from $24 to $32, and a decade later from about $16 to $20. After markups by jobbers and dealers, cowboys purchased them from about $65 to $100. The Winchester Repeating Arms Company sold some 22,000 guns in 1870, about 26,000 in 1880, and 79,000 in 1890. Its peak sales year, prior to turn of the century, came in 1899, with a total of 113,000 guns sold. Obviously, not all were bought by cowboys or used on various frontiers, but many were.[34]

Too many statistics stifle and overmuch detail destroys interest, but such were the guns commonly credited to lean, tall, lanky, hard-faced men of the ranges, whom legend ascribes with being crack shots. It is written that their lips were like strips of black paint. Dusty, sun-blackened men, so yarn-spinners tell, treated their guns like sweet virgins, cuddling them softly and gently, so that they would not turn into old bitch whores. If cowmen did not drill a meddling sheriff "neatly" between the eyes, they, getting off six rounds "instantaneously," hit him once on the right side of the chest, again higher upon the left side, and poured the remaining bullets from crotch to eyebrow. Many a victim was hit "not far below the heart."

Imaginative narratives never end. Cowboys, ruthless, brutal ruffians, shot it out—whether glad or sad or drunk or sober—in livery stables; on deserted streets of desolate towns; in rock-ribbed, dead-end canyons; around disputed *pozitos*, which were wells dug in sand washes; around poker tables where sat professional gamblers with aces up their sleeves; and, shamefully enough, in lace-curtained parlors in palaces of pleasure.

[34] Harold F. Williamson, *Winchester the Gun That Won the West* (Washington, 1952), p. 460, appendix D–1.

Their deadly guns spit across desert sands, smacked through stands of timber, and sped across pleasant pastures.

No one considered it particularly unique, even though it was unusual, if an irate mourner got off a shot across the coffin of a friend. Not even the undertaker appeared surprised. Low-down, belly-crawling, scheming horned toads got what they deserved, wherever they were. It did not matter whether they were white renegades, skulking Apaches, Comanches, or Kiowas, or homesteaders, sheepherders, rustlers, or strangers drinking quietly in a saloon. While the wounded writhed in misery and corpses sprawled grotesquely, cowboy gunmen calmly blew swirling smoke from pistol barrels. That was standard ritual. A cowboy who didn't blow smoke after an affray did not deserve to be a cowboy.

All these shootings and marvels of marksmanship, most of which must be taken with a grain of powder, are narrated both in the purple prose of pulp western magazines and of novels. Others appeared in distorted form in newspapers, or passed from liar's lip to liar's lip. Consider, for example, the case of Billie Collins, a Texan, who, earlier in life, rode the open range and tended cattle. It is well worth examining.

When older, Collins, on April 10, 1877, robbed the Texas and Pacific Railroad at Mesquite. Eventually he was arrested, jailed, and released on bond. Thereupon, Collins, with a certain degree of insight, decided he would be happier and healthier in another section of the Union. He fled to Dakota Territory. A Deputy United States Marshal tracked Collins and found him in a post office.

The deputy said, "Hold up your hands. You are my prisoner."

Collins smiled and raised his hands, saying, "How are you marshal?"

Collins, so the story unfolds, then dropped his right hand to his pistol, and, as he attempted to draw, the deputy fired, his gun being not more than a foot from Collins' breast. The ball passed through Collins' heart. The deputy, for some reason, then ran some twenty feet to hide in the post-master's cubbyhole office. When Collins was shot, he did not change countenance, but, still with a smile on his face, fired at the hidden deputy, but missed. Collins then stepped to the left a yard or so, with gun still in hand, and waited for the deputy to emerge. When he did, Collins fired again, his slug passing through the deputy's heart, and both men fell dead, on the spot.[35]

Among the amazing details of this episode, one stands out. If .44-caliber Colts or Smith and Wessons were used by Collins and the marshal, the slugs were in the neighborhood of two hundred grains. At close range, the velocity would be so terrific that upon impact the lead bullet could

[35] Charles L. Martin, *A Sketch of Sam Bass the Bandit* (Norman, 1956), pp. 162–64.

knock a man off his feet and perhaps send him reeling backwards. Few men could remain upright.

Remember that the deputy plugged Collins from a distance of not over a foot. Recall also that the marshal's bullet passed through Collins' heart. Yet Collins continued to smile, walked a yard or so, and fired at the officer, killing him. Anyone with a rudimentary knowledge of ballistics knows that Collins was a corpse, or close to being one, when he took the deputy's slug; that his smile, if he smiled, was death's grimace; that he would have been rocked backward and could not have arisen, especially to stagger a few feet, raise a heavy revolver, and kill the deputy. Both shock and slug would have taken their toll. Quickly.

At times, of course, death's macabre fandango became farce, not tragedy, and demonstrated the awkwardness with which cowboys handled weapons. One March day in 1887, Cowboy William Williams, sober, but wild-eyed and full of garbroth, rode into Fort Sill, Oklahoma. His quarry was a foreman. Williams dismounted, carefully rested his gun over his saddle, and fired. He missed the foreman, but the slug struck an army private, putting out an eye. Williams fled and was never heard from again. Two Texas cowboys, fired by their boss in 1891, determined upon revenge. Riding into town, they first filled themselves with drink and then, happily and carelessly, began shooting at bolt heads in hitching racks. They next set out to find and kill their former employer. Entering a bar, they made a slight mistake, confusing one man with another. They threw down on the wrong individual, but missed him, although one cowboy's gun "was so close that the powder burned the victim's face."[36] Even a tipsy puncher, if legend be true, should be able to do better than that, but there's no hard and fast rule governing a man and his gun.

The truth is that anyone, sufficiently sober and with strength enough to lift a heavy Colt and wits enough to point it, should hit a target at point-blank range. No fine, hairline shooting is involved in this sort of thing. Tough hombres, facing one another under leaden skies, managed to accomplish it in real life, in western novels, and, of course, on radio and television programs. Their victim was flat on his ass, as the expression goes, with his head in the grass. Snap shots sometimes paid off, although now and again they missed their intended mark and wounded or killed spectators. Stray bullets thudded into cow ponies, punched holes in canvas covers of nesters' wagons, splintered glass windows, and slit the skirts of dance hall girls if they happened to be wearing them.

In a free-for-all, snap-shooting brawl in a Fort Griffin saloon in 1877,

---

[36] W. S. Nye, *Carbine & Lance The Story of Old Fort Sill* (Norman, 1962), p. 246.

SMOKE OF A .45. By Charles M. Russell. Photograph courtesy of Amon Carter Museum of Western Art, Fort Worth, Texas.

the score among bystanders was: one attorney killed, one young man killed, one county attorney shot above the heart and critically wounded, and one deputy sheriff wounded slightly. Sometimes the results of shootings approached the humorous. A story goes that one night in Tascosa, Texas, a ranch manager took a hotel room. Suddenly, in the dead of night, he was awakened by shots in the saloon below. Hauling on his pants, he rushed down stairs. On the floor lay a seriously wounded man. Two other cowmen squatted in a corner by a barrel which spurted whiskey from a hole made by a stray bullet. The rancher, aghast, asked if the wounded puncher didn't need help. "Hell, yes," replied one of the gentlemen near the barrel, "but if we don't stop this hole all the whiskey will go to waste."[37]

All this boils down to the fact that few individuals, whether cowboys or not, were so proficient that if they notched their guns after each slaying their Colts would be whittled to nothing. Too many, inspired by a current bromide that "God made some men big and some men small, but Sam Colt made them all equal," set out to test its validity. They discovered the hard way that there was little truth in the statement. A man with a Colt who lacked the skill to handle it was no match for one who was knowledgeable

[37] *Dallas Weekly Herald*, January 27, 1887; Haley, *The XIT Ranch*, p. 198.

in its use. The revolver was clumsy and unreliable in the hands of clumsy men. The axiom applied equally to rifles.

Not too many range riders were really handy, say, with the Winchester Model 1886, a rifle with a 405- or 500-grain bullet. This rifle was a powerful weapon. Its heavy slug could penetrate about sixteen pine boards, each seven-eighths of an inch thick. It had a trajectory of about twelve inches at two hundred yards. It was an excellent weapon for long-distance work, especially bushwhacking, when there was plenty of time to rest the piece across log or rock and take careful aim. The best weapon of all for close-up massacre, of course, was the sawed-off shotgun. But, in the smoke-filled, powder-choked legend of the West, it was not considered genteel, noble, or fashionable to knock off, in a private grudge fight, an opponent with rifle or scattergun, although it was done. It was quite proper, however, to use such dealers of death on rustlers, Indians, the dirty drifter who ravaged the range owner's fair daughter, or against mobs threatening to rip a jail apart and free the sheriff's prisoner. Yet generalizations are like quicksand. One cannot, for example, sink deeper and deeper into the shooting exploits of Cowboy Will Hale without attempting to save one's self from the mire of exaggeration and half-truths.[38]

Truth can be stretched longer than a hangman's rope and, in the process, miraculously becomes falsehood. Probably not one man in a hundred, including cowboys, received sufficient instruction or practiced sufficiently to become a professional pistoleer. This has been indicated earlier, but it deserves repetition. Most learned by the by-God-and-by-gosh method, and this trial-and-error schooling resulted in cowboys accidentally wounding themselves and putting some of them securely in a Boot Hill. Newspapers repeatedly reported news of those who shot themselves while at work, while undressing to go to bed, while removing guns from wagons and carts. "It is well known," said an editor, "that most of the accidents with revolvers arise from the unintentional manipulation of the hammer: either it receives a blow, or it is allowed to slip off the thumb in cocking, or it is caught against the clothing, and particularly when it is at full cock."[39]

No statistics are available to prove how many cowboys fired a gun in anger or for vengeance. Doubtless too many did. But these, whatever their number, were fewer than those who, unfortunately enough, used weapons as toys and fired just for the hell of it. It is acknowledged generally that riders, on occasion, spurred mounts into saloons, firing haphazardly into ceilings. Others, drunk and cocky and on the prowl for dalliance with the follies of

---

[38] Will Hale, *Twenty-Four Years a Cowboy and Ranchman in Southern Texas and Old Mexico* (Norman, 1959), *passim*.

[39] *Dallas Weekly Herald*, February 19, 1887.

frontier flesh, went for weapons. For a few, that was the last move they ever made. But such antics, deplorable as they were, were not shared by all riders of the purple sage.

Many, when they arrived at drive's end and cantered into town, smelled of sweat and reeked of cattle and horses. They made for a barbershop for shave and haircut and a steaming bath in a tin tub. Afterwards, they headed for a bar-cafe for a beer or two—perhaps for a couple of jolts of brandy or rye or bourbon—and then sat to a meal not served from the rear end of a chuck wagon. Sober ones were glad enough to check guns, if they wore them, for there is no evidence that all cowboys always wore weapons when they came to town, although the majority probably did. At night they registered in a hotel to satisfy a long-felt dream of sleeping in a real bed instead of hunkering down on hard ground with a blanket over them and a saddle for a pillow. But when in bed, some could not rest, for they were unaccustomed to cornhusk or straw mattresses and pillows and sheets, so they yanked bedclothing to hard floors, and, ironically enough, slept peacefully. It was the rambunctious, maverick minority, not the average puncher, which created lurid legend.

Believe it or not, there were cowpunchers—red-blooded, vigorous men—who knew their prayers and said them; who were staunch temperance advocates; and who, in their way, celebrated secular and religious holidays. "It is a well known fact," said a commentator in 1887, "that cowmen and cowboys are almost to a man for prohibition." What the cowboy vote was in the Texas campaign against saloons was not recorded, but prohibition was defeated by ninety thousand votes. That not all ranchers were accustomed to prayer was demonstrated in January, 1887, when the Texas Livestock Association convened. When a bishop opened the first session with prayer, an editor commented: "Prayer, perhaps, is a new feature in cattlemen's conventions, and when the bishop repeated the Lord's Prayer, the cattlemen didn't follow him, but they listened reverently and prayerfully." Perlstrom, part-time cowboy and shotgun rider, recalled that in North Dakota he saw punchers, prayerbook in hand and pistol in holster, attend a revival conducted by a peripatetic preacher.[40]

There is no uncertainty about the zeal with which many ranch hands celebrated holidays. An account of Halloween festivities in the Dakota Badlands offers insight, even if colored a bit by a reporter's imagination:

> The cowboys of the Badlands favored the stars and gaudy buttes of that land of earthen gobblins with a celebration, which for brilliancy and spontaneity surpasses any thing of the kind on record. True, there were no

[40] *Ibid.*, January 15, July 16, 1887; interview with Perlstrom, Minneapolis, February 9, 1951.

75

maidens to add the feminine charm to the occasion, but the pistol decorated gentlemen of the ranges were equal to every emergency. . . . A number of the bovine guardians agreed to don the female attire, and while away the evening hours. . . . They could skim the jagged pasture land on their half breed plugs and rip the ambient air up the back with shouts and whoops and leaden balls. A general fusilade [*sic*] was indulged in, the meeting adjourning when the lamps were shot to pieces.[41]

Such a fusillade, repeated so many times along the cowboy's trail from life to quick death, does not indicate fancy shooting, but it does raise a point generally overlooked in discussions of cowboy marksmanship. In the sad saga of the West, gunshot victims were slightly wounded and recovered, seriously wounded and died, or fell lifeless, then and there. Few historians or fiction makers bother themselves too much with anatomical knowledge, with the result that an individual who was wounded and should have died lives, and he who should have lived dies. Little is known about how gunshot wounds were treated. The brevity of convalescence is nothing short of miraculous.

Consider, for example, the case of a cowboy seriously wounded in the region of the first, long rib. How does the fiction writer care for him? A rag or shirttail—grimy and dirty—is stuffed into the "gaping" wound and saturated with spirits of camphor. The patient, dripping blood which "pools" upon the ground, is given all the water he wants. Within a few hours he is sufficiently recovered to mount his faithful pony and go about his business.

Or the puncher whose chest is a bloody mass behind which is imbedded a bullet. His compassionate companions flood the wound with whiskey and force nips between clenched teeth. If whiskey is unavailable, he was given generous draughts of Dr. Betts & Betts Tonic, Electric Bitters, or Dr. Pierce's Golden Medical Discovery, each of which was heavily laced with alcohol. The wound was bandaged with whatever was handy.

There's the yarn of a cowboy who caught three slugs, one through the muscles of the upper leg, another in the upper arm, and a third one through the belly. Yet he is transported a considerable distance draped across a horse. Then he is left to his own devices. He drinks coffee and wolfs down antelope stew, and within a day or two, although still fevered, staggers on foot some eight miles, arriving at the home ranch just in time to engage in a gunfight in which three very mean bastards are killed.

Both the nature and treatment of gunshot wounds receive relatively slight attention in western literature. The flash of the gun blinds researchers to what a bullet actually did to the body. Usually, as set down in many

[41] *Bismarck Daily Tribune*, November 3, 1885.

accounts, a cowboy, if an author wishes him to survive and resume being a hero, is hit so that the slug encounters only soft tissue and will travel in a straight line through the body to exit without causing extensive damage. This is correct enough and is a safe way for an author to wound a cowboy and get him back on his feet in right smart time—if no infections develop. Shots in the hand or shoulder are favorite spots chosen by authors who wish to wound, but not slay. Even so, they are taking a chance.

A bullet striking an index finger can—and has—come out through the palm of the hand, entered the opposite shoulder, and exited from the back. A chunk of soft lead, hitting the clavicle or collar bone, would damage the traperzius, shaft, and sternal end. Nerves and blood vessels would be affected. A shot in the leg could cut the femoral or popliteal arteries. A cowboy hit in this fashion, unless professional assistance was available, might never place foot in stirrup again. A blow in the arm from a .38 or .45 handgun could well shatter the brachial artery which supplies the muscles of the front arm.

The "between-the-eyes" shot, whether the bullet hit smack in the nose or an inch or so above the eyes, worked havoc throughout the sagittal section. Depending upon the angle of fire, the missile would damage the posterior part of the eyeball, the orbital plate of the frontal sinus, the middle ethmoidal sinus, and the frontal lobe. It would fracture the frontal, parietal, and occipital bones. It might slice a vertebral artery, again depending upon angle of fire, which supplies the brain. The entrance puncture would be small and neat, but the exit wound would be massive and unsightly.

The "gut-shot," again a favorite in western literature, could well wreck colons and small intestines. A true shot in the stomach itself would damage the gastric vessels, the duodenum, and the greater omentum. Those unfortunates, plugged "right in the heart," often had the aorta destroyed. When the internal jugular vein, which receives blood from the skull and drains the face by the facial vein, was cut, the patient, as a physician put it, "was in a helluva shape." This is about equally correct for the cerebral veins and for the internal iliac vein, which drains the pelvic organs. Yet, in instance after instance in cowboy literature, a victim neither faints from loss of blood or wreckage of internal organs, nor goes into profound shock, a condition characterized by pallor, loss of consciousness, cyanosis, irregular pulse and respiration, and dilated pupils. In real life, the patient must be treated for both injury and shock.

There is little nice, neat, or clean as a whistle about violent death by gunshot. There is filth and muss, whether the victim is a cowboy or a schoolmaster, a tinhorn gambler or a buffalo hunter, a Mexican or an Indian, a friend or a stranger. To write authoritatively about cowboys—or any other group—as marksmen, one must push one's knowledge beyond abecedarian facts and discard the generally accepted. Obviously, at least an elementary knowledge of the types of weapons is desirable. Second, there must be comprehension of what guns did to the body when projectiles smashed into flesh and bone and nerves and veins and muscles and arteries.

Researchers will go to extreme lengths to ferret out the most minute details concerning the round-up, will inventory all available cattle brands, and will concentrate for hours over charts and maps. Some are knowledgeable about the Wild West show, the rodeo, the Cowboy's Association of America, the Cowboys' Turtle Association, and even the Australian Bushmen's Carnival Association.[42] Yet they apparently know little about the physical structure, except in gross fashion, of the men and women about whom they write. Anatomy seems to be a seven-letter bad word. It is no more difficult to master the rudiments of anatomy than it is to learn, for example, the component parts of a saddle or the difference between bridle and bit or between whippletrees and whang strings. If authors did not assume they were pathologists, they might not wound or kill in the unreal, comical manner they do.[43]

When historians of cowboys, for one reason or another, neglect to indicate the results of either expert or sloppy marksmanship, the sense of realism and of immediacy fades into the supposed and the imagined. Artifices become established formulas. Characters become cardboard cutouts, like targets on a pistol range. When, for example, a cowboy is shot and crumples in a dead heap, how many times, if ever, is he examined to determine if he really is dead? Who checks the breathing and the pulse? Who looks for loss of muscle tone of the eyeballs and changes in the pupils? The latter, instead of being round, may be eccentric.

Frequently, the shot cowboy is described as throwing up his hands when a bullet strikes. His weapon thuds to dusty street, muddy ground, or rocky soil. He falls with appropriate gestures, sometimes even turning a somersault while his sombrero pirouettes above him. But almost always the pistol drops. That is standard practice. Yet it is not uncommon for a person who holds a gun or a knife at the time of death to continue to clutch it tenaciously after death in what is known as cadaveric spasm. The weapon must be pried loose. Even *rigor mortis* is ignored. Generally, depending upon temperature and allied factors, *rigor mortis* develops within eight or ten hours, although there is no set schedule. An additional sixteen or more

---

[42] Clifford P. Westermeier, *Man, Beast, Dust: The Story of Rodeo* (Denver, 1948), *passim*; *see also* Russell, *The Wild West, passim*.

[43] Any edition of *Gray's Anatomy* will be helpful, as will, for example, R. D. Lockart, G. F. Hamilton and F. W. Fyee, *Anatomy of the Human Body* (Philadelphia, 1965), and LeMoyne Snyder, *Homicide Investigation* (Springfield, Illinois, 1946).

hours usually are allowed before the entire body is affected. However, some individuals dying under intense emotional tension, such as gun fights, may develop *rigor mortis* more rapidly. Despite all this, writers move long-dead bodies about as if they were rag dolls.

It matters little whether or not cowboys were the crack shots some allege them to be; for the fact remains, as indicated previously, that many sustained wounds. The majority, again to keep setting the record straight, were clumsy. The efficiency of the Colt has been exaggerated. So has the treatment given wounded punchers by physicians. Ex-army surgeons, Federal and Confederate, followed the frontier into the Great Plains and hung out shingles in areas throughout the cattle country and in towns situated at the ends of the long drives. Most learned their surgery prior to entering service. Few advanced their skills while in the army, except, perhaps, to perfect their amputating technique. Not all, by any means, were "surgically clean," although they were acquainted with and used carbolic acid as an antiseptic.

It was simple enough for men carrying black bags to set a simple, even compound, fracture of leg or arm after a cowhand was tossed from a fractious horse or was pinned against a corral's rails. It was more difficult to treat a gun-shot patient—a broncbuster, *vaquero*, or *caballero* cut down in chaparral or attempting to escape from a calaboose. Cattle-country physicians, during the 1870's, were wary about using bullet forceps and probes unless the slug lay near the wound's mouth or lodged directly under the skin. Under those circumstances, bullets were cut out. Practitioners used whiskey, laudanum (tincture of opium), or chloroform as an anesthetic.

Abdominal penetrations were left strictly alone if a surgeon determined that stomach, bladder, gall-bladder, or blood vessels were injured. The general opinion was that when bullets were lost in the belly, one need not amuse oneself hunting for them. Such judgment was based upon the fact that the overall mortality rate from abdominal wounds during the Civil War was 87 per cent. The percentage rose to a hundred when the small intestine was involved. Cowboys, unless they fell into the hands of expert surgeons, which they seldom did, faced about the same odds until procedures improved.[44] For many of them the only thing ahead was to ride the final dark trail.

[44] Harry E. Webb, "The Sad Saga of Hard-Luck Sam," *The Roundup*, Vol. 22, No. 7, (July 1974), p. 1, describes treatment of a fracture by ranch hands: "Sam wound up with an arm bone sticking out through his skin, but with the aid of some home-made splints, carbolic and whiskey we (as Bob Long said) 'growed a new arm on him.' " See also Mark H. Brown and W. R. Felton, *Before Barbed Wire* (New York, 1966), pp. 59–61; George Worthington Adams, *Doctors in Blue, The Medical History of the Union Army in the Civil War* (New York, 1952), chapter 6.

One reading western cowboy literature might easily conclude that the only physical hazards stemmed from ponies, Colts, and chippies, and that if powerful men of the painted desert hurt, it was because of falls, bullets, or venereal disease. It is only fair to balance the record. It is both possible and probable that more ill-health and pain were suffered as a result of hernias, diarrhea, dysentery, and insect bites, including those of the deadly New Mexican vinagrilla, than were caused by bullets or infected females.[45]

Post-mortem examinations in the cattlemen's country were few. What was the use? The law did not always demand them, and coroners, even if available, frequently were incompetent. Inquests, although not always held, were common enough, although some were perfunctory. Verdicts ranged from the serious to the humorous. It is regrettable that folklorists have emphasized the comical and exceptional findings of coroners' juries.

Acquaintances, perhaps weaving a bit from an excess of liquor or perhaps from genuine emotionalism (although writers prefer the former to the latter), carried corpses to local undertaking shops, where ready-made boxes were constantly in stock and coffins were made to order. Coffins, at times, were purchased in town and carted to home spreads. The Stine & McLure Undertaking Company, Kansas City, Missouri, began offering its services in 1861, long before the post-war cattlemen's frontier reached its peak to erupt—in the language of the romantics—in bloody barrages from smoking equalizers. A. M. Moore, of Dallas, did a brisk business in 1868, and McIntire & Walker, in Forney, Texas, in 1887 served both town and country. The firm was congratulated, with an unintentional humorous twist, by a newsman. McIntire & Walker, he wrote, planned to add a five-hundred-dollar hearse to their business. Then he added: "They are both live men and will undoubtedly succeed." Two years earlier, Bismarck's practical undertaker was Wm. D. Smith & Company. Small-town undertakers commonly coupled their burying business with either the furniture trade or with running a livery stable.[46]

If the deceased was an unknown drifter or if he was broke, with no friends or relatives to foot burial expenses, his horse, saddle, and gun might be kept by the undertaker, who might sell or auction them off. Normally, the dead were interred in the clothes they wore when they died, including boots. Indeed, the saying that "Cowboys worked with their boots on, died

---

[45] Although no specific study of cowboy health has been done, it is reasonable to conjecture that the range hand was subject to about the same diseases as were soldiers and laymen in the same geographic and climatic environments. Although printed before the advent of the cattlemen's frontier, helpful material may be found in Richard H. Coolidge, *Statistical Report on the Sickness and Mortality in the Army of the United States . . . From January 1855 to January 1860* (Washington, 1860), 36 cong., 1 sess., ex. doc. 52.

[46] *Dallas Weekly Herald*, November 28, 1848; October 7, December 9, 1876; January 21, 1877; *Bismarck Daily Tribune*, June 30, 1885.

with their boots on, and were buried with their boots on," has been accepted both as gospel and as a unique custom applicable only to cowpunchers. This appears to be untrue.

The custom of burying a body with shoes reaches back to Aryan tradition, when it was believed that the trail from the land of the living to that of the dead passed through regions overgrown with thorns. The dead could not undertake such a journey without shoes to protect their feet. The custom persisted in the Old World and was carried to the English New World, becoming traditional at least among the upper classes who could afford footwear. Not until about the early decades of the twentieth century was the custom discontinued by American undertakers. Until then, tradesmen, merchants, railroad workers, bankers, empire builders, and others went to the grave with shoes on their feet.

Although it was possible to remove cowboy boots from a corpse, the task was difficult. If *rigor mortis* had set in, the job was somewhat easier, but if decomposition had occurred, no one really wanted the boots, even if removed. So—it is sheer bunkum to claim uniqueness for a cowboy being buried with his boots on. Wister tells of finding the unburied bones of a murdered cowboy, adding that "lately someone went to appropriate his boots, Government boots, but on picking them up, the bones of the feet fell out on the ground. So the boots are there yet alongside of the bones."[47]

More range riders who lost their lives from accidents or from the impact of a slug from a hog leg were hastily shoved underground with scant ceremony than were buried by undertakers. They lay alone, on the home spread, beside the long drive, or somewhere on the lonesome prairie. There they rested, wrapped in their blankets, with no marker to testify to their location. There were exceptions. Adams described a grave which an outfit had fixed up, he thought, "quite nicely." A pen of rough cottonwood logs surrounded the mound, and large, flat stones marked head and foot. The grave itself was covered with smaller stones to protect it from animals. "In a tree his name was cut—sounded natural too, though none of us knew him." When, in camp near the Blue River, a cowboy was thrown by his mount and killed, his companions dug a little of the ground away beneath him, "slipped his saddle blanket under him and piled niggerheads on top." That was the best which could be done, for "The ground was hard and we didn't have no proper tools." Cowboys murdered by Indians were frequently so mutilated that there was little left to bury. Those shot in the vicinity of Fort Sill, Oklahoma, were buried in the post cemetery. When a North Dakota sheriff searched for and found the corpse of a murdered

[47] Wister, *Owen Wister*, pp. 105–106.

A DUDE'S WELCOME. By Charles M. Russell. Photograph courtesy of Amon Carter Museum of Western Art, Fort Worth, Texas.

cowboy, he found the killer had buried it, then exhumed it, and finally cut it in half in order to transport it to a more concealed location.[48]

There was good reason for rapid burial. Corpses had to be interred before decomposition advanced too far, usually before face slippage took place. When one cowboy was buried thirty-six hours after death, he was "so swollen that he had to be jammed down" in his coffin. Although embalming was practiced during the Civil War, the technique did not become commonplace until shortly before the turn of the century, and in some regions not even then. It was practically unknown in isolated, small communities on the fringe of the frontier. Corpses of bad men seem to have received better attention than those of cowboys. The bodies of Billy Clanton and of Tom and Frank McLaury, whom the Earp brothers murdered in October 1881, were displayed in handsome caskets in a window of a Tombstone hardware store before burial in Boot Hill. The corpse of Luke Short, who died in September, 1893, was embalmed. Yet most took the sun for shroud.[49]

[48] Adams, *Log of a Cowboy*, p. 276; E. C. Abbot and Helena Huntington Smith, *We Pointed Them North* (New York, 1939), p. 43; Dorothy M. Johnson, *The Bloody Bozeman* (New York, 1971), pp. 344–45; Nye, *Carbine & Lance*, pp. 246–47; Bert L. Hall, comp., *Roundup Years, Old Muddy to Black Hills* (Pierre, South Dakota, 1956), p. 307.

[49] Wister, *Owen Wister*, p. 105; Robert W. Habenstein and William M. Lamers, *The History of American Funeral Directing* (Milwaukee, 1955), chaps. 8, 9; the standard text, in its sixth edition, was *The Champion Text-Book on Embalming* (Springfield, Ohio, 1919).

Perhaps cowboys strapped on gun and cartridge belts to prove their masculinity and mask a feeling of inferiority; perhaps they carried weapons because the carrying of guns was a social folkway; and perhaps they toted Colts and Winchesters because all America was awed by death symbols. Some say the pistol and pony symbolized direct, uncomplicated action which satisfied the soul and increased men's concepts of democracy and of individual power and worth. It certainly is true that a weapon was a useful tool of the cowman's trade, just as the red lantern was to the railroad brakeman, the whip to the stage driver, the anvil to the blacksmith. But the gun was less important than the lariat. Moreover, it was recognized as deadly and dangerous. A lawyer, reporting on conditions of the Texas XIT ranch in 1887, said a "lot of men" were still wearing guns which "could not do otherwise than destroy all discipline and organization." A year later, when the rough-and-ready cow kingdom had reached and passed its climax, the XIT ranch proscribed the carrying of weapons by its employees. No cowboy was permitted to carry, on his person or in saddlebags, weapons for offense or defense. Included were pistols, dirks, daggers, slingshots, knuckles, and bowie knives.[50]

But the mold had been cast and the pattern cut. After the official closing of the frontier in 1890, more than ever cowboy legends and tales became an escape mechanism for Americans caught in the vise of a newborn, urban, industrialized society. In an increasing miasma of misinformation, the nation became beclouded with the fantastic rather than the real. It was forgotten that although the cowboy was an expert with the rope, with branding iron, with the breaking and gentling of horses, with the know-how to handle cattle, he was no damn good with a handgun. The irony is that most had no desire to be.

[50] Haley, *XIT Ranch*, pp. 110, 243.

JUST A LITTLE PLEASURE. By Charles M. Russell. Photograph courtesy of Amon Carter Museum of Western Art, Fort Worth, Texas.

The Cowboy and Sex

BY CLIFFORD P. WESTERMEIER

DURING THE CENTURY WHEN THE COWBOY EVOLVED from an unknown drover and herder into America's most enduring folkhero he acquired many attributes. His image and stature grew as he passed through the hands of the frontier journalist, dime novelist, wild-west promoter, novelist, historian, radio, motion picture- and television-producer, psychiatrist, socio-psychologist and pornographer. These hucksters, merchants of nostalgia, literators, analysts, and image-makers, helped to shape a many-sided figure which reflects their particular concern for anecdotes, humorous incidents and considerable exaggeration, yet is subject to the disciplines of the investigators. The cowboy has an enormous appeal for Americans; however, for the majority, the cowboy they know exists more on film and TV screens than in real life.

The early periodical journalists and dime novelists, in their enthusiasm for him, created a forceful image. But, as for sexual activity or relations between the sexes, this enthusiasm is prudish. One seldom, if ever, finds an incident or a single word suggestive of indecency or sexual impropriety. The periodical and dime-novel cowboy is highly moral, although descriptions of him are sensual and at times suspect. However, in all instances, virility is the keynote of much public admiration.

As early as 1867, these writers described cowboys as being "full of reserved force, [in the] prime of manhood, [and] usually tall, muscular, well-built, slim, sinewy, and with sun-burned faces." Theodore Roosevelt (1885), always an admirer of the manly and robust, praised their "lithe, supple figures erect or swaying slightly as they sat loosely in the saddle."[1]

---

[1] *New York Daily Tribune*, November 6, 1867; *Daily News* (Denver, Colorado), April 4, 1873; Alice McGowan, "A Successful Round-Up," *Overland Monthly*, Vol. XL (November, 1902), p. 460; Theodore Roosevelt, "Ranch Life in the Far West," *Century*, Vol. XXXV (February, 1888), p. 502.

Such descriptions are journalistic templates, the forerunners of the body-beautiful, the he-man cowboy of cinema and TV.

By 1871, the image took on a new dimension when a correspondent of the Topeka *Daily Commonwealth* wrote: "They drink, swear, and fight, and life with them is a round of boisterous gayety and indulgence in sensual pleasure."[2] More emphatically, cowboy Bruce Siberts reminisced (1890–1906) that most of the cowboys "were burned out with bad whiskey and disease; [some during the winter months] were pimps, living off some cheap prostitutes. . . . Most of them had a dose of clap or pox and some had a double dose. All in all, most of the old-time cowhands were a scrubby bunch."[3]

Thus, described on the one hand by admirers as a prime example of prowess much like the "Marlboro cowboy," and on the other by critics who tagged him as foul-mouthed, drunken, corrupt, and lecherous, the word "cowboy" was often synonymous with all that was good or all that was bad.[4]

Who is *the* American cowboy? Lewis Atherton answers in part:

"One must recognize that he continues to be a composite of many men, a nameless hero in recognition of the fact that his deeds were not beyond the powers of virtually anyone willing to exert his energies. . . . As a hero of the American folk, he is truly all of them in one."[5]

To tamper with the image of a folk hero, a historic formula, a legend, and, most of all, that of the American cowboy heritage is probably more dangerous than the proverbial where "fools rush in . . . ." Perhaps the subject of sexuality does not deserve the attention it is given, but whatever conclusion is reached regarding its relation to the cowboy—bad taste, sensationalism, iconoclasticism—it did exist in his life, and it is a part of American social history.

Probably, the orderly way to look at cowboy sexuality would be *to be* a cowboy. Since this is not possible, logic would direct us to examine the records left by those who were or are cowboys. Very important also, an investigation of the popular trends in image- and myth-making can be most informative. Thus, with less scientific acumen, and certainly with greater detachment than a Kinsey or a Masters or Johnson, need one tread care-

2 "The Texas Cattle Herder," *Daily Commonwealth* (Topeka, Kansas), April 15, 1871, p. 15.

3 Walker D. Wyman, *Nothing But Prairie and Sky* (Norman, 1954), pp. 100–101.

4 Clifford P. Westermeier, *Trailing the Cowboy* (Caldwell, Idaho, 1955), pp. 22–56. Note: Carl B. Bradley, the "Marlboro cowboy," former wagon boss for the 6666 Ranch at Guthrie, Texas, was killed when his horse slipped and kicked the cowboy on the way down. "Cigarette Ad Cowboy Dies in Horse Mishap," *Denver Post*, May 9, 1973, p. 13.

5 Lewis Atherton, *The Cattle Kings* (Bloomington, 1961), p. 248.

fully? If the legend, hero, and formula represent all men, then all their deeds, good or bad, are within the realm of consideration.

On May 12, 1870, page one of the Abilene *Chronicle* listed, among various ordinances, those guiding the welfare of the community—those regarding gambling, drunkenness, deadly weapons, and places of prostitution. All of these support the contention that in cattle towns there was much law and also much disorder. A cowboy in the last decade of the past century reminisced, "Rum, cards, and women are the epitaphs in the cowboys' graveyard. Some bunches all three, and some cuts one out of the herd and rides after it till he drops. . . ."[6] Joseph G. McCoy includes tobacco but drops cards from the unholy trinity, although he ignores neither cards nor dancing as vices.[7]

One cannot deny the basis of the chroniclers' variant images of the cowboy. First, there was the hard-working, dedicated, and fun-loving man on the range, or in the camps, where women, cards, and rum were conspicuously absent; secondly, the wild, wanton, wayward man in the cattle towns where, in the minds of the righteous, every weakness was fostered. However, women, cards, and liquor were, to a considerable extent, causes of trouble both for the cowboy and for westerners in general.

Since the cowboy shared with the sailor a public image based on escapades after long periods of privation, he is best described as a hard-working man of restricted and sober habits who, after several months in the saddle, had built up a head of steam not unlike the seaman heading toward port. Unfortunately, in his heyday and thereafter, the fact-fiction cowboy accepted the myth of both images as a reality, which resulted in a tragic struggle to be his own man.

Actually, his failings were not three but four: drinking, gambling, lechery, and violence—the latter a natural outcome and often companion of all the former. Of these, however, lechery is often alluded to but is the least detailed activity of his frenetic pleasures.

A correspondent for the distant *Washington Star* wrote in 1878: "In the cow towns these nomads in regions from restraint of moral, civil, social, and law enforcing life, the Texas cattle drover . . . loiter and dissipate sometimes for months and share the boughten dalliances of fallen women."[8]

If virtue was almost unknown in the cattle towns and vice was flaunted indiscriminately, then the saloon, dance hall, and redlight districts were

---

[6] Julian Ralph, "A Talk with a Cowboy," *Harper's Weekly*, Vol. XXXVI (April 16, 1892), p. 376.

[7] Joseph G. McCoy, *Historic Sketches of the Cattle Trade of the West and Southwest* (Kansas City, Missouri, 1874), p. 85.

[8] "Social Influences in the West," *Washington Star* (Washington, D.C.) January 1, 1878, p. 2.

necessities—veritable Edens of evil. Hogtowns and hog ranches were adjuncts of many cow towns and of isolated ranches, as well as roadside stopping places between communities.[9]

Regardless of size, cattle town or big city, the pleasure palaces lured the free-wheeling, rollicky cowboy. Charles A. Siringo, according to J. Frank Dobie, was the first genuine cowboy to reveal in print the special deviltries in which a cowboy cutting high jinks could be involved.[10] Siringo, on arrival in Chicago with a carload of cattle, headed for the parlor houses with their large, glittering, diamond-dust mirrors and the tinsel tarts. In one grand fling on the very first night he rid himself of his year's wages.[11]

Teddy Blue (E. C.) Abbott, with the aid of Helena Huntington Smith, reveals much more about cowboy philandering with shopworn chippies and parlor house madams. For instance, Cowboy Annie, who operated from a house in Miles City, carried a little book listing all her clients' names. Never accepting failure, she urged Teddy to join the growing list, "Now just make all the brands in it, Teddy."[12] Willie Johnson, the madam of an Omaha house patronized by Abbott, after being beaten up, complained: "I don't care for the black eye, Teddy . . . but he called me a whore."[13]

Novelist Owen Wister, before fashioning the irresistible Virginian as a "slim young giant, more beautiful than pictures . . . . ,"[14] created Lin McLean, who was "supreme in length of limb and recklessness,"[15] a callow "box-headed" youth conscious of his sprouting adolescent hair. Lin was injured in a riding accident; however, surgical skill and the boy's good health resulted in rapid healing, so he was able to enjoy hospital privileges.[16] Accordingly, "the disobedient child of twenty-one . . . slipped out of the hospital and hobbled hastily [across a bridge] to the hog ranch, where whiskey and variety awaited for the languishing convalescent. Here he grew gay and soon was carried back with the leg refractured."[17]

The youthfulness and virility of the men, devoid of normal comforts, and the scarcity of women drove them to seek outlets in the seedy surroundings provided by dance halls, saloons, and cribs, all anxious for their patron-

---

[9] Forbes Parkhill, *The Wildest of the West* (Denver, 1957), p. 30.

[10] Charles A. Siringo, *A Texas Cowboy, or Fifteen Years on the Hurricane Deck of a Spanish Cow Pony* (New York, 1950). Introduction by J. Frank Dobie, p. x.

[11] Charles A. Siringo, *Riata and Spurs* (Boston, 1927), p. 62.

[12] E. C. Abbott ("Teddy Blue") and Helena Huntington Smith, *We Pointed Them North* (Norman, 1962), p. 105.

[13] *Ibid.*, p. 109. *See* Siringo, *A Texas Cowboy*, p. x.

[14] Owen Wister, *The Virginian* (New York, 1902), p. 4.

[15] Owen Wister, *Lin McLean* (New York, 1897), 128.

[16] *Ibid.*, pp. 7, 115, 128.

[17] *Ibid.*, p. 129.

age. Those who had not gained experience were accosted by sporting women or their pimps on the streets; and, fascinated by the flamboyantly dressed procurers, they followed them to the places of business.

Bruce Siberts, whose story Walker Wyman captures in *Nothing But Prairie and Sky*, maintains that the women of Pierre, South Dakota, were of two kinds, "the sporting ladies as they called themselves, and the wives who tried to raise families decent-like."[18] Among the former, Nigger Jenny, never particular about her clientel, is the source of many stories. One concerned a drunken cowboy's criticism of her kinky hair. In answer she said, "White man, what you expect for fifty cents—sealskin."[19]

The Abbott, Siringo, and Siberts-Wyman books, all basically reminiscences, are franker about individual cowboy sexuality and the women they met in the bordellos than all other cowboy and range chronicles yet produced. The cowboy is now an individual and no longer a faceless generalization. Most of his escapades are described as "cutting loose" and having "a little fun." He is still pictured as a healthy young animal, forgivable for seeking out the nautch-joints. Upon being solicited, his arrogant question and boast, in contempt for the man on foot, might include the sly stipulation: "Can I do it on horseback?" One writer suggests: "Unhorse a cowboy and you unman him!"[20]

After months on a dusty trail, home-ties broken, lonely, frustrated by his companions and the beasts he herds, his only consolation a tobacco sack, coarse, badly-cooked food, bitter black coffee and brackish water, the cowboy saw the Hide Park across the tracks as living. In Dodge City such a man "might break all the ten commandments in one night, die with his boots on, and be buried on Boot Hill in the morning."[21]

Contemporary newspapers shared in the creating of the range cowboy's sexual image. Not unlike the published reminiscences, they, too, stress cattle-town philandering. Classic instances, usually accompanied by violence, are found in the journalism of the so-called cowboy territories and states.[22]

A news item, captioned "A Lark," found in the *Denver Daily Times*, April 26, 1877, relates the frolic of four Texas cowboys who shot up a house occupied by Negro women on Wazee Street. Then a visit to a Chinese residence ended in the shooting of one of the Celestial patrons, and, after a chase by two officers, the quartet ended in the cooler.

[18] Wyman, *Nothing But Prairie and Sky*, pp. 142–43.

[19] *Ibid.*, p. 143.

[20] Donald Mackay, "The Cow-Puncher at Home," *Munsey's*, Vol. XXVII (August, 1902), p. 760.

[21] Stanley Vestal, *Queen of Cowtowns Dodge City* (New York, 1952), pp. 1–2.

[22] Westermeier, *Trailing the Cowboy*, pp. 109–149.

In Hunnewell, Kansas, a prostitute was the object of a night's wrangling that resulted in a killing. Two men met "high noon" fashion, and one put a bullet through the other.[23] In Denver, a house of ill-repute was the scene of a fight when several soldiers were thrown out by cowboys. The angry and disappointed soldiers returned armed, and rounds of shots were exchanged, with one soldier seriously injured. Cryptically, the reporter ended his account, "The soldier will probably die."[24]

High-jinks also took place in Cheyenne. The *Cheyenne Democratic Leader* reports a shooting in a house over Frankie, the mistress of the victim. Before the law arrived, an undressed cowboy was last seen running down the street, believing he had killed Frankie's lover.[25]

In many of these early accounts there appears to be a fascination for the violence of the incident rather than its cause—the drunken brawls over whores and cards, or both.

As the cowboy followed his calling he seldom came in contact with decent women. His work did not encourage family relationships nor a normal pattern of dating, courtship, marriage, and family. Married cowboys in the early days were not the rule, because wanderlust, extended absence, the somewhat arrogant attitude of self-importance, and a poor wage did not lend themselves toward domesticity. Around the cowboy grew an aura of self-sufficiency by which he excluded all others. Douglas Branch wrote: "Love in the cow-country was a brusque thing, an incident not the aim of life in this woman-starved country with its iron traditions of clanship between men."[26]

Will Wallis of Laramie, quoted by C. L. Sonnichsen in his study *Cowboys and Cattle Kings*, makes a very important and revealing appraisal which holds good for the old-time and modern cowboy: "The old-time cowboy was most respectful of women as long as they kept their place. If they let down the bars, one of those boys would go the limit."[27]

Larry McMurtry, from a long line of cowboys and ranchers, and author of *Horseman, Pass By* (motion picture *Hud*), adds to the sexual image of the cowboy: "Even the most innocent cowboy was scarcely good enough for a good woman, and the cowboy who was manifestly not innocent might never be good enough, however much he might crave one."[28]

It may be exaggerative to say that the graveyards of the cattle towns

---

[23] *Caldwell Commercial* (Caldwell, Kansas), July 7, 1881.

[24] "Soldiers and Cowboys Fight," *Denver Republican*, September 11, 1892.

[25] "A Brawl," *Cheyenne Democratic Leader*, August 28, 1885.

[26] Douglas Branch, *The Cowboy and His Interpreters* (New York, 1961), pp. 157, 201.

[27] C. L. Sonnichsen, *Cowboys and Cattle Kings* (Norman, 1950), p. 46.

[28] Larry McMurtry, "Take My Saddle From the Wall," *Harper's*, Vol. CCXXXVII (September, 1968), p. 45.

were filled with victims of rutting cowboys in a drunken haze battling for shopworn women, but certainly the women they consorted with were not made for domesticity. For decent women, the cowboy's animal drives, obscenity, crudeness, and arrogance were unbearable. While his respectful gallantry toward ladies has become legend, his role of cavalier did not extend to the inmates of brothels who might cheer him on as he shot at lewd pictures on the wall.

Sonnischen clarifies this situation: "Most confusion on this subject would be eliminated if people would remember that cowboys were human beings. There were all sorts and conditions. No two were alike. Put two or three of them alongside each other, and the point becomes clear and unmistakable."[29]

Actually, mention of cowboys' sexual activities appears in very few autobiographical works, but more often in newspaper accounts.

A similar void exists concerning his sexual language. In any case, there are, at best, only a few healthy goddams, affectionate sons-of-bitches, and far from prayerful Jesus Christs interspersed with endless expletives. Earthy, obscene, and lewd as it may be, the cowboy's peculiar and descriptive sexual language is still missing after half a century of published lingo, western words, and so-called salty lexicons. "Salty" is the best descriptive of what has been written since, including, Ramon Adams' *Cowboy Lingo* (1936). Oaths, curses, profanity, blasphemy, and obscenity spewed easily from the cowboy's mouth, often without evil or wicked intent, for much depended on the time and place in which they were used. However, when sturdy and lusty profanity and Anglo-Saxonisms become, in the hands of bowdlerizers "gol-derned," "son-of-a-gun," "dern right," "shucks," and "heck," the cowboy becomes mighty lily-livered.

But in this age of permisiveness in literature, theater, motion pictures, magazines, and even in newspapers—including those found on most campuses—there was bound to appear a writer gutsy enough to corral some of these gems. Edgar R. Potter, in his small book *Cowboy Slang* (1971), enlarges the published vocabulary of the range with humorous, sly and blue expressions. Typical of the argot heard around a bunkhouse, branding corral, or simply the campfire are these pristine examples: "Must think her butt is a gold mine since everybodys' a diggin' at it," "A man that stood up before he was weaned," "Like a steer, he can still try," "It now takes him all night to do what he used to do all night," "She wasn't even fit for a drinkin' man to hole up with," "One of them widder's as always wants her weeds plowed under."[30]

[29] Sonnichsen, *Cowboys and Cattle Kings*, p. 89.
[30] Edgar R. Potter, *Cowboy Slang* (Seattle, Washington, 1971), p. 12.

More recently, and far removed from the bunk house, the Lotus Fortune Cookie factory of San Francisco got into the heady business of making adult and X-rated oriental delicacies containing philosophical range lusties. Fat Fong now say: "Cowboy who make love to girl on hillside not on level;" also Fat Fong say: "Cowboy who makes love on horseback not get much of a ride."[31] Furthermore, should the question be asked, "Are you in the mood for love?" the experts on aphrodisiac foods now have given away the cowboy's secret for overcoming impotency. Cowboys who bellied up to the bar demanding sarsaparilla were not sissies, the drink was the traditional remedy. Interestingly enough, male hormone pills are now manufactured from it.[32]

Cowboy versions of cowboy songs, according to N. Howard (Jack) Thorp, "were full of the vernacular of the range and it wasn't always parlor talk, [some of the words] would have burned the readers' eyeballs if printed."[33] These couplets—prurient and sexual—have been bowdlerized and expurgated into innocuousness in order to perpetuate the strong, pure, masculine, and sentimental image.

Probably, "Bucking Bronco," the classic of such songs, lent itself more readily to the skills of the vulgar composers of the bawdy. Several of the stanzas are as follows:

> My love has a gun that has gone to the bad,
> Which makes poor old Jimmy feel pretty damn sad;
> For the gun it shoots high and the gun it shoots low,
> And it wobbles about like a bucking bronco.

> My love had a gun that was dirty and long
> But he wore it to visit the lady gone wrong
> Though once it was strong and it shot straight and true
> Now it wobbles and buckles and it's red, white and blue.

> Lie still ye young bastard
>   Don't bother me so
> Your father's off bucking
>   Another bronco.[34]

However, the song-tamperers are tame in comparison to the sexual image of the cowboy as verbalized in limericks which are the epitomes of

---

[31] "X-Rated Fortune Cookies," *Boulder Daily Camera* (Boulder, Colorado), April 5, 1972, p. 17.

[32] Evelyn Smith, "Violets, Vinegar & Lemonade," *Family Circle*, Vol. LXXVII (November, 1970), 138.

[33] N. Howard (Jack) Thorp, in collaboration with Neil M. Clark, *Pardner of the Wind* (Caldwell, Idaho, 1945), pp. 41–42.

[34] N. Howard (Jack Thorp and Austin E. and Alta S. Fife, *Songs of the Cowboys* (New York, 1966), p. 124.

bawdiness. Like the songs, they were based on key words—riding, bucking, rawhide, gun, saddle, etc., all of which are suggestive of sexual activity. Gathered over a period of years are the following:

There was a cowboy named Hooter,
Who packed a big six-shooter,
When he grabbed the stock
It became hard as a rock,
As a peace-maker it couldn't be cuter.

A cowboy named Bill from Dallas,
Sported a tremendous phallus,
Mainly of callous,
He worked without malice,
In a Fort Worth sporting palace.

Now a cowboy named Jim from Forth Worth,
And his tool of notable girth,
Went to the palace
And used it as ballast,
Swinging back and forth with mirth.

Young cowboys had a great fear,
That old studs once filled with beer,
Completely addle'
They'd throw on a saddle,
And ride them on the rear.[35]

Since so much of the old-time cowboy's image relies on written, rather than actual, experience and oral history, one should not ignore the works of modern image-makers. Nowhere has this image been enlarged and colored more than at the hands of writers and film and TV producers. The motion pictures designated as "Westerns" cover all aspects and characters, but include, at most, only two dozen truly cowboy films during almost seventy years of production. However, in the minds of fans cowboy films are interchangeable with Westerns. The classic cowboy-Western script with hero, heroine, villain, endangered homestead, the chase, and hideout captivated fans for nearly half a century until the appearance of the "New Western."

Our present generation has now witnessed the "messaged Western, comic Western, neurotic Western, adult Western, anti-Western, sociological Western, homosexual Western, Italian, Japanese, and Maoist Western and, now the 'funky' Western." The myth that the old West was a time when all aspects of life were clean, pure, and uncomplicated is shaken.[36]

[35] Contributed by various collectors for use in this particular study.
[36] "Funky Western Funnier than 'High Noon,'" *Denver Post*, November 30, 1972, p. 101.

Frankly, there is really nothing new about the "New Western." The mythology of the unstable hero, the seamy side-kick, the golden-hearted villain, the cowardly cavalry officer, the sadistic killer, and the crusty old cowboy caught in the corral of obsolescence "are derived more from America's mythic oracle, whose home is Hollywood, than from scientific data."[37] Among the cowboy's innumerable film virtues and characteristics: he has no past, he has few friends, he never starts a fight and always wins, he never draws first. This same cowboy may be classed as a sexual puritan, for he shows little desire for women and seldom, if ever, kisses one. "He might be asexual."[38]

To avoid losing identity and relevance, the motion picture and TV producers and writers engage in a mad scramble for conflict and human interest stories. One writer suggests that sophistication can be added to the original formula without losing the vigor of the outdoor epic.[39]

In 1962, George Fenin and William Everson concluded the section "teen-age and adult markets" in their splendid book *The Western*: "So far the West seems to have remained free of drug addiction and homosexuality, but with the new 'free adult screen,' one wonders for how long."[40] And it wasn't long; even before the decade had passed, both were in evidence.

European film critics of Westerns note that in the past two decades many of the characters portrayed and the themes explored are "rich with clinical complexities never suspected by adoring fans."[41] Harry Schein, Swedish critic, in his monograph "The Olympian Cowboy" (1955), suggests that the hero of the motion picture *Shane* is not Zeus, who, disguised as a human being, visits the earth to cavort with its women, but an American saint, the cowboy who died in the Civil War and sits at the right hand. He is a leather-bound angel with a gun . . . ."[42]

More significant, Schein also detects in the blameless life of the cinema cowboy a "sadistic dislike for women."[43] Evidence of this is found earlier (1942) in the film *The Outlaw*, wherein the young hero,

after prolonged abuse, humiliates the woman by choosing, in a tossup between her and a fine horse, the horse. In a priceless homosexual castration fantasy, the father figure of the film shoots off the ear lobes of the young man when

[37] James Carroll, "Contemplation," *National Catholic Reporter*, December 24, 1974, p. 6.
[38] *Ibid.*
[39] George Eells, "TV Western Craze How Long Will It Last?" *Look*, Vol. XXIV (June 24, 1958), p. 70.
[40] George N. Fenin and William K. Everson, *The Western* (New York, 1962), p. 339.
[41] "Le Western," *Time*, Vol. LXVI (July 4, 1955), p. 70.
[42] Harry Schein, "The Olympian Cowboy," *The American Scholar*, Vol. XXIV (Summer, 1955), p. 319.
[43] "Le Western," *Time*, Vol. LXVI, (July 4, 1955), p. 70.

he dares to defend himself. The pistol in Westerns is by now accepted as a phallic symbol.[44]

Thus the post-war Western gradually moved away from scenic and naïve grandeur toward social consciousness and psychological exploration. Westerns and cowboy films now begin with sunsets rather than end with them, and no longer does the trusty steed respond to a dutiful whistle of a loving master. Thin plots are sensationalized by padding with sadism, sodomy, and a series of genital collisions. Nowadays one does not need a tour guide for these trips, but a head shrinker.

This becomes more obvious if gambling, a long-time recognized cowboy pastime, is subjected to analysis. For instance, Sigmund Freud, in his classic paper "Dostoevsky and Parracide" (1928), was the first to assume a sexual basis in gambling.

> Freud penetratingly analyzed the great Russian writer's character and attempted to explain his passion for gambling with compulsive neurotic states and held that the childhood determinant of gambling was a repetition of the compulsion to masturbate . . . the "vice" of masturbation was symbolically transformed and given expression, for play is an equivalent of the old compulsion to masturbate; "playing" is the actual word . . . .[45]

Furthermore, the language of the gambler relies on many sexual and scatalogical terms which are evident in card games. Queen cards are referred to as "whores" and "bitches;" a player has another player "by the balls" when an unbeatable hand is held. The dice player's argot includes such terms as "craps," "to come," and "the come line," and number ten is refered to as "Big Dick." It is not uncommon for the gambler to suggest "I would sure like to get a piece of Lady Luck."[46]

Alfred C. Kinsey, in his study *Sexual Behavior in the Human Male* (1948), points out additional findings: "The highest frequencies of the homosexual we have ever secured anywhere have been in particular rural communities in some of the remote sections of the country."[47] Kinsey lists among possible reasons: Boys on isolated farms have few companions other than brothers, male cousins, neighbors, and older farm hands. Contact with sisters and other females is carefully regulated by family and community moral codes. Furthermore, most farm activities are masculine oriented.[48]

[44] Schein, "The Olympian Cowboy," *The American Scholar*, Vol. XXIV (July 14, 1955), p. 312.

[45] Darrell W. Bolen, M.D., "Sexual and Nonsexual Factors in Gambling," *Sexual Behavior*, Vol. I (October, 1971), p. 78; Sigmund Freud, "Dostoevsky and Parracide," *Collected Works of Sigmund Freud*, edited by James Strachey (New York, 1959), Vol. V, p. 241.

[46] Bolen, "Sexual and Nonsexual Factors in Gambling," *Sexual Behavior*, Vol. I (October, 1971), p. 79.

[47] Alfred C. Kinsey, *Sexual Behavior in the Human Male* (Philadelphia, 1948), p. 457.

[48] *Ibid.*

Beyond this, there is a fair amount of sexual contact among the older males in Western rural areas. It is a type of homosexuality which was probably among pioneers and outdoor men in general. Today it is found among ranchmen, cattle men, prospectors, lumbermen, and farming groups in general—among groups that are virile, physically active. These are men who have faced the rigors of nature in the wild. They live on realities and on a minimum of theory. Such a background breeds the attitude that sex is sex, irrespective of the nature of the partner with whom the relation is had. Sexual relations are had with women when they are available, or with other males when the outdoor routines bring men together into exclusively male groups. Such a pattern is not at all uncommon among pre-adolescent and early adolescent males in such rural areas, and it continues in a number of histories into the adult years and through marriage.[49]

Stanley Vestal in his study of early Dodge City uncovered only one case of cruelty to animals, one case of brutal flogging, and "scarcely any of sexual perversion among other crimes of violence."[50] *The Cattle Towns* by Robert R. Dykstra is no more enlightening on the subject of deviation. Big Nose Kate Fisher [Elder], a paramour of Doc Holliday, a coarse and crude prostitute, was accused by members of her profession of engaging in questionable sexual practices. Henry Sinclair Drago believes that "it certainly couldn't have been her looks that made Doc provide her with Bed and Board for years."[51]

Cowboys attending dances noted for a lack of females tagged their male partners with a scarf tied to the arm (heifer branded) without suggesting any abberation. In *Reminiscences of a Ranchman*, Edgar Beecher Bronson describes the antics of a six-foot-two blond giant, Jake De Puyster, in "drag" at a dance at "The Cowboy's Rest," Ogallala, Nebraska. Dressed in scrounged feminine apparel, he and his buddy Buck joined an unfilled dance set, and "that first quadrille made 'Miss De Puyster' the belle of the day and night...."[52]

Stuart Henry in *Conquering Our Great American Plains* comments on Marshal Wild Bill Hickok's "feminine looks and bearing . . . and his hermaphroditism [Hickok, no cowboy in any sense of the word, accordingly] conducted himself as if courting this confusing, epicene pattern . . . his looks surprise one. That softly rounded contour, that rather angelic countenance, were quite opposite of the then, rawboned Texan model."[53]

[49] *Ibid.*, pp. 457, 459; *See* "A Sex Poll (1973)" *Time* Vol. CII (October 1, 1973), pp. 63–64.

[50] Vestal, p. 68.

[51] Harry Sinclair Drago, *Wild, Woolly & Wicked* (New York, 1960), p. 304.

[52] Edgar Beecher Bronson, *Reminiscences of a Ranchman* (New York, 1908), p. 270.

[53] Stuart Henry, *Conquering Our Great American Plains* (New York, 1930), p. 288.

Almost forty years later, Larry McMurtry, previously referred to, in *Harper's*, September, 1968, offers opinions relative to the cowboy's masculinity:

> I would not wish to make the point crudely, but I do find it possible to doubt that I have ever known a cowboy who liked women as well as he liked horses, and I know that I have never known a cowboy who was as comfortable in the company of women as he was in the company of his fellow cowboys.
>
> This is not, I think, the result of repressed homosexuality but of repressed heterosexuality, complicated by a commitment to a heroic concept of life that simply takes little account of women.[54]

The saddle-sore hero of yore, the American Cowboy, is surrounded by many Freudian symbols because of his costume, horse, gun, and solitary life activities. Again, referring to McMurtry:

> The master symbol for handling the cowboy is the symbol of the horseman. The gunman had his place in mythology of the West, but the cowboy did not realize himself with a gun. Neither did he realize himself with a penis, nor with a bankroll. Movies fault the myth when they dramatize gunfighting, rather than horsemanship, as the primary skill. The cowboy realized himself on a horse, and a man might be broke, impotent, and a poor shot and still hold up his head if he could ride.[55]

Each week, indecisive cowboy film heroes work out their psychological hangups, which would last Freud a lifetime. Now "when someone pulls a gun everyone else wonders what's the matter with the guy? Is he impotent or something? Why does he hang around with the boys all the time? How come he can only make it with prostitutes? . . ."[56]

Millions of Americans identify with the cowboy-myth hero, and this identification extends from the President of the United States and Secretary of State Henry Kissinger down to the ordinary citizen. Former President Nixon, a staunch admirer of John Wayne and Westerns, spoke of getting out of Vietnam, "as a cowboy, with guns blazing, backing out of a saloon."[57] In an unbelievable interview, Kissinger, our Lochinvar, conscious of his own solitary characteristics, commented: "I've always acted aloof. Americans admire that enormously. Americans admire the cowboy leading a caravan alone astride his horse, the cowboy entering a village or city alone on his horse. . . ."[58] What incredible saddle-buddies—himself and Kissinger!

[54] McMurtry, "Take My Saddle From the Wall," *Harper's*, Vol. CCXXXVII (September, 1968), p. 45.

[55] *Ibid.*

[56] Roger Ebert, "Miss Those Old Movie Cliches? There's New Batch," *Denver Post* "Roundup," November 5, 1972, p. 11.

[57] Carroll, "Contemplation," *National Catholic Reporter*, December 4, 1974, p. 6.

[58] Martin F. Nolan, "Kissinger: a Tragic Cowboy," *Rocky Mountain News*, December 25, 1972, p. 43.

Furthermore, throughout the world, and particularly in Europe, the term American is synonymous with cowboy. For instance, Germans are wild about Wild West. Their cowboy and Indian clubs are evidence of this admiration and their western outfitting stores are stacked with cowboy gear and clothing. Among the male toiletries is "Rodeo After Shave" which emphasizes the rugged virility of the cowboy and is advertised as "Rodeo: For Men who like it hot. . . ."[59] A deodorant and anti-perspirant advertisement for women, "Lasso," features a girl sporting a big hat and holding two cans of the product, six-shooter fashion[60]—a definite relationship to cowboy power and sexuality, pistols, the obvious phallic symbol.

The assassination of President John F. Kennedy with a mail-order weapon focused attention on a serious and controversial law enforcement problem. Kenneth Boulding, internationally known economist on the faculty of the University of Colorado, noted that "guns and missiles are phallic symbols, which is one reason for their popularity. Fear of impotence causes a feeling of need for power which is equivalent to orgasm."[61] Furthermore, our frontier tradition fosters the American's love for guns. It is estimated that there "are 200,000 members of 'quick draw clubs' using real guns and wax bullets."[62] Every adult watching Westerns knows that guns and virility go together, and he has much satisfaction in knowing that if he does not possess the latter he can obtain the former.

Wallaby Hornblower, chief lobbyist for the National Cheap Handgun Association, informed columnist Art Buchwald that "the gun is a sex symbol. . . . Most American men who own handguns have virility problems. The gun is an extension of their manhood. . . . If you take the gun away from a man in his country, you're emasculating him."[63] In 1874 Joseph G. McCoy simply said, [The cowboy] "would rather fight with pistols than pray. . . ."[64] However, J. Frank Dobie characterizes the cowboy: "He was a healthy animal . . . anything but a gun-toting, swaggering murderer ready to shoot the daylight out of the first man he met."[65] Psychologist Karl Heiser believes that men may be "displaying sexual impotency by opposing gun-control legislation, [and that] our society has many sexually inadequate

---

59 Observed while traveling on European Faculty Fellowship, 1967. *See* Thomas Freeman, "The Cowboy and the Astronaut—The American Image in German Periodical Advertisements," *Journal of Popular Culture*, Vol. VI (Summer, 1972), pp. 90–91.

60 *Ibid.*

61 Dianne Sadok, "U.S. Needs Exchange—Boulding," *Colorado Daily* (Boulder, Colorado), February 23, 1968, p. 3.

62 Cynthia Lowry, "Death Dealing Weapons," *Boulder Daily Camera*, June 11, 1964, p. 17.

63 Arthur Buchwald, "Sex and the handgun are like peas in the pod," *New Mexican* (Santa Fe, New Mexico), June 13, 1971, p. D 4.

64 McCoy, p. 85.

65 J. Frank Dobie, *A Vaquero of the Brush Country* (Boston, 1946), p. 100.

men and some drive 'fast, powerful cars,' to make them feel sexually potent while others use guns as sex symbols."[66]

With the "dawning of the naked man" the cowboy could not escape the addition of the facet of nudity being added to his image. According to Mark Twain: "Clothes make the man. Naked people have little or no influence in society."[67] Still, motion picture and TV producers strip the cowboy to the waist as proof of strenuous labors, mainly of violence done to him.

Total male nudity became legitimate in 1967, when dancer Rudolf Nureyev appeared in *Vogue* magazine in the altogether. That same year Frank Protopapa boyishly advertised men's underwear, and early in 1972 French couturier Yves Saint-Laurent posed with horned rimmed glasses to launch his new cologne for men.[68] But none of these individuals reached the sensational status of Burt Reynolds following his debut as *Cosmopolitan* magazine's (April, 1972) centerfold pin-up boy, though he "outstripped" that caper when he appeared in the December *Playboy* wearing a football shirt above the waist and below is in the buff.[69]

A rash of exposures followed. The Ladies Home Companion nude male calendar;[70] also, Men For Women, a firm featuring picture posters of unclad males compiled by a group of enterprising women,[71] and the *Harvard Lampoon*, the nation's oldest college humor magazine, featured a parody of the Reynold's escapade with a nude Henry Kissinger centerfold—at least his head superimposed on the body of probably some collegian.[72]

When Miss U.S.A. contestants were questioned about an all-male ideal they listed several. Vermont's entry drooled ecstatically over the TV and film star of "Cheyenne": "Clint Walker—he's got a beautiful body."[73]

Allegedly, Robert E. Kintner, White House aide for President Lyndon B. Johnson and the former president of the National Broadcasting Company, introduced the sex-and-violence-formula to boost the TV ratings. According to a witness during the hearings of the Senate Juvenile Delin-

[66] "Sex Rears Head in Gun-Law Tiff," *Denver Post*, August 21, 1968, p. 26.

[67] *See* Tom Gavin, "Old, Old Story . . . Only Hairier," *Denver Post*, August 18, 1972, p. 25; "The Many Sides of Mark Twain," Compiled by the Editors, *Readers Digest*, Vol. CIII (August, 1973), p. 230.

[68] Lloyd Shearer, ed., "Intelligence Report," *Rocky Mountain News*, "Parade," June 18, 1972, p. 12.

[69] Hy Gardner, "Glad You Asked That," *Rocky Mountain News*, January 15, 1973, p. 54.

[70] "Nude Male Calendar," *Denver Post*, June 23, 1972, p. 40; "Turning the Calendar," *Time*, Vol. XCIX (September 4, 1972), p. 67.

[71] "Firm sells male pin-up posters," *Rocky Mountain News*, October 17, 1972, p. 43.

[72] "Bad nudes on the diplomatic front," *Rocky Mountain News*, October 17, 1972, p. 43.

[73] "All-Male Beauty Contest Leave Girls Undecided," *Boulder Daily Camera*, May 20, 1967, p. 1.

quency subcommittee, Kintner advocated a shirts-off policy and ordered that an episode of "Overland Trail," presenting a long scene with the cowboy in a bath tub, be the first to be shown on the home screen. The witness testified, "I think he [Kintner] felt "Cheyenne" was the greatest western ever produced up to that time [and that] he thought that Clint Walker was an exciting man, a towering human specimen, very attractive to women. . . . I think that sex has the connotation of implying both the sexes; . . . Clint Walker was an example of a sex symbol."[74]

A year later (1968) the film *A Man Called Gannon* had what no other Western had—a couple of nude love scenes. Nudity was bound to come to that genus. In addition, *Gannon* had a cowboy relationship between one man and another beyond Boy Scout devotion.[75] Actually, many of these so-called "new" trends are repeats of what has gone on for some time. Jack Elam's characterization of a jerky psycho in *Rawhide* in 1951 is repeated by Bruce Dern twitching his way through John Wayne's later film *The Cowboys*. Strains of homosexuality showed in *My Darling Clementine* in 1956—a dozen years later so did *Warlock*, and a 1970 release *Doc*, falls in the category of the "new" trend.[76] In that film the famous gun-fight at the OK Corral lasted approximately 32 seconds—as in real life—but more significant is the triangle, with Doc making a choice between the two, Wyatt Earp and Kate Fisher [Elder], and what they represent.

The basic theme of *The Hired Hand*, the tale of an itinerant cowboy, again reveals "that a woman is only a women but a saddle-buddy is man's best friend."[77] The film *Will Penny* portrays a grizzled, range-weary saddle tramp who meets a trouble-beset woman as he approaches the sunset of a lonely life, and, according to a critic, "Its tradition . . . is the West, not the Western,"[78] but it did feature the inevitable you-must-take-a-bath scene.

"Joe Buck is Texas-born and New Mexico-bred, strong in the trousers and weak in the head."[79] Joe, the son and grandson of prostitutes, is the make-believe cowboy of the originally X-rated Oscar winner *Midnight Cowboy*. With neither cows, blazing guns, nor grandeur of scenery, this appalling story of a male stud—hetero and homo—not only fascinated myriads of cowboy worshippers but added a conglomerate of admirers to the growing multitude of devotees. However, this much praised and damned motion picture had redeeming "social merit" and won enthusiastic, although quali-

[74] Jack Anderson, "Sex, Violence on TV," *Denver Post*, May 20, 1967, p. 10.
[75] Dick Kleiner, "Nudie Western Makes Debut," *Rocky Mountain News*, January 14, 1968, p. 7.
[76] David Elliott, "Who Killed Movies' Western Hero?" *Denver Post* "Roundup," June 18, 1972, p. 11.
[77] Judith Crist, "The Week's Movies," *TV Guide*, Vol. XX (December 2, 1972), p. A–9.
[78] "Will Penny," *TV Guide*, Vol. XX (December 16, 1972), p. A–53.
[79] "Joe's Journey," *Time*, Vol. LXXXVI (September 3, 1965), p. 86.

fied, support from the National Catholic Office of Motion Pictures as well as the International Catholic Film Bureau award.

The lure of the word "cowboy" is strong. Columnist Abbey Van Buren, the oracle of the perplexed, received the following query:

> "DEAR ABBEY: Nobody believes me, but when I went to see "Midnight Cowboy," I honestly thought it was a Western. It won the Academy Award so I thought it was worth seeing. Well, after awhile, I realized it wasn't the kind of movie I thought it was, so I went to the box office and asked for my money back. The girl selling tickets said she was sorry but I had seen nearly the whole movie and she couldn't give me my money back. How about that?
>
> GYPPED

> "DEAR GYPPED: I don't know how many minutes make a legal movie, but four and a half innings make a legal ball game. Next time ask to see the Manager.[80]

Long before the movies sullied the cowboy by casting him as an anti-hero, sadist, sodomist, and homosexual, the pornographers found that here was a ready-made sex symbol—a man's man with all the equipment to satisfy the desire and differences of readers and audiences. Such a pictorial sortie into the sordid is *Bronco*[81] which began with carefully posed, and then later air-brushed, nudies at the time when any adult had the right to buy, read, and view within his home whatever he wished. Thus, these stalwart models continued posing in the buff—booted and spurred—with big hats and belted with a brace of low slung six-shooters—the contention being that the cowboy shoots mainly because he has a loaded gun and is better with it than anyone else around.

The Colt Studios produced two such albums entitled *Manpower!* "Studs of the Wild West," featuring a procession of prodigious penises. According to the editors:

> In dealing with the most viril aspects of the masculine image, it was inevitable that the American Cowboy should appear as our prime subject. . . . Some things are just right together. This "rightness" is apparent within the following pages as you enter this world of dust, jeans, chaps, stirrups, boots, leather —and men. Because that's where Colt is—where the men are![82]

Another pictorial, *David Goes Cowboy*, is the extreme of hardcore pornography.[83]

Selective writings of a western pornographic nature extend from the shoddy *Gay on the Range* (1967) by Dick Dale, "back when men were

---

[80] Abigail Van Buren, "Dear Abbey," *Boulder Daily Camera*, September 29, 1970, p. 10.
[81] Miscellaneous photographs from collection of cowboy pornography.
[82] *Manpower!* "Studies of the Wild West," (New York, n.d.) Foreword.
[83] Collection of cowboy pornography.

"Adult Reading"—paperback cover illustrations, 1968. Illustrations courtesy Clifford Westermeier.

men ... more or less"[84] to Richard Amory's libidinous "literature" the Loon Song trilogy. With the appearance of his second book, *Song of Aaron*, the publisher's squib insisted that it is "this generation's most eagerly awaited book ... The spectacular sequel to the best-selling underground sensation ... *Song of the Loon*."[85] Recently, *Song of the Loon* appeared in full color as a motion picture with an all-male cast.[86]

In 1968, advertisements quoting film critic John Wasserman of the *San Francisco Chronicle* and plugging the film *Lonesome Cowboys* by Andy Warhol commented: [It] "is a magnificent and very funny satire of the American West that is liberally seasoned with our favorite 4, 8, 10, and 12-letter words and a cornucopia of nudity and sexual carryings-on that is—in combination—perhaps unprecedented."[87]

It is touted by other critics as the "true story of what it was like to live the life of a cowboy in the Old West. . . . a story of men among men . . . a

[84] Dick Dale, *Gay on the Range* (San Diego, 1967).
[85] Richard Amory, *Song of the Loon* (San Diego, 1967).
[86] [Advertisement], *Denver Post*, February 14, 1973, p. 31.
[87] *New York Times*, May 14, 1969, p. 10–1).

Newspaper advertisements of X-rated and triple X-rated motion pictures of 1970–73 vintage. Illustration courtesy Clifford Westermeier.

wild troupe of homosexual cowboys, a transvestite sheriff, and a woman who would undo them all."[88] Philip Hartung, critic for *Commonweal* suggests it be titled, *Homo on the Range.*[89]

[88] [Advertisement], *Colorado Daily*, April 17, 1970, p. 8; "Warhol Spoofs the West," *Rocky Mountain News*, April 7, 1972, p. 62; Dan Wakefield, "No Thrills, Lotta Laughs," *Atlantic*, Vol. CCXXIII (April, 1969), p. 140.

[89] Philip T. Hartung, "The Screen," *Commonweal*, Vol. XC (July 25, 1969), 465.

Along the porno-alleys of our cities are found such films as *Uprising*—the first triple X-rated Western; *Girls in the Saddle, San Francisco Cowboy*, and *Meat Rack*, which is claimed to begin where *Midnight Cowboy* left off.[90] The film *Magnificent Cowboys*, with an all-male cast, produced for the deviate fan, and *Hot Spur*, from Olympic International films,[91] might well be entitled *Horny Hombres, Rape Ranch*, or *Tit for Tat*. Of this latter film one might well ask how the belted, booted, spurred, holstered, Levied, hatted, and rope-toting cowboys rape anything, let alone rope a steer!

These tawdry skin flicks truly live up to their advertising as films of blatant rawness and suggest that in the cowboys' world women were the only thing cheaper than life. *Le Monde Weekly*, commenting on much of modern film-making says: "The object nowadays is to turn out films for *voyeurs*—they are not new, but they are not art, they are simply sex for the poor."[92] In light of the price of admission this statement is suspect, but in many instances the greatest obscenity is the admission fee.

From the dawn of his era, the cowboy suffered from overexposure. He rapidly became one of the most notable stereotypes of the West, and in the passage of a century all media of communication have treated these stereotypes. Now the working cowboy is the forgotten man of novels, cinema, and TV, while the fictionalized image dominates the scene to the extent that his real-life counterpart is obliterated. Although his occupation has been whittled down, his image has grown steadily as a misfit hero of an age long past. Symbolizing the adventuresome spirit, the cowboy became the center of a cult which enshrined him in the hearts of millions of admirers.

History dictates that the cowboy must go, but what the image-makers are doing in order to sustain him is a regretful commentary. It was between the pages of western thrillers that the post-Civil War generations found the romance they craved. They found it in those writings of the unusual and spectacular, and accepted it as reality. However, they were no more improbable than the motion picture and TV fare which have continued to perpetuate the fictional cowboy as the most popular American figure of the West and the fictional West as the most American part of America. At best, it has enabled all to be a part of that last grand image of the West.

Turned into a machine, the cowboy and his code, mythic as they might be, have been destroyed. Stricken with the disease of this century, the cowboy retains the least significant tool of his trade—a gun, the sexual symbol of an individual's dictatorial presence. The American West was the last locale in which the individual remained supreme, but the cowboy, a stark

90 "Adult Entertainment," *Rocky Mountain News*, October 19, 1971, p. 48.
91 "Adult Entertainment," *Denver Post*, November 30, 1972, p. 101.
92 "Skin, Sweat and Leers," *Le Monde Weekly* (Paris, France), November 18, 1970, p. 8.

symbol of individuality, apparently is no longer necessary for survival. Thus, the flame of the old West, which was the storehouse for our fantasies, is no longer burning.

Yet, the fictional betrayal of the West and its most romantic figure probably will never be completely displaced by realism, because the man on horseback *without* cows has become the symbol of the West. It was an escape from reality, even though it exploited a greater reality. This fictionalization met the increasing public demand for a wild and wooly West with a gallant hero until the souls of both were eliminated. The symbolic qualities for, and influence on, youngsters and adults no longer exist.

It is probably true that the cowboy existed more in the minds and works of the image-makers than in real life; but there was a very human man other than the one fabricated and foisted upon our country, who belied the illusion found in novels and on screens. In many ways what has happened to the cowboy is what is happening to America now—both no longer appear squeaky-clean.

Cowboys on arrival in the big cities resorted to the pleasure palaces "with their large glittering diamond-dust mirrors and tinsel tarts." (Illustrated by Terence Duren) *The American West* by Beebe and Clegg. Illustration courtesy Clifford Westermeier.

DICK RANDALL

The cowboy who became known as the "father of dude ranching" in Montana. Photograph courtesy of Burlington Northern Railroad.

The Cowboy and the Dude

BY LAWRENCE R. BORNE

THE COWBOY, AND THE CATTLE INDUSTRY that made him a folk hero, came out of Texas in the aftermath of the Civil War. With the simple combination of a supply of cattle in Texas, a demand for beef in the North, and the rapid growth of western railroads, a new style was added to an old industry. The Long Drive became part of American folklore as driving cattle to Kansas railheads conjured up images of hard-riding cowboys, wild cowtowns, and fast-gun marshals.

The cattle industry was not static, however, and changes soon broadened the trade. New markets opened in New Mexico and on the northern plains as soldiers and miners looked for supplies of beef while they hunted Indians or gold. Cattle and cowboys followed these new markets, and soon both were spread throughout the far West. Unknown to the cowboy, or to his employers, the stage was being prepared for the introduction of the dude ranch, an institution that would prove to be an additional impetus to opening the West to the East.

The word "dude" acquired a new meaning in the West, and most dictionaries do not give much of a clue to this unique concept. Most equate the word with a fancy dresser; "dandy" is usually the closest synonym agreed upon. "Dude" entered Western slang to mean a visitor whose attire was fancy compared to the cowboy's working clothes[1] and, for a time in Wyoming, it meant anyone who came there wearing a white collar.[2] Eventually it indicated anyone who was not a resident of the region he was visiting.[3] It did not necessarily denote ignorance, softness, or being a

---

[1] Brooke Burnham, "Are Some Dude Ranchers Flying Under False Colors?" *The Dude Rancher*, Vol. XXII, No. 1 (January, 1953), p. 14.

[2] *The Wyoming State Journal* (Lander), June 16, 1926, p. 6.

[3] *Wyoming State Tribune* (Cheyenne), July 20, 1929, p. 1, Vertical Files, Ranches and Ranching, Dude Ranches #2, Wyoming State Archives and Historical Department, Cheyenne.

"greenhorn" or "tenderfoot," but rather a visitor who hired someone to guide him, or cook for him, or who paid to stay on a ranch.[4]

There is probably no way to identify the first person who visited the far West simply to enjoy it, rather than to seek furs, gold, or other wealth. Long before the cattlemen arrived, visitors had been coming in order to enjoy the western climate and scenery. One example was Rufus Sage, who, in 1842, was a tourist in the Middle Park area of Colorado.[5] Another was Bill Sublette, the mountain man, who decided in 1844 to take some invalids to Brown's Hole in northwestern Colorado for a summer outing.[6] The mountain men themselves admitted that one of the reasons they entered the fur trade was to see the western United States.[7]

But this type of visiting and adventure was not dude ranching; rather it was an indication that the West held attractions whose value would be slowly recognized and exploited.

Cattlemen were not concerned with scenery and adventure, but rather with beef and markets. Their interest was certainly justified, as the industry boomed through the 1870's and into the 1880's, and profits soared—some in fact and some only on paper. Raising cattle in the West became so attractive that thousands of people and millions of dollars of investment money flowed to the trans-Mississippi West from the East and from foreign nations. Among the many who came were the Eaton Brothers of Pittsburgh, Pennsylvania, men who would help initiate the dude ranch. The Eatons had suffered some financial difficulties in the East and decided in the late 1870's to "make their fortune" in western ranching.[8] They had the backing of some wealthy Pennsylvanians and established several ranches near Medora, in Dakota Territory, where they raised horses and cattle.[9] The Custer Trail Ranch, run by Howard Eaton, became the brothers' headquarters.[10]

It also became the regular vacation spot for a seemingly endless supply of Eastern friends who learned of the gracious western hospitality that existed in a land where good hunting was also available.[11] While the Eatons welcomed their visitors and enjoyed their company, they soon realized that

[4] M. Struthers Burt, *The Diary of a Dude Wrangler* (New York, 1924), p. 60.

[5] Robert C. Black III, *Island in the Rockies: The History of Grand County, Colorado, to 1930* (Boulder, 1969), pp. 22–23.

[6] Bernard DeVoto, *The Year of Decision, 1846* (Boston, 1943), pp. 54, 65.

[7] Robert E. Riegel and Robert G. Athearn, *America Moves West* (5th edition, New York, 1971), pp. 312–14.

[8] Hermann Hagedorn, *Roosevelt in the Bad Lands* (Boston, 1930), pp. 109–10.

[9] C. L. Sonnichsen, *Cowboys and Cattle Kings: Life on the Range Today* (Norman, 1950), p. 164.

[10] Charles, Alden, and Willis were the other three brothers; Charles apparently remained in the East.

[11] Hagedorn, pp. 25, 109–10. See also Joseph P. Sullivan, "A Description and Analysis of the Dude Ranching Industry in Montana" (unpublished Master's thesis, School of Forestry, University of Montana, 1971), p. 11.

Howard Eaton (on right, with outstretched arm), generally considered to be the founder of dude ranching. Courtesy J. E. Haynes, St. Paul, Minn.

the profit they were making on their stock was being swallowed by the cost of entertaining their friends. At first they thought the answer was to have the guests pay only their share of the expenses, but they soon realized that a new business opportunity had opened to them.[12] The visitors were willing, and even anxious, to pay for their entertainment, and the Eatons saw that they could make a profit with a guest ranch just as they did with horses and cattle. In 1882 they accepted their first paying guests.[13]

Thus the Eatons are generally credited with being the founders of the dude ranch industry; they and their cowboys were soon spending much of their time taking care of dudes in addition to horses and cattle.[14] Riding, hunting, and fishing were the chief attractions for guests at Eatons', the same appeals which, incidentally, drew Theodore Roosevelt out West to become a neighbor of the Eaton Brothers.[15] While these forms of relaxation would always be important to dude ranch visitors, another factor, and a totally unexpected development, began in 1885, when wealthy Eastern parents decided to send to the ranch their offspring who "were over-addicted to strong drink."

[12] Burt, pp. 60–63.
[13] Eaton Ranch Collection, Custer Trail Ranch Guest Register for the Years 1883 through 1903, Western History Research Center, University of Wyoming, Laramie.
[14] Charles G. Roundy, "The Origins and Early Development of Dude Ranching in Wyoming," *Annals of Wyoming*, Vol. 45, No. 1 (Spring, 1973), p. 16.
[15] Brochure, "Eatons' Ranch Wolf, Wyoming," p. 3. Clippings File, "Dude Ranches–Wyoming," Western History Department, Denver Public Library.

A less-likely place to avoid the temptation of alcohol could scarcely be imagined, since Medora housed more than a dozen saloons, and drinking was considered almost the patriotic duty of the local populace. While the Eatons kept liquor from these Eastern-banished guests, the Medora saloon-keepers discovered a new and interesting market. The dudes regularly returned from town with all the alcohol they could carry "without and within, and the cowboys round about swore solemnly that you couldn't put your hand in the crotch of any tree within a hundred yards of the Eatons' ranch-house without coming upon a bottle concealed by a dude being cured of 'the drink.' " At Bill Williams' saloon in Medora, "Eatons' dudes" could always provoke a laugh when everything else failed to rouse a comment.[16]

The Eatons survived this use of their ranch as a place of cure for alcoholics and built a prosperous business that is still operating. They did not, however, cause an instant switch to dude ranching among western ranchers. The cowboys and others around Medora could afford to laugh at the dudes, for cattle and horses were still the way to make money in the Badlands, as well as in the rest of the Plains in the early and mid-1880's. But the soaring profits would not continue forever, since serious problems were developing in the western cattle business. Vast outside investment created a large number of cattle companies and a critical problem developed in the Northern Plains—overgrazing. There were simply too many cattle being put on the limited grasses available. Most western land belonged to the federal government, but in practice this meant the land was controlled by those strong enough to hold it. Some cattlemen realized that overgrazing was a serious threat to continued use of the land, but they were unable to halt it, even through their Cattlemen's Associations.[17]

Overgrazing eventually would combine with a natural disaster to change the western cattle industry. The collapse of the boom came when the legendary winter of 1886–87 hit the Plains. The story of this winter has been told many times: bitter sub-zero temperatures, never-ending snow-storms, and layers of ice covering both feed and cattle. When warm weather finally arrived in March, it revealed utter disaster; losses of 50 to 60 per cent of the cattle were common, while some ranches lost as much as 90 per cent of their herds. Some cattle companies were completely destroyed, others would have to reorganize, and the range cattle industry would never again be the same.[18]

One of the less-noticed by-products of this change was the growth of

[16] Hagedorn, pp. 110, 260–61.

[17] Lewis Atherton, *The Cattle Kings* (Bloomington, Indiana, 1961), pp. 156, 165.

[18] For example, see: Ernest S. Osgood, *The Day of the Cattleman* (Chicego, 1966) pp. 218–22.

the dude ranch, a neglected but significant institution in Western history. It would become the method of introducing the West to many outsiders, and it would also be an economic salvation for many ranchers and cowboys. And the dude ranch, while beginning in the northern plains, would spread throughout the West and return eventually to the cowboys' home, Texas.

An excellent illustration of the cowboy's plight in this era is the story of Dick Randall, a man who became known as the "father of dude ranching" in Montana. Randall came from Iowa to Montana Territory in 1884, when he was eighteen years old. He made friends quickly and became a cowboy, thus fulfilling a dream that had lured hundreds of boys and men from the Midwest and East. After the severe winter of 1886–87, however, he and his friends could not find jobs as cowboys and had to seek new work. In the fall of 1887 they went out as packers with some hunters; Randall enjoyed this new occupation and continued to guide hunters for the next fifteen years. He eventually bought some land on Cedar Creek, northeast of Gardiner, and began the OTO Ranch.[19] Here his hunters stayed for a few days or weeks in preparation for their trips; they recommended the OTO to friends who wanted a place to visit, and soon Dick Randall had many non-hunting guests, also. He had become a dude wrangler.[20]

The former cowboy built the OTO into a thriving operation in the early twentieth century and became one of the charter members of the Dude Ranchers' Association in 1926.[21] He continued his ranching until his retirement in 1934.[22] The winter of 1886–87 thus turned Randall in the direction of a new occupation that he followed most of the rest of his life.

Another impetus to dude ranching was the appearance of the "remittance man" in the West. The dictionary described him simply as one "who lives abroad supported by remittances at home."[23] Mary Shawver, a co-owner of one of the early Wyoming dude ranches, gave him a more appropriate Western definition as

> the embarrassment to some family in the east; he may be a real or a fancied one. He may have an unquenchable thirst, his mental IQ may at times lean a little toward the minus side; it may be any number of things that Sister may think impedes her progress toward the inner circle of the Astorbilts.[24]

19 L. W. (Gay) Randall, *Footprints Along the Yellowstone* (San Antonio, 1961), pp. 65–69.

20 "Dude Wrangler" meant either the man who took care of the dudes or a dude who came West; in this article it is used in the first sense.

21 Randall, *Footprints Along the Yellowstone*, pp. 74–75.

22 L. W. (Gay) Randall, "The Man Who Put the Dude in Dude Ranching," *Montana*, Vol. X, No. 3 (July, 1960), p. 41.

23 *Webster's New World Dictionary of the American Language* (College Edition, New York, 1962), p. 1230.

24 Mary Shawver, *Sincerely, Mary S.* (Casper, Wyoming, n.d.), pp. 6–7.

Whatever the reason for this banishment, the remittance man was sent West, often stayed permanently, and sometimes became a noted Western citizen. While learning to adapt to the West, he needed a place to live, and ranches were among the few possible choices. The money these men brought was needed in the West, hence many ranches improved their food and lodging to satisfy these newcomers.[25]

Such a man was Clement Bengough, son of a wealthy English family. His only fault, or embarrassing trait, was an overwhelming shyness that made even the most elementary social contacts in England painful to him; this finally drove him to the United States as a remittance man in late 1886 or early 1887, when he became one of the first dudes in Wyoming.[26] The location that Bengough chose was the Sanders 91 Ranch, twenty-five miles west of Laramie. Two Englishmen, Neil Gresley and John Robbins, owned it and sought men from England who wished to experience western life and learn the cattle business. Preferring to call their visitors "learners" instead of "dudes," they charged $500 a year to teach the young men how to ride, rope, and brand. Bengough was one of the first of these "learners," and he provided Gresley and Robbins with an added income from his regular remittances from England.

Bengough was certainly not the typical Westerner; the home he left in England was an estate called The Ridge, Wotton-under-Edge, and contrasted sharply with the crude accommodations he found in the West. He kept a library in his western log cabin, occasionally wrote a check in Latin, and kept eleven vicious Siberian wolfhounds for his hunting expeditions. After a year or two as a "learner," he bought his own land and got along well with his neighbors in Wyoming, where he lived till his death in 1934.[27]

Bengough and other remittance men thus helped the Western economic situation. The hard winter of 1886–87 had forced ranchers to adjust, and some of them decided that accepting paying guests was a satisfactory way to tide themselves over some difficult times. A few years later the Panic of 1893 caused more hardships and forced additional ranchers to accept dudes to keep themselves in business.[28]

Dude ranching followed no orderly plan of development; like Topsy,

[25] E. C. Abbott, *We Pointed Them North: Recollections of a Cowpuncher* (Norman, 1955) pp. 4, 138.

[26] Handwritten account of Clement Bengough by his niece, Evelyn Rosa Bengough, Sept. 25, 1970, Biographical Manuscript File: Bengough, Clement Stuart, Western History Research Center, University of Wyoming.

[27] Robert H. Burns, Andrew S. Gillespie and Willing G. Richardson, *Wyoming's Pioneer Ranches* (Laramie, 1955), pp. 238–48.

[28] Interview with John G. Holzwarth, August 15, 1971. Mr. Holzwarth operated the Neversummer Ranch near Grand Lake, Colorado, from 1919 until 1973; he is one of the oldest dude ranch operators in the state.

it "jes growed" was the way one rancher explained it.[29] Some ranches became dependent on dudes to the near exclusion of other business interests, while other ranches ignored the dude business completely. The area around Jackson Hole, Wyoming, was one that benefitted immensely from the dude business. It seemed to be on the verge of economic collapse in the early twentieth century, but there were many dudes who wanted to hunt there, and the local residents became dude wranglers or guides from simple economic need. This type of business was a mixed blessing to the Jackson Hole area, however, since the unlimited hunting nearly led to the extinction of the big game. Eventually the hunting was controlled, and one of the area's best resources was preserved.[30] Another area that saw heavy dependence on the dude business was Cody, Wyoming. Here Billy Howell and Mary Shawver developed Holm Lodge to cater to travelers to Yellowstone Park; this ranch is generally believed to be the first one in America that was totally dependent on the dude business. Cody was also the site of other ranches and lodges that served the tourist trade.[31]

Customers for the dude ranches seemed to be abundant, since the West continued to appeal to outsiders despite the decline of mining and stock raising as spectacular, money-making industries. The main attractions were hunting, fishing, and sightseeing, and pack trips lasting as long as forty-five days were a popular way of enjoying all three of these in the early days of dude ranching.[32] The ranch would serve as the base camp or starting point, as the trips went to the scenic areas the guests wished to see. And each group of satisfied visitors soon became the ranches' best advertisers, since they spread the word to others seeking a measure of adventure or excitement in a new vacation spot.[33]

Of course, all these activities required horses for the dudes, and cowboys or wranglers to care for both. As Oliver LaFarge explained, every good dude ranch needed

> men who will ride twenty-four hours straight and think nothing of it, who can tough it out for a week hunting horses, with no bedding and little grub, who can handle animals and, if need be, people through every accident of rain and storm and sand.

[29] Charles H. Cooper to Charles Donnelly, President Northern Pacific Railway, November 10, 1927, Northern Pacific Railway Company Records, President's File #201–1, Research Center, Minnesota Historical Society, St. Paul.

[30] *The Ft. Collins Express*, Oct. 17, 1906, pp. 5, 8. Letter to the Editor from W. B. Shepard.

[31] *The Dude Rancher*, Vol. XXI, No. 3 (July, 1952), p. 8.

[32] Neil Morgan, "Hey, Dude!" *Western's World: The Magazine of Western Airlines*, Vol. 4, No. 3 (June/July, 1973), p. 43.

[33] Mildred A. Martin, *The Martins of Gunbarrel* (Caldwell, Idaho, 1959), p. 218. See also Arthur N. Pack, *The Ghost Ranch Story* (Philadelphia, 1960), p. 23.

Mary Roberts Rinehart at Eaton's Ranch in Wyoming. Her writings helped popularize dude ranching in the early twentieth century. Photograph courtesy of Burlington Northern Railroad.

And LaFarge also noted that "you can bet a pile of blue chips as long as his rope" that the men who did this were cowboys.[34]

Such stalwart workers were needed, for instance, when Dick Randall led a pack trip through Yellowstone Park with 173 guests from the San Francisco Sierra Club; the trip required forty workers and nearly two hundred horses and mules. Pack trips were not the only activity, however, that required cowboys; as the number of guests increased on a particular ranch, all ranch operations had to be enlarged. More beef, chickens, dairy products, and vegetables were required; and most of this had to come from the ranches themselves, since they were too far from towns to be supplied easily. And cowboys had to become more diverse in order to handle all these jobs on the dude ranch.[35]

[34] Oliver LaFarge, "They All Ride," *Vogue*, Vol. 87, No. 9 (May 1, 1936), p. 97, Northern Pacific Railway Co. Records, President's File #2001, Burlington Northern files, St. Paul.
[35] Randall, *Footprints Along the Yellowstone*, pp. 69–71, 75–76.

Three states emerged as the leaders in the early days of dude ranching: Wyoming, Montana, and Colorado. Typifying this trend was the fact that the Eaton brothers moved their ranch to the Big Horn mountains near Sheridan, Wyoming, in 1904; the move was prompted by the depletion of rangeland in North Dakota and by guests who wanted more varied vacation activity, especially pack trips to Yellowstone Park and into the Big Horn Mountains.[36] Mountains and scenic areas that were or would become National Parks were thus the early drawing points for these first dude ranches. Yellowstone National Park[37] was obviously a big attraction for guests of ranches in both Wyoming and Montana, while Rocky Mountain National Park[38] became a significant site for Colorado visitors. Dude ranches preceded the establishment of the latter park, since many visitors learned of the scenic attractions before the federal government set the land aside for the Park.

In Colorado, for instance, Henry Lehman, a German immigrant, had started a ranch near Granby in the Middle Park area of the state; it became a stopping point for travelers on their way to Grand Lake, the southern entrance to the area that would become Rocky Mountain National Park.[39] By the early 1890's Lehman's ranch was a well-developed dude operation.[40] Similarly, other dude accommodations were added to ranches in the vicinity of Estes Park, the eastern entrance to the Rocky Mountain Park area.[41]

Hunting, spectacular mountain vistas, and access to parks thus gave these three states a lead in attracting visitors and creating dude ranches. But desert and canyon scenery soon beckoned others farther south, as Arizona and New Mexico joined the dude business, particularly as the sites for ranches that provided winter vacation spots.[42] Dude ranching eventually developed in the other western states, too; Texas apparently first became involved in the 1920's, when ranchers near Bandera discovered that "you can run more dudes to the acre than you can cattle."[43]

Cowboys, and others who considered themselves original pioneers in the West, reacted to the growth of dude ranching in various ways. Some, like Dick Randall and Howard Eaton, took to dude ranching as the proverbial

[36] *Casper Star-Tribune*, Dec. 22, 1968, p. 9. *See also Sheridan Journal*, May 17, 1929, pp. 1, 7.

[37] Established in 1872.

[38] Established in 1915.

[39] Nell Pauly, *The Day Before Yesterday* (Apple Valley, California, 1972), p. 105.

[40] Black, p. 218.

[41] *Denver Times*, June 25, 1899, p. 17.

[42] Raymond J. Raddy, "Dude Ranching is Not All Yippee!" *The Western Horseman*, Vol. XVII, No. 4 (April, 1952), p. 16.

[43] Jerome L. Rodnitzky, "Recapturing The West: The Dude Ranch in American Life," *Arizona and the West*, Vol. 10 (Summer, 1968), p. 114.

Some dudes and their horses at the Ox Yoke Ranch, Emigrant, Montana. Photograph courtesy of Burlington Northern Railroad.

duck does to water. Another man who reacted similarly was Charles Moore, who was born and reared near Fort Washakie, Wyoming, where his father was the post trader. Moore was sent to a secondary school in New Jersey, but he spent his summer vacations in Wyoming with his classmates from the East. After finishing high school, he returned to Wyoming, where he trapped and hunted and worked as a cowboy.[44] Moore left the West again when he went to the University of Michigan and obtained a law degree, but he yearned to make his living in the outdoors. He remembered how his eastern classmates had enjoyed their summers in Wyoming, so he returned there and began taking boys on pack trips. He started in 1907 and gradually built a successful "packing" operation. Relatives of the boys wanted a place to stay when they came to get them at the end of the summer trips; Moore, therefore, built cabins to accommodate these relatives, and from these cabins he started the CM dude ranch. The ranch soon dominated his time

[44] Clipping from unidentified newspaper "CM Is Second Oldest Dude Ranch in State," n.d., Charles Cornell Moore Memorial Collection, unprocessed material, Western History Department, Denver Public Library.

Horses have long been the center of attention on dude ranches. Photograph courtesy of Burlington Northern Railroad.

and he ended the boys' pack trips to concentrate on it.[45] What is especially significant is that the dude business gave Moore his opportunity to return to the West and the outdoor life that he had known in his youth.

Not everyone reacted as enthusiastically as Moore, Randall, and Howard Eaton; some Westerners looked at dude ranching suspiciously and/or ridiculed it. The dude-ranch men were actually among the most far-sighted Westerners, since they understood that raising stock would not always guarantee economic success in certain areas of the West. Many Westerners, however, had to be convinced of this fact.[46] Struthers Burt, a writer and successful dude rancher, tried to explain this to his ranch hands; he insisted that they should still consider themselves cowpunchers, since they led basically the same life their fathers and grandfathers had. And they should retain the cowboys' customs and clothing, since both were practical and picturesque. The fact that they were picturesque also meant that

[45] *Ibid.*, Typed statement by C. C. Moore, "Frontier Notes," and typed statement, "Charles Cornell Moore."
[46] Burt, p. 49.

Easterners would travel a long way to see them and to try to experience something of Western life.[47]

In addition, the dude wrangler did not have to consider himself an underling or inferior to the dudes. He could meet them on a footing of equality, even though he served them, because his way of life was so strange to the outsider. Instead of their becoming his boss, he became theirs, because of their dependence on him.[48]

The work required of a dude wrangler differed somewhat from that of a cowboy, even though it was similar in some respects; both certainly had to ride well and know horses. Knowing the horses was critical for the dude wrangler, for he had to be able to mount properly all types of guests, from the most timid to the expert, old and young, male and female[49]—all with an astonishing variety of temperaments.[50] Finding suitable animals was especially difficult in the earliest days of dude ranching, since the ranchers had to rely on cow horses and Indian ponies.[51] Some of these animals were so rank that they were dangerous, even to the cowboys, and had to be killed.[52] And horses were used extensively on dude ranches—on pack trips, for shorter sight-seeing jaunts, and even to transport the guests to the ranches.[53]

Horses, and everything related to them, were thus the backbone of the dude wranglers' work. But this was not all that was needed, since wranglers were expected to have skills never dreamed necessary for the cowboy. Playing a guitar and singing, for instance, were desirable characteristics. The image of a guitar-strumming cowhand sitting near a campfire may seem to be a myth of the movies, but on a dude ranch he was often a reality.[54] Ranch guests, especially women, expected such entertainment, and astute ranch owners supplied it whenever possible. In addition, dudes were notorious for asking questions on every conceivable subject, and the wrangler was expected to have a practical knowledge of geology, plant life, animals, wildlife management, and forest conservation.[55]

[47] Rodnitzky, "Recapturing The West: The Dude Ranch in American Life," *Arizona and the West*, Vol. 10 (Summer, 1968) pp. 124–25.

[48] *Ibid.*, p. 122.

[49] Raddy, "Dude Ranching is Not All Yippee!" *The Western Horseman*, Vol. XVII, No. 4 (April, 1952), p. 36.

[50] Struthers Burt, "Western Horses and Eastern Riders," *The Dude Rancher*, Vol. XVII, No. 2 (April, 1948), p. 39.

[51] Leta Tompkins, "Dude Horse," *The Western Horseman*, Vol. XVII, No. 4 (April, 1952), p. 14.

[52] Frank A. Tinker, "Whatever Happened to Dude Ranches?" *Catholic Digest*, Vol. 38, No. 9 (July, 1974), p. 103.

[53] *The Dude Rancher*, Vol. I, No. 2 (March, 1933), p. 6.

[54] Randall, *Footprints Along the Yellowstone*, pp. 75–76.

[55] Rodnitzky, "Recapturing the West: The Dude Ranch in American Life," *Arizona and the West*, Vol. 10 (Summer, 1968), p. 122.

Such a variety of duties for the cowboy-turned-wrangler prompted an anonymous author to write a piece of verse titled "The Wrangler's Lament." After listing some of his trials and tribulations with dudes, the imaginary wrangler concludes:

> I'm a tough, hard-boiled old cowhand
> with a weatherbeaten hide,
> But herdin' cows is nuthin' to teachin'
> dudes to ride.
> I can stand their hitoned langwidge an'
> their hifalutin' foods—
> But you can bet your bottom dollar I'm
> fed up on wranglin' dudes![56]

There was the possibility that there was even more unpleasant work for the wrangler than that described by "The Wrangler's Lament," or in previous examples. In an article titled "Is Dude Ranching the Answer in Rangeland?" Tacetta Walker explains this possibility:

> Did you ever see a cowboy that could be induced to go near a milk cow in the good old days? Go to the dude ranch now and watch him in his high-heeled boots and wide brimmed hat, a milk bucket on his arm going jauntily down the path to the corral where the gentle "moo" of the Jersey greets him.

Fresh milk was needed for the comforts of the dudes so cowboys had to milk cows![57]

A long and humorous commentary on cowboys turning dude wranglers appeared in a song written by Gail Gardner, a long-time cattleman in Arizona. In the 1920's cattle prices were low, and the ranchers could not afford to hire cowboys, so many were forced to go to work on dude ranches. Incidents concerning one of his cowboy friends prompted Mr. Gardner to write "The Dude Wrangler."

> I'll tell you of a sad, sad story,
> Of how a cowboy fell from grace,
> Now really this is something awful,
> There never was so sad a case.
>
> One time I had myself a pardner,
> I never knowed one half so good;
> We throwed our outfits in together,
> And lived the way that cowboys should.

[56] Basil Woon, *None of the Comforts of Home—But Oh, Those Cowboys!* (Reno, 1967), n.p.

[57] *Wyoming State Tribune*, Dec. 19, 1936, p. 2.

119

He savvied all about wild cattle,
And he was handy with a rope,
For a gentle-well reined pony,
Just give me one that he had broke.

He never owned no clothes but Levis,
He wore them until they was slick,
And he never wore no great big Stetson,
'Cause where we rode the brush was thick.

He never had no time for women,
So bashful and so shy was he,
Besides he knowed that they was poison,
And so he always let them be.

Well he went to work on distant ranges;
I did not see him for a year.
But then I had no cause to worry,
For I knowed that some day he'd appear.

One day I rode in from the mountains,
A-feelin' good and steppin' light,
For I had just sold all my yearlin's,
And the price was out of sight.

But soon I seen a sight so awful,
It caused my joy to fade away,
It filled my very soul with sorrow
I never will forgit that day.

For down the street there come a-walkin'
My oldtime pardner as of yore,
Although I know you will not believe me,
Let me tell you what he wore.

He had his boots outside his britches;
They was made of leather green and red,
His shirt was a dozen colors,
Loud enough to wake the dead.

Around his neck he had a 'kerchief,
Knotted through a silver ring;
I swear to Gawd he had a wrist-watch,
Who ever heard of such a thing.

Sez I "Old scout now what's the trouble?
"You must have et some loco weed,
"If you will tell me how to help you,
"I'll git you anything you need."

120

Well he looked at me for half a minute,
And then he began to bawl;
He sez, "Bear with me while I tell you
What made me take this awful fall."

"It was a woman from Chicago
Who put the Injun sign on me;
She told me that I was romantic,
And just as handsome as could be."

Sez he, "I'm 'fraid that there ain't nothin'
That you can do to save my hide,
I'm wranglin' dudes instead of cattle,
I'm what they call a first-class guide.

"Oh I saddles up their pump-tailed ponies,
I fix their stirrups for them too,
I boost them up into their saddles,
They give me tips when I am through.

"It's just like horses eatin' loco,
You can not quit it if you try,
I'll go on wranglin' dudes forever,
Until the day that I shall die."

So I drawed my gun and throwed it on him,
I had to turn my face away.
I shot him squarely through the middle,
And where he fell I left him lay.

I shorely hated for to do it,
For things that's done you cain't recall,
But when a cowboy turns dude wrangler,
He aint no good no more at all.[58]

Mr. Gardner's song illustrates humorously some of the antagonisms between cowboys and dude ranching. While it is humorous, there was a certain amount of seriousness about this conflict. Obviously, some cowboys and others in the cattle business were critical of dudes, and there was considerable reluctance by some cowboys to become dude wranglers. As Pete Smythe, Denver radio personality and ex-dude rancher, explained it, animals are easier to handle than people. In addition, horses and cattle don't talk back or play politics, they are not consciously unkind, and they can be herded.[59]

[58] Letter from Gail Gardner to the author, Aug. 19, 1974. "The Dude Wrangler" is on pp. 12–13 of a booklet titled *Orejana Bull For Cowboys Only*, published by the Desert Caballeros in Wickenburg, Arizona, in 1935 and 1950.
[59] Pete Smythe, *Pete Smythe: Big City Dropout* (Boulder, 1968), p. 208.

However, the reaction of most cowboys to dude ranching seemed to be somewhere between total acceptance and outright rejection. The cowhand's work was never a bed of roses, and sometimes a dude wrangling job looked pretty good after the hard work and long hours the cowboy endured. Some men alternated between cattle and dudes, finding the company of one a pleasant change from the other.[60] As various changes came to cattle ranches, the more modern cowhand might even envy the dude wrangler, who wears the traditional cowboy clothes, carries a rope, and gets paid more money, while the cowhand drives a tractor, sprays insecticide, and harvests hay.[61] A professional group of wranglers eventually emerged, as some men grew up in the western cow country and saw dude work as a type of job cowboys sometimes took. They traveled north in the summer to work on the mountains ranches and south in the winter to work on those that were cold-weather vacation spots. And they became more than just another ranch worker; their personalities and popularity with the guests became a vital factor in a ranch's success.[62]

This was not too surprising, since the guests identified ranch life with the cowboy. He was the heroic figure that drew many of them to the West, and so his personality and attitude often determined their enjoyment and the length of their stay on the ranch.[63] Sometimes this fascination with cowboys went so far that marriage resulted; many women went to dude ranches enthralled with the image of cowboys, and occasionally the irresistible cowboy met the enthralled female. While many such marriages soon foundered on the rocks of reality, some proved successful.[64] One involved a Boston girl who went to a New Mexico ranch, where she met and married a Texas cowboy. The couple then were able to build their own successful dude ranch in New Mexico, since she had the Eastern contacts to attract guests, and he had the knowledge to run the ranch properly.[65]

Ranch owners thus lost some of their more personable wranglers; in a sense it was a case of being too successful in creating an image, for they emphasized the cowboy in their advertising. The man credited with being the first dude rancher, Howard Eaton, portrayed such an image before the

[60] LaFarge, "They All Ride," *Vogue*, Vol. 87, No. 9 (May 1, 1936), p. 138.

[61] Rodnitzky, "Recapturing the West: The Dude Ranch in American Life," *Arizona and the West*, Vol. 10 (Summer, 1968), p. 125.

[62] Raddy, "Dude Ranching is Not All Yippee!" *The Western Horseman*, Vol. XVII, No. 4 (April, 1952), p. 38.

[63] Rodnitzky, "Recapturing the West: The Dude Ranch in American Life," *Arizona and the West*, Vol. 10 (Summer, 1968), p. 123.

[64] Frank A. Tinker, "Puttin' Up The Dudes," *Westways*, 65, No. 11 (November, 1973), p. 53.

[65] Pack, pp. 11–12.

turn of the century. One of the visitors to Eaton's North Dakota ranch described him as one "who sat a horse as though he were centaur and looked a picturesque and noble figure with his clean-shaven cheeks, blue shirt, and neckerchief with flaming ends."[66] Cowboy clothing, mannerisms, and customs were not affected by these early dude wranglers, but they were emphasized because the dude ranchers understood their appeal to the distant visitors. Charles Moore described incidents that illustrated Easterners' fascination with the dude wrangler, also. During one pack trip into Yellowstone Park, he was closely observed at one of the visitor spots by several little girls. After some hesitation they finally approached him and asked if he were "real or imitation."[67]

The dude wrangler has also made his entry into the field of fiction, and here, too, a romantic, cowboy-type image has been presented. One interesting example is a book for children featuring Jim Dawson, wrangler on the Lazy R Ranch, somewhere in the southwestern United States. Dawson is an excellent horseman, cook, guitar player, singer, and storyteller; of course, he is an ex-cowboy who dislikes cities, possesses excellent health, and is a good shot with a six-gun. He is extremely attractive to women, but has no desire to marry; he is a fountain of folklore, common sense, and practical knowledge.[68] What an image for the wrangler to match!

Another fictional portrayal came from the pen of Caroline Lockhart. Her hero was Wallie Macpherson, an Easterner who journeyed west to "prove" himself. After failing in his attempt to homestead 160 acres of dry, plains land, he became a cowboy and bought the land with the wages he earned. While he had become a skillful cowhand, he eventually turned his 160 acres into a dude ranch in order to make more money. While Macpherson does not possess the same set of qualifications as Jim Dawson, he does perform his share of spectacular feats to demonstrate his grit and determination. And it is interesting that he had to become a cowboy and learn to "ride and shoot and handle a rope with the best of them" before becoming a dude wrangler.[69]

So the cowboy-dude wrangler developed in reality and in fiction as the West was opened to tourism by means of the dude ranch. Dude ranching began in the latter part of the nineteenth century and reached its peak sometime in the 1920's or 1930's. Since then, and especially in the last

[66] Hagedorn, p. 110.

[67] Typed statement, "Charles Moore, Round-up, Sunday, July 27, 1952," p. 4A, Charles Cornell Moore Memorial Collection, unprocessed material, Western History Department, Denver Public Library.

[68] Gene Hoopes, *Tales of a Dude Wrangler* (San Antonio, 1963).

[69] Caroline Lockhart, *The Dude Wrangler* (Garden City, N.Y., 1921), p. 150.

fifteen years, dude ranches have declined in numbers and popularity. One reason for this has been the fact that the federal government has purchased many of the oldest ranches that were within the boundaries of the National Parks; rising land values have encouraged owners to sell to the government and have discouraged the building of new ones. Restrictions by government agencies (the Occupational Safety and Health Administration for example), and inflation have also hurt dude ranching.[70] And, as the number of dude ranches is reduced, the number of wranglers who can make dude work a permanent job is naturally reduced.[71]

The decline of dude ranching does not, however, mean its demise; it still offers a different type of vacation to the city dweller and hence provides economic benefits to many Westerners. Visitors have enjoyed dude ranches for the same reasons they liked Western stories and films, rodeos, and Wild West shows. They were, and still are, a fundamentally American institution that resemble nothing else.[72] Continuity of the dude ranch is symbolized by Eaton's Ranch, where the current operator is the granddaughter of Alden Eaton and the workers are descendants of the original hired help.[73]

In a sense, dude ranches are comparable to rodeos. Although they differ in many ways, both present the cowboy in his image as an American folk hero. Rodeo has certainly been pictured this way often, since rodeo cowboys travel widely, compete in violent and dangerous sports, and maintain a high degree of independence.[74] While dude wranglers will probably not replace rodeo cowboys as the accepted successor to the "old-time cowboy," they do present the image of the cowboy to thousands of western visitors each year.

Their jobs are not as dramatic as those of the rodeo participant, but then, seldom was the cowboy's, either. Dude wrangling is not the pathway to great riches or personal fame, but then, neither was "riding fence" or trailing Longhorns.

The dude ranch is probably a permanent American institution, despite its decline and changes; and, while it exists, it will need wranglers, who will

[70] John F. Turner, "Delights and Dilemmas of Dude Ranching," *Wyoming Wildlife*, XXXVI, No. 7 (July, 1972), p. 23.

[71] Anne Chamberlin, "Big Dude Drive in the Crazies," *The Saturday Evening Post*, Vol. 240, No. 15 (July 29, 1967), p. 33.

[72] Rodnitzky, "Recapturing the West: The Dude Ranch in American Life," *Arizona and the West*, Vol. 10 (Summer, 1968), p. 123.

[73] Chamberlin, "Big Dude Drive in the Crazies," *The Saturday Evening Post*, Vol. 240, No. 15 (July 29, 1967), p. 33.

[74] One of the clearest statements of this idea is in the 1974 documentary move, 'The Great American Cowboy." See also Clifford P. Westermeier, *Man, Beast, Dust: The Story of Rodeo* (Denver, 1947), pp. 353, 408.

The Cowboy's Bawdy Music

BY GUY LOGSDON

OVER THE PAST SIXTY YEARS MUCH HAS BEEN WRITTEN about cowboy ballads and songs, particularly those associated with the origin of the range cattle industry and the trail-driving days. However, very little attention has been given to the total music of the cowboy, such as the instruments he used and the obscene elements in his songs. Little interest has been shown in the progressive travels and image of cowboy music in the twentieth century. And too many scholars seem to think that the "real" cowboy and his culture died when the last of the old-time cowboys died, when, in fact, cowboy music is very much alive and well in both traditional and popular culture.

Cowboy songs first were printed in collection form in 1908 in Estancia, New Mexico, by N. Howard "Jack" Thorp in his small, fifty-page, paper-back book, *Songs of the Cowboys*. It was reprinted with extensive notes and commentary by Austin E. and Alta S. Fife in 1966, by Clarkson N. Potter, Inc. The first edition is extremely rare, but it was reproduced in facsimile form in the Fife edition. It also includes Thorp's article "Banjo in the Cow Camp," which is a description of cow camp activities as experienced by Thorp. This reprint edition is the most important single title about cowboy music to be printed.

The best-known collection was printed in 1910 as the effort of John A. Lomax, under the title *Cowboy Songs and Other Frontier Ballads*, by Sturgis & Walton It went through reprintings in 1911 and 1915. In 1916 a new edition included a few additions, and by 1938 it had enjoyed nine more reprintings, when a new enlarged edition was published. The 1938 edition is still being reprinted; MacMillan has published the title since 1918.

In his "Collector's Note," Lomax wrote that sharp yells were utilized "to stir up lagging cattle" and that the night guards "improvised cattle lullabies which quieted the animals and soothed them to sleep." He also

127

admitted that he edited and restructured some of the songs, for "the volume is meant to be popular." The popularity and impact on cowboy songs was extensive, for many songs collected in oral tradition since Lomax published his collection have been word for word with his versions. It is not uncommon for cowboy singers to say that they own or have used the Lomax book.

Also, the image of the cowboy, i.e., singing while he worked, possibly gained impetus from the Lomax statement about song utility. Even though no commentary about the individual songs was made by either Lomax or Thorp in their original publications, Lomax made them in his 1938 edition, and more romanticized concepts about the cowboy emerged. Also, Lomax originally gave limited credit to his sources, but having been criticized by Thorp for using songs that were written by him with no credit, Lomax gave specific credits in 1938.

Lomax edited another collection, *Songs of the Cattle Trail and Cow Camp*, that was published by MacMillan in 1919, in which he made a distinction between songs that emerged from and were sung by the cowboys and poems that were composed by poets and were printed in newspapers, magazines, and books. This volume was composed of the poets' efforts, even though some of the poems had been set to music and were sung by cowboys, of which an example is Larry Chittenden's "Cowboys' Christmas Ball." The poets included Chittenden, Charles Badge Clark, Henry H. Knibbs, Arthur Chapman, and others.

An enlarged edition of Thorp's *Songs of the Cowboys* published by Houghton Mifflin appeared in 1921, and for those known, Thorp gave credit to the poet. Alice Corbin Henderson wrote the introduction, in which she expressed the belief that the origin of the song was not as important as the "use" of the song. To Thorp and Henderson the spirit of a song could possess the folk element, which was made obvious when cowboys took the poem, set it to music, and absorbed it into their traditions. This method of use or absorption was and is a vehicle by which so much romanticization of the cowboy and the West moved into their songs and lore. Henderson made a strong distinction, yet a close relationship, between the early oral tradition songs and the printed songs by poets who, due to the folk process, quickly lost their identity. If the cowboy sang it, its origin was unimportant.

Musical notation was omitted from both Thorp editions; obviously it was impossible to include notation in the first volume, but music could have been included in the second volume. Also, even though he did sing, Thorp was a poet, not a musician, and his emphasis was on telling a story, not on musical accuracy. It can be assumed that his life as a cowboy taught him that many great recitations of the song-stories were performed with great skill and gusto by cowboys with limited musical ability. Even today some cowboy singers have a limited ear for the music and sing with a limited range and accuracy; their strength is word memory and talking a good song. In contrast to the performer with a strong word memory is the cowboy who knows many tunes and sings beautifully but does not know as many verses as the one with a good word memory. No thorough study has been made about these folk memory skills or about folk creativity.

Lomax made a few tunes available to his first edition; notation was provided with piano accompaniment by Henry Leberman. In the 1938 edition Edward H. Waters drew on many sources for a melody line for the songs, if one could be found. Lomax was a poet with a strong Harvard University literary background, but, as with Thorp, he did sing. Some of the Lomax melodies, as with the restructured words, became the fixed melodies for the songs, and it can be assumed that if the words were altered for poetic purposes then the tunes also were altered for musical purposes. The primary problem was the limited ability of musicians to adequately indicate slides, trills, non-standard intervals, and other characteristics of the folk singer.

Other collections were to follow, but none had the impact of Lomax. Charles A. Siringo, authentic cowboy-author, published in Santa Fe in 1919 a paperback titled *The Song Companion of A Lone Star Cowboy*; it contained thirteen songs on forty-two pages. It was actually intended to be a companion to Siringo's book about cowboy life, *A Lone Star Cowboy*.

Charles J. Finger compiled *Sailor Chanties and Cowboy Songs*, another small paperback published by Haldeman—Julius Company, Girard, Kansas, in 1923; on sixty pages it contained his narrative of experiences and his collected songs. This was followed by an enlarged collection and narrative, *Frontier Ballads*, published by Doubleday Page & Company in 1927. In this volume Finger wrote the melody line as well as his ear and training allowed. In his introduction he wrote, "Neither cowboys nor sailors . . . are given to the singing of what have been called occupational songs." Instead they sing songs that fit the emotion of the moment, oftentimes the popular sentimental songs of the day. Finger romanticized about himself, not about cowboy singing.

In 1931, Alfred Knopf, Inc. published Margaret Larkin's *Singing Cowboy*; each song was introduced by a short narrative with much romanticized nonsense. For the song "I Ride An Old Paint" she wrote, "This is a typical riding song—it lopes along gently to the rhythm of the horse." Anyone who has ridden a loping horse knows that you do not sing. Also, Larkin included extensive piano accompaniments that were arranged by Helen Black.

In 1933 the Naylor Company in San Antonio published what has become an often reprinted volume, *Cowboy Lore*, by "The Singing Cowboy,"

Jules Verne Allen. He was a working cowboy and a rodeo cowboy from Texas, who was one of the first cowboy singers to be recorded by RCA Victor, and he became a radio performer in the 1920's. Allen was another romanticizer, but he did not elaborate about each song as did Larkin. He did state that Mrs. G. Embey Eitt of San Antonio wrote the melodies exactly as he sang, and she set them to piano accompaniment.

Other collectors were pulling material together, among whom were J. Frank Dobie, Louise Pound, Robert W. Gordon, J. D. Robb, and many more, but no new major contributions were published until the Fife edition of Thorp's *Songs of the Cowboys* in 1966. This was followed in 1969 when Clarkson N. Potter, Inc., published Austin E. and Alta S. Fife's *Cowboy and Western Songs: A Comprehensive Anthology*. While this is an excellent collection, the same problem of working over the words and tunes to make a better version exists. However, the Fifes do indicate which stanzas were added or changed. The melody lines with guitar chords were printed for each song, and notes and commentary precede each song. The Fifes represent the finest of the cowboy ballad scholars today.

The Fifes edited another title, *Heaven On Horseback: Revivalist Songs and Verse in the Cowboy Idiom*, published in 1970 by the Utah State University Press as Volume 1, No. 1 of their Western Texts Society Series. Much commentary is made about the utilization of sacred music for texts and melodies.

Two large collections gleaned primarily from printed sources and dealing with the West in general were printed almost back to back. Irwin Silber edited *Songs of the Great American West*, and MacMillan published it in 1967. Richard E. Lingenfelter, Richard A. Dwyer, and David Cohen edited *Songs of the American West*, which was published by the University of California Press in 1968. Neither volume added any substance to cowboy song scholarship, even though some speculative narratives were written for each volume.

By no means were cowboy songs limited to book collections, for songs, poems, and essays were printed in newspapers and magazines through the years. An important article by Sharlot M. Hall, "Songs of the Old Cattle Trail," appeared in *Out West* (pp. 216–21) March, 1908. A number of articles have appeared in the *Journal of American Folklore* and in the Publications of the Texas Folklore Society series. Dane Coolidge, author of many books about the West, contributed "Cow Boy Songs" to *Sunset* (pp. 502–510), November, 1912. The great Arizona cowboy Will C. Barnes authored "The Cowboy and His Songs" for *The Saturday Evening Post* (pp. 14–15, 122–28), June 27, 1925. And the work of John I. White, in recent years, in tracing the origin of many songs and the lives of many of the poets has been of great value. His articles have appeared in numerous journals and newspapers.

The Barnes article is the most realistic of all, for he wrote that the lyrics of the cowboy ran "from sacred hymns to some of the commonest doggerel imaginable." He decried the statements about the songs expressing the virtues and sentiments of the noble, pastoral cowboy by stating that "the songs the cowboy sang were those he picked up from all sorts of sources —mainly saloons, barber shops, cheap shows and others of his kind." Many of the songs were "manhandled in a most brazen, reckless manner" when the words were localized, and the source of the most popular cowboy themes were written by non-cowboy poets who romanticized the cowboy's life. Needless to say, very few of the collectors and scholars have quoted Barnes.

The poets who have been most popular are William Lawrence Chittenden *Ranch Verses* (1893), Charles Badge Clark *Sun and Saddle Leather* (1912), and Arthur Chapman *Out Where the West Begins* (1916). Many other poets turned out one or two poems that were published in a local paper and picked up by cowboy melody makers. Two cowboy poets of significance were "Jack" Thorp—who authored "Little Joe the Wrangler" while in the mountains of New Mexico in 1898, and Curly Fletcher, who wrote "The Strawberry Roan" about 1915. These two songs enjoy as much popularity as any, with the possible exception of "The Cowboy's Lament," a traditional cowboy ballad, which is better known as "Streets of Laredo." Another popular song, "When the Works All Done This Fall," was written by the Montana cowboy poet D. J. O'Malley in 1893.

The origin of cowboy songs has been of limited concern for the second, third, and fourth generation of cowboys and collectors who accept the romantic image of the cowboy and protect it. However, the first generation of cowboys only sang a few occupational songs, which were mostly lyrical. Most of the great ballads or narratives came from the second generation or, as stated previously, from the non-cowboy. The influence of Lomax, with his belief in the communal origin of the songs, lingers to some extent, and the romantic notion that cowboy songs emerged from work still persists. However, the identity of the author of many of the best ballads dispels the communal theory; the exceptions are seen in authentic first-generation lyric songs such as "The Old Chisholm Trail," where many short stanzas were made up on the spot.

The first generation of cowboys worked too hard to consider itself to be romantic; it was their sons who had the time to reflect and make images. Also, with age most people seem to forget the hard, bad experiences and reflect about the good times; thus the tendency to exaggerate to grandchildren creates a different experience.

A manuscript by John A. Lomax was published in 1967 by the Encino Press, Austin, under the title *Cow Camps and Cattle Herds*. From cowboys he quoted much supportive material for his theories, but a strong contradiction entered when he quoted "no song was ever as popular in the seventies among the cowboys as 'When You and I Were Young, Maggie.'" This seems to support the statements of Barnes about what cowboys sang.

The function of the songs is another point of contention, in that most of the aforementioned people accepted the theory that there were actual work songs that fitted the gait of the horse. It is highly improbable that much singing was done on horseback except at a slow walking pace. Also, the work was hard, dusty, non-rhythmic activity, and to think that a cowboy, face covered with a kerchief, eating dust, trailing cattle, could sing, is ludicrous. Horseback riding is just not conducive to singing. However, musical yells were used for driving cattle.

Night herding was slow, quiet riding; therefore a cowboy could sing or whistle in a soft manner. In this capacity the songs were work songs, and there are some beautiful night herding songs written by later-generation cowboys. But there are not many traditional ones; instead church songs were mostly used in this way.

Cowboy songs and songs sung by the cowboy were mostly for entertainment, to pass time around the campfire, in the bunkhouse, at stag dances, and in saloons. The songs were sung to other men, rarely to animals, and they often were raunchy.

Another problem with cowboy songs and the romantic image lies in the expurgation of texts by the collectors. Thorp and Lomax allude to expurgation by making non-committal statements about many songs that in print would curl the pages of the book or singe the hair on a cow's tail; then they quickly move on to other subjects. It is impossible to visualize men grouped together for long periods of time without at least off-color subjects being discussed and being the source of laughter, and, in most situations, the language and stories become blatant obscenity. Until recent times it would have been impossible to get the songs printed, but if a scholarly collection of obscene cowboy songs were published today, it would be a major contribution to cowboy song scholarship.

As a collector, I found two old-time cowboys in Arizona who sang obscene cowboy songs. One informant was seventy-nine and had been reared on a ranch and knew no work other than cowboying. He referred to his obscene songs as his "ugly" songs; some of them could more appropriately be called "gross obscenity." Themes usually dealt with phallic size and virility, venereal disease, and sodomy. Nothing was left to the imagination.

When asked if he sang these songs to his cattle, he replied indignantly, "No, we sang church songs to the cows; these songs were sung for other cowboys, usually at stag dances." A stag dance was what it implies, a dance without women, where the cowboys drank, danced, and raised hell. But by no means is it intended to imply that all cowboys were of this type. However, enough were to warrant a serious study of the non-romantic obscene cowboy ballad.

But singing was not the only music of the cow camp. Musical instruments were also important. Popular belief associates the guitar with the cowboy, particularly with his singing, when, in fact, his singing was usually unaccompanied. The favorite instrument was not the guitar but the fiddle, followed by the banjo. The guitar was down the line in popularity. The fiddle was the instrument of the cowboy because it could be carried with greater ease and in less space in a chuckwagon or in a pack, and it was the over-all most popular folk instrument. Also, no cowboy on a spirited cow pony is going to let the reins hang loose while he plays an instrument—thus another romantic concept does not fit the working conditions of the cowboy.

The cowboy loved to dance, and the fiddle supplied the accompaniment for dancing. The best account of cowboys dancing is found in Joseph G. McCoy's Historic *Sketches of the Cattle Trade*, which was published in 1874 and is generally considered to be the first personal account of the trail-drive days. McCoy wrote:

> . . . that institution known in the west as a dance house, is there found also. When the darkness of the night is come to shroud their orgies from public gaze, these miserable beings gather into the halls of the dance house, and "trip the fantastic toe" to wretched music, ground out of dilapidated [*sic*] instruments, by beings fully as degraded as the most vile. . . . Few more wild, reckless scenes of abandoned debauchery can be seen on the civilized earth, than a dance house in full blast in one of the many frontier towns. To say they dance wildly or in an abandoned manner is putting it mild [*sic*]. (p. 139)

Dancing was described as wild and was probably a mixture of reels, balances, and swinging with some waltzes. The cowboy "enters the dance with a peculiar zest, not stopping to divest himself of his sombrero, spurs, or pistols," this is a tradition carried on today at western dances where the cowboy seldom takes off his hat even to dance. The cowboy's "eyes lit up with excitement, liquor and lust." McCoy did not describe an organized, nice square dance, and he did not support the romantic concept of the cowboy.

McCoy did support the night herding practice of singing which was "in a voice more sonorous than musical." Also, they would settle the cattle during or after any disturbance by "standing at a distance and hallooing or singing to them. . . . Singing hymns to Texan steers is the peculiar forte of a genuine cow-boy, but the spirit of true piety does not abound in the sentiment." (p. 101)

Another cowboy writer who spoke of dancing and the fiddle was Andy Adams in *The Log of a Cowboy*, published in 1903 by Houghton Mifflin:

> By the time I was twenty there was no better cow-hand in the entire country. I could besides, speak Spanish and play the fiddle, and thought nothing of riding thirty miles to a dance. (p. 7)

In *The Trail Drivers of Texas*, compiled by J. Marvin Hunter from the members of the Old Time Trail Drivers' Association during 1920–23, reprinted by Argosy-Antiquarian in 1963, one man told that:

> . . . I learned to play the fiddle, but there was only two tunes that I could play to perfection, one of which was "Seesaw" and the other was "Sawsee." Often I have taken my fiddle on herd at night when on the trail, and while some of my companions would lead my horse around the herd I agitated the catguts . . . those old long-horned Texas steers actually enjoyed that old time music." (p. 838)

That the cowboy sang and danced and loved the fiddle is obvious throughout many of the printed accounts of the cowboy, but to think that the cowboy culture died with the old timers is wrong. Instead, the culture has continued through the perpetuation of the old songs, with the added direction of songs from recordings and "B" grade cowboy movies, of rodeo cowboy songs, and of western dance music. Also, cowboys and rodeo cowboys continue to write songs that enter the singing tradition. One such writer is the former cowboy, now movie star, Slim Pickens, who sings and writes primarily for his friends.

The rodeo is the only sport to have its origin in an industry, so it is natural that some of the traditions of the range cattle industry would extend into the sport. Rodeo cowboys have to kill time from show to show. Singing and story telling are often employed. The most significant contribution to cowboy music since Thorp's first book is Glenn Ohrlin's *The Hell-Bound Train*, published by the University of Illinois Press in 1973. Ohrlin has worked as a cowboy and as a rodeo cowboy since 1940, and his book reflects the traditional influence as well as the many rodeo songs that exist. He tells how some of the rodeo songs were created, and he has written some lyrics that he later collected as traditional songs. This is the only book in which rodeo songs have been published.

The "B" grade cowboy movies had more to do with shaping the modern image of the cowboy than any other source, with the possible exception of Zane Grey. Most certainly they shaped concepts about cowboy

134

singing, i.e., the cowboy on horseback strumming a guitar and singing "Riding Down the Canyon" or "I'm Back in the Saddle Again."

The first singing cowboy in the movies was Ken Maynard, who had been a cowboy before turning actor, and he played both the fiddle and the guitar in his movies. Two articles, "The Ken Maynard Story" by Ken Griffis and "The Songs of Ken Maynard" by William Henry Koon, are in the Summer, 1973, No. 30 issue of the John Edwards Memorial Foundation's *JEMF Quarterly* (pp. 67–77). It was in Maynard's movie *In Old Santa Fe*, 1934, that Gene Autry was given a bit singing part, and this started his movie career and the musical western. Also, it started the new concept of the cowboy and his songs.

Gene Autry's success was followed by movies with Dick Foran, Roy Rogers, Tex Ritter, Eddie Dean, and other lesser-known singers. All were supported by musical groups that ranged from Bob Wills and His Texas Playboys, the Sons of the Pioneers, and Foy Willing and the Riders of the Purple Sage to groups brought together only for a specific movie. And each movie had songs composed for its title and theme. Some of these songs were thought to be old cowboy songs, when, in fact, very few traditional songs were used.

Gene Autry had made his reputation on records and over the radio as "Oklahoma's Yodeling Cowboy" before he became a movie star. Other singers put on a cowboy hat and sang new songs about cowboys and were considered to be cowboy singers. Numerous music folios and much sheet music were published in order to capitalize on the interest in western music; the image was being romanticized more and more. Some of these song books included traditional songs, but most of them were new compositions. Many of the recording, radio, and movie cowboys had their own song books, such as Tom Mix, *Western Songs* (1935), Gene Autry, *Famous Cowboy Songs and Mountain Ballads*, Nos. 1 and 2 (1932 and 1934), Buck Jones, *Songs of the Western Trails* (1940), Al Clauser and His Oklahoma Outlaws, *Original Mountain and Range Songs* (1937), and many, many more. Some of these songs were taken by the "real" cowboys as songs they liked, particularly a few of the Sons of the Pioneer songs.

One recording and movie singer must be considered as a performer who moved with ease back and forth from traditional to pop material, Tex Ritter. He was always popular with working and rodeo cowboys as well as with country-western music fans everywhere. His recording of "Blood On the Saddle" created a new "traditional" song. It was written by Everett Cheetham in the 1930's, but from the Tex Ritter recording it was picked up and is sung by some as an old cowboy song. Tex also recorded some rodeo songs, such as "Bad Brahma Bull," as well as many traditional songs. No

Gene Autry, singing movie cowboy. Photograph from the collection of Guy Logsdon.

other commercial artist maintained ties to traditional music as did Tex Ritter.

Since the cowboy loved to dance, this tradition continued throughout the Southwest; the early twentieth-century cowboy loved all kinds of dancing, some square dancing, polkas, waltzes, two-steps, schottisches, and round dancing or body contact dancing. The early house dances evolved into western swing dances with a specific style of fiddling and instrumentation and with a strong rhythm section.

Bob Wills is considered to be the "Daddy of Western Swing." As a west Texas cotton farmer-fiddler, he was hired to play house dances. The house dances might have had people dancing in as many as three rooms, and they usually danced three round dances, a waltz, and a square. Each square set was called individually by a dancer in the square, very much different from the square dance of today. In 1929 Wills and Herman Arnspiger, a guitar player, teamed up in Fort Worth. Eventually, with Milton Brown, a singer, they became the Light Crust Doughboys with "Pappy" O'Daniel, one of the most popular radio groups in the Southwest.

Bob was fired by O'Daniel, and after trying two other cities, he landed in Tulsa with his band in 1934. Bob Wills and His Texas Playboys soon were playing six dances a week within driving distance from Tulsa, for they also had two live radio shows a day over KVOO. They became the most popular dance band in the Southwest as a string swing band with a strong dance rhythm.

Other string swing bands were organized with Spade Cooley, "The King of Western Swing," bringing together musically the best of all the groups in the 1940's. But Bob was the most popular. The term "western swing" was not used until Foreman Phillips, a promoter-disc jockey, used it to describe Spade Cooley in 1942. The best of the bands included Johnnie Lee Wills and His Boys, Leon McAuliffe and His Cimarron Boys, Tex Williams and his band, Merl Lindsay and His Oklahoma Night Riders, and Hank Thompson and the Brazos Valley Boys. Many lesser known, but good, bands worked, and still work, the Southwest.

The big bands started breaking up in the mid 1950's, because of television and rock music competition. But smaller western swing bands continue to play dances every Saturday in hundreds of dance halls throughout the Southwest. Of the big name bands, Hank Thompson is the only one who has continued. He still plays nearly two hundred dances a year and is a rodeo dance favorite. Very few, if any, of his dances are not sold out in advance.

A short discography is necessary for any study of cowboy music. Two albums from "The Ballad Hunter Series" with John A. Lomax (AAFS L49 and AAFS L50) and "Cowboy Songs, Ballads, and Cattle Calls From Texas," edited by Duncan Emrich (AAFS L28), represent the best field recordings available; they are sold through the Music Division of the Library of Congress. The first of the commercial recordings in the 1920's by RCA Victor have been reissued as "Authentic Cowboys and Their Western Folksongs" (LPV–522). One of the best albums is Harry Jackson's "The Cowboy: His Songs, Ballads and Brag Talk" Folkways Records (FH–5724). Sons of the Pioneers albums are essential to any collection; the best are "The Sons of the Pioneers" John Edwards Memorial Foundation (JEMF 102) and "Riders In the Sky" RCA Victor (ADL2–03363). The singing and collecting of Glenn Ohrlin are available on "The Hell-Bound Train," University of Illinois, Campus Folksong Club (CFC 301). A privately-pressed album, "George Gillespie Sings Campfire Songs of the Old West," is good, but nearly impossible to find.

Others are: Slim Critchlow, "Cowboy Songs," Arhoolie Records (5007); two anthologies from the Arizona Friends of Folklore, Flagstaff, "Cowboy Songs" and "In An Arizona Town"; Woody Guthrie and Cisco

Houston, "Cowboy Songs," Stinson Records (SLP–32); Johnny Baker, "Songs of the Rodeo," Audio Arts, Wheaton, Ill.; Chris LeDoux, "Rodeo Songs—Old and New," American Cowboy Songs, Nashville, Tenn.; Rex Allen, "Boney Kneed Hairy Legged Cowboy Songs," JMI Records (4003) Nashville, Tenn.; the best of Tex Ritter, a highly recommended set, is titled "An American Legend," Capitol Records (SKC–11241); many Bob Wills albums are available, but the best is "The Bob Wills Anthology," Columbia Records (KG–32416) and the most recent, but without Bob, is "Bob Wills and His Texas Playboys For the Last Time," United Artists Records (LA216–J2). Hank Thompson has numerous records still available, for his career is still going strong.

The Cowboy in Indian Territory

BY ARRELL M. GIBSON

> Come along boys, and listen to my tale.
>   I'll tell you of my travels on the Old Chisholm Trail
>   . . . Oh, a ten-dollar horse and a forty-dollar saddle—
>   and I'm goin' to punchin' Texas cattle.
> I woke up one morning on the Old Chisholm Trail
>   Rope in hand and a cow by the tail.[1]

THE COWBOY DOMINATED THE BONANZA AGE of Western development, 1866–1900, as the most popular folk-hero type in the drama of this unprecedented national development. His image as a spirited, daring drifter, moving from ranch to ranch, a "soldier of fortune" serving "the man who paid and fed him," continues to titillate wide popular interest and nostalgic regard for an age that is past. The Indian Territory was the setting for the denouement scene of the American frontier—stockmen and nesters engaged in the final contest for control of the land, and the cowboy played a leading role in this action.[2]

The cowboy was first introduced to the Indian Territory after 1866 in response to the phenomenal postwar surge in stock raising. Texas ranges, largely untouched by foraging Union and Confederate armies, were crowded with beef animals locally valued at only $3 to $5 per head. In the East, beef was scarce and expensive. An animal ready for slaughter sold for about $40. During 1866, Texas cattlemen attempted to take advantage of this favorable market condition and began to drive their cattle north to railheads on the Missouri border for shipment to Eastern markets. The northward passage crossed Indian Territory, and this region became a

[1] J. Marvin Hunter, compiler and editor, *The Trail Drivers of Texas* (New York, 1963), Vol. 2, p. 931–32.
[2] Ellsworth Collings and Alma Miller England, *The 101 Ranch* (Norman, 1937), p. 32.

great cattle highway, laced with north-south trails connecting Texas ranches and northern railheads.[3]

Indian Territory's principal stock concourses were the East Shawnee Trail, West Shawnee Trail, Chisholm Trail, and the Dodge City or Great Western Cattle Trail. The East Shawnee Trail initiated at Colbert's Ferry on Red River, coursed north to Boggy Depot in the Choctaw Nation, then generally followed the Texas Road to Baxter Springs, Kansas, and terminated at the Sedalia, Missouri, railhead. The West Shawnee Trail forked at Boggy Depot and ran northwest to Abilene and other emerging railhead towns in Kansas. The most famous cattle highway in the West was the Chisholm Trail, named for Jesse Chisholm, a mixed-blood Cherokee trader who, during the Civil War, blazed a freighter's trace from the mouth of the Little Arkansas River near Wichita into the Leased District in southwestern Indian Territory. Cowboys used this route to move cattle to Abilene, Caldwell, and Wichita. The Chisholm Trail began at Red River Station and generally followed the 98th meridian into Kansas. The fourth Indian Territory cattle highway, the Dodge City or Great Western Cattle Trail, crossed Red River at Doan's Store and proceeded across western Indian Territory to Dodge City. Texas drovers moved over three hundred thousand head of cattle up the trails in 1870, twice that number the following year, and, during the first ten years of the northern drive, over 3 million head crossed Indian Territory to the Kansas cow towns.[4]

Each spring, Texas ranchmen assigned cowboys as trail drivers to move their steer herds to northern railheads, a task which provided most of them their first exposure to Indian Territory. The trail driving assignment was exciting, dangerous, and punishing in its demands on the drovers, but even the ultimate hazard or hardship was of no consequence when measured against the prospect of a bacchanalian frolic at the end of the trail in the rip-roaring cow towns of Kansas.[5]

These riders were "true knights of the plains, inured to the hardships of the range," each attired in colorful and functional regalia which included a broad-brimmed sombrero to protect the head from the sun's heat, driving rain, and blizzard's icy blast of sleet and snow. A decorative neckerchief, which doubled as a jaunty tie or a face cover to mask the dust raised by milling cattle, embellished the drab chambray shirt. Chaps over denim

---

[3] See Edward E. Dale, *The Range Cattle Industry* (Norman, 1930), for a study on the origins of the range cattle industry.

[4] Basic works on the cattle highways of Indian Territory include Sam P. Ridings, *The Chisholm Trail: A History of the World's Greatest Cattle Trail* (Guthrie, 1936), and Wayne Gard, *The Chisholm Trail* (Norman, 1954).

[5] The glamour of the Kansas cow towns is depicted in Floyd B. Streeter, *Prairie Trails and Cow Towns* (Boston, 1936).

pants protected legs from stabbing thorns when pursuing errant cattle through sand-plum thickets. Hand-tooled boots with elevated heels held the feet firmly in the stirrups and provided bracing when the rider had to dismount and work cattle and horses with a rope on the ground. He carried a "Fish Brand" slicker tied behind the high-pommeled stock saddle. His range equipment included a braided lariat, coiled and tied to the front of the saddle, a Colt .45 single-action Frontier Model revolver with a seven-and-a-half-inch barrel, generally carried in the saddle bag, and a .44 Winchester rifle nestling in a boot holster behind the saddle. For his work on the trail the cowboy received $30 and board a month, his trail boss, $75.[6]

A drover crew consisting of trail boss and eight to twelve riders, a cook, chuck wagon, and remuda containing an average of five mounts per rider, was assigned to each trail herd, ranging in size from fifteen hundred to three thousand animals. Beeves from the Texas ranges, called "long-horns" and "yellow backs," were a mix of Anglo-American and Spanish cattle breeds which produced large, tough, wide-foraging cattle, capable of withstanding the hardships of open-range existence. "The Texas steer was no respecter of unmounted cowboys, but for the man on horseback he had a wholesome fear. Separately, neither man nor horse had any more chance in the herd, or on the open range, than among so many wolves. With their long, sharp-pointed horns these steers rent man or horse with ease and the fights among themselves had all the ferociousness of wild beasts."[7]

Just before the march toward the Red River crossing into Indian Territory, cowboys marked each animal in the trail herd with a road brand. During the early days of the drive, drovers pushed the herd at twenty to thirty miles a day to wear the animals down. Thereafter, the pace slowed to ten or fifteen miles a day, the overall march from the ranch to the railhead requiring about three months. After the herd had become accustomed to trail routines, at the beginning of each day's drive cowboys strung the herd out over a two- to three-mile area, "drifting" the animals and permitting them to graze. At mid-morning, riders bunched the herd, forced the lead steers into a trot, and moved the column at a more rapid rate. At midday, the procession stopped on the trail at the chuck wagon for the noon meal. The afternoon march continued at a steady pace, the column halting at twilight at the night camp site selected by the trail cook with his chuck wagon. During the night, shifts of riders guarded the herd, each cowboy moving slowly around the resting steers, singing to soothe the animals and to discourage a stampede. Drovers dreaded the stampede. Besides the deadly risk of life and limb in attempting to turn the lead steers, if the herd got out

[6] Collings and England, *The 101 Ranch*, p. 59.
[7] *Ibid.*, p. 55.

of hand cowboys had to spend many tiring hours, sometimes days, without food or rest while hunting scattered cattle and regrouping the herd. Texas cattle spooked easily, "some trifle, the sound of a cracking stick, a flash of lightning, the restlessness of some steer, every head was lifted, and the mass of hair and horns, with fierce, frightened eyes, was off."[8]

Besides stampedes, hazards facing the cowboy on the cattle concourses of Indian Territory included threat of Indian attack and treacherous river crossings. During the early years of trail driving the federal government was in the process of concentrating the fierce Kiowas, Comanches, Cheyennes, and Arapahoes on reservations in western Indian Territory. These tribesmen were not completely vanquished until 1874, and until then drovers faced the regular threat of lightning-swift raids from mounted warrior bands. After their conquest, these tribesmen continued to prey on the cow columns, deliberately stampeding herds, stealing horses, and exacting a tribute of several beeves for the privilege of crossing their reservations.[9]

Indian Territory cattle trails running on a north-south line crossed the region's eastward flowing streams—the Red, Canadian, North Fork, Cimarron, Salt Fork, and Arkansas rivers. Most of the trail drives occurred during the spring and early summer, when the grass was prime for sustaining the herds. This was the region's rainy season, and frequently drovers found these streams out of their banks. Cowboys rated the Canadian, Cimarron, and Salt Fork the worst on the trail. Sam Ridings, an Indian Territory cattleman, explained that these streams "flow over beds of sand, and are subject to extensive rises during which time they are impassable for days, sometimes weeks. During rises the force of flowing water causes the bed of the river to shift, and for some time after the water subsides this sand is unsettled and loose. Persons or animals crossing it will sink . . . . This is called quicksand." Cowboys pulled bogged animals from the river bed with spliced lariats and ganged teams of horses.[10]

A trail driver in Andy Adams' *Log of a Cowboy* averred that the Canadian exceeded all other Western rivers for treachery. "Well in all my experience in trail work . . . I never saw as deceptive a bottom in any river. We used to fear the Cimarron and Platte, but the . . . Canadian is the girl that can lay it over them both."[11]

Rain, lightning, boggy ground, swollen rivers, and nervous cattle on the verge of stampede made drovers' work a nightmare. Trail boss George Duffield commented that during a storm on the Arkansas crossing his men

[8] *Ibid.*, p. 56.
[9] Arrell M. Gibson, *Oklahoma: A History of Five Centuries* (Norman, 1965), pp. 253–58.
[10] Ridings, *The Chisholm Trail*, p. 39.
[11] Andy Adams, *The Log of a Cowboy* (Boston, 1931), p. 163.

were in the saddle without sleep for sixty hours, with time only for hasty rations of bread and coffee. "Dark days are these to me. . . . Hands all Grumbling & Swearing—everything wet & cold. . . . Am not Homesick but Heart sick." The inevitable stampede and scattered herd caused him to admit that he was "in Hel of a fix."[12]

The cowboy enterprise of trail driving in Indian Territory faded during the late 1870's with the entry of railroads into the Southwest. By 1880, Texas cattlemen were provided local transportation service to Eastern markets. Thereupon, the Indian Territory entered its second stage in the cattle industry, that of intensive ranching, which engaged cowboys on a more or less permanent basis and in larger numbers, in contrast to the small number employed in trail driving each year before 1880.

Bonanza profits from ranching in the postwar period led to the expansion of ranching onto the lush public domain pastures of the Great Plains. Cattle corporations dominated this vast range kingdom for about a decade. Then large numbers of homesteaders, the scorned nesters, entered the Great Plains; filed on 160-acre tracts; fenced the ranges, watering points, and cattle trails; plowed the grasslands; and forced many of the cattle companies to evacuate the public domain ranges. Several displaced ranchmen moved their herds to the choice grasslands of Indian Territory.[13]

By 1880, large-scale ranching was well established in Indian Territory. Cattlemen negotiated grass leases with the Cherokee, Choctaw, Chickasaw, Creek, and Seminole governments, but the available pastures in these Indian nations were limited, since many of the tribesmen already were established in ranching and required the grass for their own livestock. Cattlemen had their greatest success in finding new ranges on the reservations in western Indian Territory. By 1890, a portion of every reservation west of the domains of the Five Civilized Tribes was under lease to cattlemen. In the Kiowa, Comanche and Cheyenne and Arapaho reservations virtually every acre of grass was leased to ranchmen.[14]

During 1882, through their agent John D. Miles, the Cheyennes and Arapahoes negotiated an agreement with seven cattle companies for use of 3 million acres of their reservation at two cents per acre per year. The syndicate grazed two hundred thousand head of cattle on the vast Indian reservation range. Their operation included publishing a newspaper, the *Cheyenne Transporter*, its columns devoted largely to articles of interest to

---

[12] "Driving Cattle from Texas to Iowa: George C. Duffield's Diary," *Annals of Iowa*, Vol. 14 (April, 1924), pp. 250–58.

[13] The ranchman-nester contest for control of the public domain is detailed in Roy M. Robbins, *Our Landed Heritage* (Princeton, 1942).

[14] Gibson, *Oklahoma*, p. 282.

stock raisers, such as brand registration and identification, and the problem of stock theft.[15]

The most extensive ranching enterprise in Indian Territory during this period was in the Cherokee Outlet, containing about 6,500,000 acres of choice grassland. In the late 1870's, cattlemen began occupying, more or less permanently, certain ranges in the Outlet. The number increased each year, with the result that this sixty-mile-wide ribbon of grassland, extending from the Arkansas River on the east to the 100th meridian, became one of the most famous ranges in the West.[16]

Cherokee Nation officials at Tahlequah soon learned of this appropriation of their land by cattlemen and sent representatives west with authority to collect grazing fees. At first the annual levy was twenty-five cents per head, later increased to forty-five cents per head. The grazing tax collected from Outlet stock growers became such an important source of revenue for the Cherokee government that the treasurer of the nation came each year to Caldwell, Kansas, established an office, and sent his deputies riding through the Outlet to collect the grazing fees.

In order to gain exclusive use of the Outlet and to protect their ranges from rustlers, Outlet cattlemen met at Caldwell, Kansas, in 1883 and established the Cherokee Strip Livestock Association. Its membership consisted of over a hundred individuals and corporations owning over three hundred thousand head of cattle. A five-year lease at $100,000 a year was negotiated with the Cherokee Nation for the exclusive use of the Outlet. This lease was renegotiated in 1888 for $200,000 a year. Association officers hired brand inspectors to police the range for rustlers and to inspect and record livestock shipments, adopted roundup schedules and rules, surveyed and mapped the Outlet, assigned particular ranges to members, and set rules for fencing the ranges.[17]

By the early 1880's, perhaps three thousand cowboys were employed in Indian Territory stock raising enterprises. Most of the men worked on established ranches in the Kiowa Comanche Country, the Cheyenne Arapaho Reservation, and Cherokee Outlet. However, many cowboys continued to be employed in some form of local trail driving. These latter-day drovers were based at temporary ranch camps situated in the Unassigned Lands and on the Sac and Fox Reservation, Osage Reservation, and Quapaw Reservation. The Unassigned Lands, a 2-million-acre tract situated in

15 *Ibid.*, p. 283.

16 *Ibid.*

17 William W. Savage, Jr., *The Cherokee Strip Live Stock Association: Federal Regulation and the Cattlemen's Last Frontier* (Columbia, 1973), is the definitive work on this ranching combine.

the center of Indian Territory and outside the jurisdiction of any Indian nation or tribe, was a popular grazing area because there was no charge for grass use. Some ranchmen wintered cattle in the Unassigned Lands. Local cowboys guarded these herds until early spring, then drove the animals to Kansas railheads for shipment to Eastern markets.[18]

Buyers from the Missouri and Kansas border towns also hired Indian Territory cowboys to ride with them to the Texas ranches to buy cattle. During the early 1870's, George W. Miller of Newtonia, Missouri, leased a tract of grassland in northeastern Indian Territory from the Quapaw tribe. Money was scarce in the Southwest when Miller made his first cattle buying trip to Texas in 1871. To overcome this problem, Miller prepared for the Texas sojourn by sending his riders across southwest Missouri, trading local farmers horses for hogs. Miller's crew slaughtered the hogs, cured the meat, and carried ten wagon-loads of hams and bacon to San Saba County, Texas. There Miller's cowboys traded "fifty pounds of hog meat" for each steer. His crew delivered a herd of nearly a thousand beeves to the Quapaw Reservation pasture. This venture by Miller in 1871 provided the basis for the fabulous 101 Ranch which he subsequently established on the Ponca Reservation in the eastern portion of the Cherokee Outlet.[19]

Joe Nail of Caddo, Choctaw Nation, dealt in horses, mules, and cattle. Each spring he hired a crew of cowboys and a trail cook, loaded the chuck wagon with food, supplies, and a safe containing gold and silver—"nobody would accept a check" or paper money—and set out across southern Indian Territory. Regular stops at the small ranches netted a herd of from two thousand to three thousand steers, which his riders delivered to the shipping pens on the Katy Railroad, a north-south line which was completed across eastern Indian Territory during 1872.[20]

By 1880, agents from the St. Louis and Kansas City Commission Company came to the Southwest each spring to buy cattle. Customarily they hired riders from the Indian Territory and traveled on a circuit across the Cherokee Outlet, Unassigned Lands, into the Chickasaw Nation, and across Red River into north Texas, buying cattle. Drovers collected and held the cattle purchased by the commission agents, eventually driving the herds to railroads for shipment to market. A single commission agent might negotiate for sixty thousand head of livestock in a single year.[21]

Some Indian Territory cowboys were employed on ranches in the

---

[18] See Evan G. Barnard, *A Rider of the Cherokee Strip* (New York, 1936), for an account of ranch life in the Unassigned Lands.

[19] Collings and England, *The 101 Ranch*, p. 6.

[20] L. F. Baker Interview, Indian-Pioneer Papers, Vol. 4, p. 215.

[21] Ridings, *Chisholm Trail*, p. 303.

Cherokee and Creek nations, which specialized in finishing steers by winter feeding. Hay, harvested from lush prairie meadows, and corn, produced on rich river bottom farms, converted lank longhorns into prime slaughter critters in less than four months of concentrated feeding. These specialized ranches in eastern Indian Territory, each handling up to a thousand head of steers each season, were ancestors of the modern Oklahoma feed lots.[22]

A profitable employment for Indian Territory cowboys was working for beef contractors. Each year federal officials expended substantial sums for the purchase of dressed beef to provide rations for reservation Indians and for troops at Fort Sill, Fort Reno, and Fort Supply, guarding the recently conquered tribesmen. The contract to supply beef for the Cheyenne Arapaho Agency called for fifteen hundred head of cattle each year at $7.25 per hundred weight. Small ranchmen, most of them based in the Unassigned Lands, served as the beef contractors, and according to the testimony of their riders, these frontier businessmen had few scruples. The beef contract required that the contractor make regular deliveries of dressed beef to the agency headquarters for issue to the Indians. In addition, he was obligated to present the hides from the slaughtered animals for inspection by the government agent. One account relates that the contractor's cowboys delivered the beef and hides as required, then, at night, returned to the hide yard and slipped away with the hides. This contractor was reported to have "used the same hides as long as he could." He allegedly filled his contract of fifteen hundred steers each year "and never butchered over four hundred head of his own cattle." One cowboy working for this contractor admitted that "We always had a running iron with us and if steers accidentally got with us we ran his brand to match.... Our boss always paid us for all extras we got in this way." He added that "I would never brand a cow in the increase of the moon for the brand would grow, but if the branding is done on the decrease of the moon your brand will always be just the size of your iron. I always carried a running iron on my saddle to straighten out brands" until officials "made it against the law."[23]

Although commission agents, local buyers, and beef contractors engaged several hundred Indian Territory cowboys each year, most of the hands were employed by the cattle companies operating under lease arrangements on the Indian reservations and in the Cherokee Outlet. Ranchmen regarded their tenure in Indian Territory as temporary, believing it only a matter of time until the reservations would be opened to settlement by homesteaders. They "expected to be run out any time so they did not

[22] Andrew L. Rogers Interview, Indian-Pioneer Papers, Vol. 4, pp. 77, 337.
[23] T. D. Dave Adams Interview, *Ibid.*, Vol. 1, pp. 232, 236.

spend any money for lumber to build" permanent improvements on their Indian Territory ranges.[24]

Most ranchmen with Indian Territory interests resided in the border towns of southwest Missouri, southern Kansas, and northern Texas. Cowboys herding their cattle on the reservation ranges lived in tents, crude cabins, or dugouts. The most common Indian Territory ranch house was an excavation in a red clay bank, covered with cottonwood poles placed close together and covered with willow brush and packed soil. The windowless shelter front was walled with cottonwood logs and included a slab door. A rock fireplace in one corner of the dugout provided heat for cooking and warmth. In the early days of Indian Territory ranching, stockraising was an open range enterprise, and during most of the year riders camped in the open with the cattle, the cowboys stationed about four miles apart to keep the animals on established ranges.[25]

Cowboy duties included working at community roundups each spring and autumn. The spring roundup was a time for branding calves, separating herds, and returning stock to home ranges. Fall roundups largely were for collecting steers for market.[26]

Glidden-process barbed wire, patented in 1873, was widely adopted across the West by the close of the decade. Ranchmen used barbed wire for two purposes. In the early years of its application, cowboys raised drift fences, on an east-west line, eight to ten miles apart to keep cattle "within reasonable bounds." Cattle customarily drifted from the north to the south, particularly during winter blizzards. Stock from ranches on the Salt Fork might by spring be in the Washita or Red River valley. Drift fences checked some of this southward movement. Gradually, stockmen fenced their leased ranges, using both four-wire and six-wire enclosures. Thereafter, cowboys, the line riders, patrolled the fences, repaired broken sections, watched for strays, and threw back the herds.[27]

A cowboy's life on the Indian Territory ranges was demanding and harsh in all seasons, particularly in winter. From November to March, "blue northers," the deadly blizzards, were a constant threat. These fierce storms brought chill wind, sub-zero temperatures, sleet and snow, and required special vigilance by riders to keep cattle from drifting into the fences where they would for a certainty stack up and freeze to death. Besides riding between line camps over the range, throwing drifting cattle back from

[24] John Gault Interview, *Ibid.*, Vol. 33, p. 285.

[25] *Ibid.*, p. 281.

[26] Collings and England, *The 101 Ranch*, p. 62.

[27] Arrell M. Gibson, "Ranching on the Southern Great Plains," *Journal of the West*, Vol. 6 (January, 1967), p. 145.

the fences, and chopping ice in the ponds and rivers to provide water for thirsty stock, winter work for cowboys included "wolfing." Predatory wolf packs, "lobos or loafers," preyed on cows, calves, and colts. On a grown cow, lobos cut the hamstrings so the animal could not run or fight, then they moved in for the kill. Ranchmen paid a bounty of up to twenty dollars for each lobo pelt. One bounty hunter, with the cowboy penchant for exaggeration, claimed the largest wolf ever bagged in Indian Territory. The creature's "hide covered as much space as a yearling steer. His head was as large as a young lion."[28]

Grass fires were an eternal threat to Indian Territory stock. Some were set by lightning, others by man, accidentally or deliberately. Once underway and fanned by the ubiquitous Plains wind, a grass fire might burn over several hundred square miles before cowboy firefighters quenched it. Ranch hands attempted to check grass fires with fire guards, backfiring, and drags. The fire guard was a series of four to six furrows plowed on the range perimeter. Backfiring was a common method for containing range fires. A cowboy ignited a backfire by pulling an oil-soaked rope, tied to his saddle horn, through the grass. Firefighting crews hauled water barrels in buckboards to the fired range and attempted to beat out the blaze with water-soaked gunny sacks. They also used saddle blankets, slickers, and occasionally a cattle drag—a dead cow, slit open and dragged on a lariat by riders along the fire line.[29]

Summer's heat and drouth complicated the cowboy's life on the Indian Territory ranges. The summer of 1888 was rated as one of the worst drouth periods in the history of the Cherokee Outlet. Parson Barnard, a veteran Indian Territory cowboy, recalled that the "grass burned as brown as if it had been in an oven. The heat during the days of July and August was so intense that many cattle went blind for about a month. A thin, white scum formed over their eyeballs and at last caused blindness. This lasted four weeks or more, and it seemed to run through almost all the cattle. The Cimarron River was just a bed of sand and teams were used to scrape holes in the sand so that stock could get water."[30]

Working spooky Texas-bred cattle was never easy for the Indian Territory cowboys. Attempts by ranchmen to improve herd quality by introducing Shorthorn, Hereford, and Angus bulls on the reservation ranges produced problems of stock segregation and no few comical incidents for

---

[28] Barnard, *Cherokee Strip*, p. 121.

[29] Gibson, "Ranching on the Southern Great Plains," *Journal of the West*, Vol. 6 (January, 1967), p. 150.

[30] Barnard, *Cherokee Strip*, p. 126.

the hands. Parson Barnard recalled that the most vicious animals he ever attempted to work were "fifty wild Spanish bulls that they drove up from the coast country in Texas. These cattle were so wild that they grew moss on their horns. The broncos and Spanish mules were nice, gentle animals compared with the Spanish bulls. Some of the bulls were as black as tar and as curly as a buffalo, and looked as long as a passenger car. They fought their own shadows and had wicked horns. They must have been bred for Mexico's bull-fighting ring rather than for the range."[31]

The Indian Territory cow camps attracted many human types. This was a big country, surveillance was difficult, and it was attractive to men with a past. Many "riders of the owlhoot trail" hired on as hands for the Indian Territory cattle companies. The code of the range required one to protect his *compadres*. Thus when word passed that United States deputy marshals from Judge Isaac Parker's federal court at Fort Smith were prowling the country on an outlaw dragnet, the renegades hid in the brush. A "red undershirt on the top of the horse corral near the gate" indicated that "all was clear."[32]

Parson Barnard, who doubled as camp cook, laundered his *compadres'* clothing at a charge of ten cents a garment and earned $5 each washday. One of his customers, Jim Hame, had only one shirt to wash each month, and Barnard explained that Hame's annual laundry bill was only "a dollar and twenty cents." Barnard boiled the clothes in a large kettle then threw them "over some brush to dry." He explained that he boiled the clothes to kill "all foreign animals" in the garments. Visiting riders often carried graybacks (lice) which infested the camp bed gear. The only way to check the graybacks was by boiling the clothes.[33]

Life in the scattered cow camps of Indian Territory was made more bearable by simple cowboy amusements. In the crude ranch shelters the hands sang and played cards, checkers, and pranks on one another. Bronc riding and steer roping contests, swapping guns, and shooting matches were popular pastimes. Cowboys delighted in "inducing greenhorns to mount broncs which nobody could ride." Bronc riding was the favorite range sport. Old time bronc busters related that these horses "were wild and mean but that made it more fun for us." Indian Territory cowboys also hunted turkey, deer, and wild horses. They told of capturing wild horses by a carefully placed bullet from a Winchester at long range, "creasing it on the top of the withers." This would knock the animal senseless, and while he

31 *Ibid.*, p. 105.
32 *Ibid.*, p. 93.
33 *Ibid.*, p. 126.

was out, riders roped the horse, put a hackamore on him and led him to the ranch corral.[34]

Isolation was nearly complete. The only towns were the settlements of the Five Civilized Tribes in eastern Indian Territory and the border towns of Missouri, Kansas, and Texas, which hands might visit once each season. In the great domain of western Indian Territory the only urban-type settlements of any consequence were at the military posts and Indian agencies. Scattered throughout the ranching territory were tiny trading settlements, stockaded from the 1870's when Indian raids were an ever-present threat. These forted villages each consisted of a store and saloon and doubled as stage stop and trading post. They included Doan's Store on Red River, Silver City on the Canadian River crossing of the Chisholm Trail, and Bison and Pond Creek Station on the northern leg of the Chisholm Trail. Storekeepers at these frontier settlements served as postmasters. They knew all the men in the country and would send mail to different ranches, the ranchmen passing the letters on until each finally reached its destination. The envelope of each letter was inscribed with the brand of the ranch where it was to go.[35]

In their isolated state, Indian Territory cowboys missed female companionship. Women were scarce in this cattle country. Two young women resided at the Anderson cattle camp near Pond Creek Station. The girls owned an organ, and cowboys from all over the western Indian Territory visited their camp to talk with them and to listen to the music. Barnard claimed that the only grindstone in western Indian Territory was at the Anderson camp, and "we rode as far as fifteen miles to grind our axes." When the foreman said the axe needed sharpening, "there was a scramble among us to see who could get to the axe first. It always took a whole day to do this job."[36]

Dancing was by far the most popular indoor sport for Indian Territory cowboys. They would ride twenty-five or thirty miles to the Skelton Ranch dance, frolic until three o'clock in the morning, "then return to their ranches and have something to talk about for weeks." Bill Miller, a champion cowboy dancer who moved with the grace of a panther, scorned the clumsy terpsichorean movements of his *compadres*—"All you cowpunchers are just locoed when ladies are around." Miller added that "most of the boys danced like bears around a beehive. . . . They were afraid of getting stung."[37]

The ranchmen's prescience that it was only a matter of time until their

[34] L. F. Baker Interview, Indian Pioneer Papers, Vol. 4, p. 217.
[35] John Gault Interview, *Ibid.*, Vol. 33, p. 281.
[36] Barnard, *Cherokee Strip*, p. 136.
[37] *Ibid.*, pp. 114–15.

150

Indian Territory ranges would be opened to settlement by homesteaders soon was fulfilled. This process of metamorphosing the grasslands of central and western Indian Territory from cattle ranges to 160-acre farms began in 1889, when the federal government authorized settlement in the Unassigned Lands. Because the eventual opening of Indian Territory had been popularized by the Boomers, and the Unassigned Lands represented a small settlement area (about 2 million acres), government officials responsible for the opening realized that there would be many more homeseekers than claims available. To equalize opportunities, it was decided to settle the area by a novel procedure—the land run. And federal officials were not disappointed, for during late April, 1889, over fifty thousand persons gathered on the perimeter of the Unassigned Lands to make the race for the ten thousand homestead claims and townsite lots.[38]

Many Indian Territory cowboys, who had "got that free and easy out of their systems, and were ready to settle down," prepared to participate in the land run. Parson Barnard and fifteen comrades were from this group. He admitted "We cowpunchers had never farmed, and looked at settling down on a farm just as a chance to make a little easy money. Consequently, we were not as much excited as some of the other people, who had families and knew what a home meant." He stated that "Our plan was to stick together, and to stick after we got our claim. We knew where we wanted to go, but knew nothing whatever about the number of the sections or quarter sections, township or range. That was Greek to cowpunchers. We wanted bottom land on the Creek where we would have water and pasture. We wanted no wells to dig, and no wood to haul, at least for any great distance."[39]

Soldiers guarding the line gave the signal at noon, April 22, and the race was on. Barnard commented that "The noise made by so many horses and wagons and rattletraps bumping over the prairies, and the yelling of the crowd, made a rumbling noise which sounded very much like ten thousand head of cattle on a stampede."[40]

Barnard and his companions filed on sixteen adjacent quarter-sections on Turkey Creek. Then, he said, the "real trouble of holding our claims began. . . . Just staking a claim did not hold it. We had to let many others, who claimed they had done the same thing, know we were the first ones on the claims. Hundreds of people were passing, and we were kept busy riding like the devil seeing to it that others did not stop on our claims." The cow-

[38] Gibson, *Oklahoma*, pp. 293–94.
[39] Barnard, *Cherokee Strip*, pp. 140–41.
[40] *Ibid*.

boys stuck together and successfully bluffed intruders off their claims. In one heated verbal contest with a claim jumper on his Turkey Creek claim, Barnard disputed that the intruder had preceded him in driving the claim stake. Thereupon the man made the proposition to Barnard that they divide the tract, each taking eighty acres. The crusty Indian Territory cowboy answered "it was a hundred sixty acres or six feet, and I did not give a damn which it was." Barnard was braced by his heavily-armed comrades which caused the intruder to withdraw.[41]

Successive land openings after 1889 liquidated the great cattle ranges of western Indian Territory. However, many ranchmen survived in the post-homesteader age by leasing large blocks of grassland from allotment Indians. By 1900, George W. Miller's 101 Ranch in northern Oklahoma Territory extended over 110,000 acres of choice range leased from Ponca Indian alottees. The tenacity in adversity of pioneer ranchmen enabled them gradually to recover and re-establish stock raising in the territory, and provided the foundation for the Sooner State's principal industry. Many cowboys who had abandoned herding cattle to work homestead claims returned to the rehabilitated ranches and rode the diminished ranges as of old.

The legacy of Indian Territory cowboys is rich and varied. They must rate credit for being among the first Anglo-American settlers in western Indian Territory. They continued their range skills on Oklahoma ranches after statehood and indelibly stamped the Western image on Oklahoma culture. And they transmitted the color and action of the frontier to great audiences in the eastern United States and Europe, in that many former Indian Territory riders were recruited as performers for the Wild West shows which were popular between 1900 and 1930. Their range skills of bronc riding and steer roping and bulldogging became popular spectator sports, culminating in the modern rodeo. Likewise, Indian Territory cowboys were pioneer actors in some of the first Western motion pictures, which were produced on Oklahoma ranches.

The heritage of the Indian Territory cowboy was recovered from oblivion in 1920 by the creation of the Cherokee Strip Cowpunchers Association. Its four hundred members met each year on Cowboy Hill in the buffalo pasture of the 101 Ranch for the reunion which the members called the "annual round-up." Old riders "brought their equipment for camping out," and around the campfire exchanged stories and "sang songs that they sang while riding the range." Their sessions "ran far into the night with stories of the round-up, brushes with the Indians, necktie parties for rustlers, and all the memories that were connected with chaps, lariat, and

41 *Ibid.*, pp. 141–42.

spur."[42] The ultimate tribute to the Indian Territory cowboy is the location of the National Cowboy Hall of Fame and Western Heritage Center in Oklahoma City.

[42] Collings and England, *The 101 Ranch*, p. 156.

The Cowboy Myth

BY WILLIAM W. SAVAGE, JR.

AMONG THE GIMCRACKS AND KNICKKNACKS of three centuries of American popular culture, the figure of the cowboy surely occupies a unique position. He is anomalous and contradictory, a trifle which, unlike other trifles, suggests substance. His one-dimensional image implies both height and breadth, but of depth there is none. He is the subject of no great work of art or literature or music, but his status among the ephemera of popular culture elevates him to the lofty levels of myth and legend. His mark—his brand, if you will—is everywhere on everything. His place in the American mythology, as expounded from drugstore to network and points between, is somewhere above the President and below the Christ. Now, approximately a century after his birth as a cult object, he is what is known as heritage; and, no matter what one makes of him as an item in the intellectual baggage of the American people, it is certain that he cannot be taken lightly.[1]

---

[1] Instructive on the subject of the cowboy myth are Douglas Branch, *The Cowboy and His Interpreters* (New York, 1926); Mody C. Boatright, "The American Myth Rides the Range," *Southwest Review*, Vol. XXXVI (Summer, 1951), pp. 157–63; David B. Davis, "Ten Gallon Hero," *American Quarterly*, Vol. VI (Summer, 1954), pp. 111–25; George Bluestone, "The Changing Cowboy: From Dime Novel to Dollar Film," *Western Humanities Review*, Vol. XIV (Summer, 1960), pp. 331–37; and Robert V. Hine, *The American West: An Interpretive History* (Boston, 1973), Chapter 9. *See also* Bart McDowell, *The American Cowboy in Life and Legend* (Washington, 1972) and William H. Forbis and the Editors of Time-Life Books, *The Cowboys* (New York, 1973) for conflicting assessments of the place of the cowboy in American history. Of interest also is John Wayne's foreword in Ed Ainsworth, *The Cowboy in Art* (New York and Cleveland, 1968), p. vii. The cowboy image is closely linked to popular music, and on that subject see Bill C. Malone, *Country Music U.S.A.: A Fifty-Year History* (Austin, 1968), chapter 5; Robert Shelton and Burt Goldblatt, *The Country Music Story: A Picture History of Country and Western Music* (Secaucus, N.J., 1966), chapter 7; and Glenn Ohrlin, *The Hell-Bound Train: A Cowboy Songbook* (Urbana, 1973). Useful surveys of the cowboy in American cinema include William K. Everson, *A Pictorial History of the Western Film* (Secaucus, N.J., 1969) and Alan G. Barbour, *The Thrill of it All* (New York, 1971).

"Cowboyin'," an old hand remarks in a recent motion-picture blend of myth and reality, "is somethin' you do when you can't do nothin' else."[2] The same is often said of other lines of endeavor, to be sure, but in the case of the historical cowboy, the man-child of the rangeland from 1865 to 1890, it is nevertheless an accurate perception. His was a sorry lot. The meanest sort of drudgery occupied his waking hours, and his only steadfast companions were tedium and fatigue. One need not belabor the point. He who doubts its validity need only examine the record. That alone is sufficient explanation of the historical cowboy's supreme unfitness as a subject for, say, literature. It makes clear the reason why the best cowboy books are history books and why the worst are novels that attempt authenticity.

To the cattle industry, Andy Adams' *Log of a Cowboy* may indeed bear the same relationship that *Moby Dick* bears to whaling (although those who say so would have us ignore the world of difference between the books themselves), but Adams' characters are prosaic and consequently his work fails as fiction. Subsequent modifications of the cowboy's image resulted in the equation of cowhand with gunhand that has become America's most firmly entrenched literary convention. Drab fellows on horseback grew progressively more interesting to wider and wider audiences because, packing iron, they could shoot wildlife, Indians, passers-by, and each other, in print or in Technicolor, without fear of popular recriminations or repercussions. Only a spate of political assassinations in the 1960's could stanch the flow of blood, and even then only on the screens of the nation's television sets. On newsstands and in theaters, cowboy gore oozed and oozes still.[3]

So there is a difference between the reality of the historical cowboy and the myth of the good man who defends truth and right for the edification of small children and sells beer and cigarettes to an older, but not necessarily wiser, audience. The delineation of that difference usually occupies more scholarly attention than it deserves, which is indicative of the fact that the beating of dead horses is a thriving pastime in academe, but the only meaningful distinction is that, of the two, the myth and the reality, the myth is by far the more important.[4]

The cowboy was a hired man, an individual without capital who was in

[2] *The Culpepper Cattle Co.* (1972), directed by Dick Richards.
[3] See Joe B. Frantz, "The Frontier Tradition: An Invitation to Violence," in Hugh Davis Graham and Ted Robert Gurr, editors, *Violence in America: Historical and Comparative Perspectives* (New York, Toronto, and London, 1969), pp. 127–54; and Roger Field, "The Technology of TV Violence," *Saturday Review*, June 10, 1972, p. 51.
[4] Joe B. Frantz and Julian Ernest Choate, Jr., *The American Cowboy: The Myth and the Reality* (Norman, 1955) is typical. It contributes little of substance and reaches no conclusions. See also William W. Savage, Jr., "Western Literature and Its Myths: A Rejoinder," *Montana, the Magazine of Western History*, Vol. XXII (October, 1972), pp. 78–81.

the employ of an individual with capital. In other words, the cowboy was not a cattleman.[5] Cattlemen possessed the financial backing and the entrepreneurial skill necessary to make the cattle business a viable industry, and were thus an integral part of the history of western American economic development. Cowboys, on the other hand, tended cattle, an occupation that classified them as unskilled laborers. The basic requirement for employment as a cowboy was an ability to remain atop a horse. (The argument is frequently advanced by devotees of the historical cowboy that it was just this liaison with horses that set him apart. A mounted man, they claim, is socially and economically superior to a man afoot. It is doubtful, however, that anyone since Crécy and Agincourt has wasted much time worrying about the superiority of horsemen, except perhaps horsemen themselves.) Anyone who could stay in the saddle could be a cowboy, and anyone usually was—frail Easterners, pampered Britons, effete Frenchmen, small children, old men, anybody at all. In fact, some contemporary observers noted that the best cowboys were Indians, a bit of intelligence studiously ignored by most exponents of the Anglo-American, Afro-American, and Mexican-American schools of cowboy studies.[6] But who the cowboys were is less important than what they were, and in comparison with cattlemen they comprised a class of men almost wholly without historical significance.

As symbol or myth, however, the cowboy is of transcendent importance. The single most dramatic event in American history was the conquest, within a century of independence, of the continent; and rather than the trapper, trader, explorer, soldier, or farmer, the cowboy represents this event in the popular mind. He is the focal point of public identification with an exciting, even a glorious, past. His image, whether or not it is a truthful representation, is accepted because it has much to do with our conception of ourselves and because it suggests that our nation, in preserving the emotional vestiges and the artifacts of cowboying, still contains the intangible stuff from which heroes are made. We believe deeply, all evidence to the contrary notwithstanding, that the individualism of which Turner spoke has always been, and still is, a valid factor in American life, and that the cowboy was the grandest individual of them all.[7]

[5] The point is strongly made in Lewis Atherton, *The Cattle Kings* (Bloomington, 1961).

[6] James S. Brisbin, *The Beef Bonanza; or, How to Get Rich on the Plains* (New edition, Norman, 1959), p. 66.

[7] Promoters and publicists of Evel Knievel's September 8, 1974, jump of the Snake River Canyon, possibly the non-event of the decade, found it advantageous to suggest that Knievel possessed not only cowboy origins (meaning Montana) but also cowboy characteristics (meaning that he would do what he said he would do). While its "science editor," Jules Bergman, reviewed Knievel's career on a program entitled "Evel Knievel: One Man, One Canyon," aired on the evening of September 5, the American Broadcasting Company provided musical background—a harmonica rendition of "The Cowboy's Lament."

As technology separates and isolates more and more people from traditional ways of life, and as the complexities of contemporary society transform them into what David Riesman called other-directed personalities, Americans increasingly internalize what they conceive the nineteenth-century westering experience to have been. Call it the preservation of heritage, call it nostalgia, call it what you will, it contains a fantastic amount of cowboy lore, either real or imagined, that offers temporary psychological —and sometimes physical—escape from a twentieth century somehow unnatural in its demands on body and soul.[8] On one level, the cowboy is a symbol of chivalry, courage, honor, and loyalty—virtues we wish were abroad in the land in greater profusion, virtues we know we ourselves possess and wish we could demonstrate for the general good. On another level, the cowboy is a symbol of all that we are not. He is colorful, decisive, active, glamorous, unfettered, exciting, uncommon, mobile, independent, and confident. Like us, he moves through a world he did not make, but, unlike us, he can resolve his conflicts at their most fundamental levels and ride on, unmolested. That is to say, the cowboy exists in a primordial state and may, accordingly, simply destroy his antagonists, if he cannot intimidate them into submission. We, in civilized societies, are unable to attain this ultimate resolution, maintaining order, as we do, through systems of intermediaries. But we buy cowboy hats and cowboy boots, and we pretend.[9] Great numbers of us buy guns, and that is where the pretense ends and the potential begins.

The violent reality of the six-gun is the matrix that unites the various levels of the cowboy myth. To discuss it is to wheel into view the whole history of weaponry and its application by Western (in the grander sense) man. There is the argument, of course, that in the New World firearms were not weapons at all, but tools—tools for harvesting game.[10] Yet, whatever effect they had on deer, wild turkeys, and other edible fauna, firearms have served European and Anglo-American society as instruments for the subjugation of technologically inferior peoples. Red, white, black, brown, or yellow, he who has no firearm is technologically inferior to anyone who

[8] Michael Harrington has described the disquieting effect of the disparity between "technological capacity and economic, political, social, and religious consciousness" in *The Accidental Century* (Baltimore, 1966), p. 41. Physical escape has something to do with dude ranches, and the people who run them seem well aware of the reasons for their popularity. See Jack Hines, "West," *The Dude Rancher*, Vol. 41 (Summer, 1972), p. 3.

[9] On the subject of western attire, see *Tack 'n Togs Dealer Roundup Report No. 2* (Minneapolis, 1972), pp. 3–6. According to this survey, there were nearly twice as many chaps sold in the southeastern United States in 1971 as there were in the entire Great Plains region. In fact, there were more chaps sold on the Pacific Coast and in Alaska and Hawaii than in Texas, Oklahoma, Arkansas, and Louisiana combined. And more western vests were sold in New York, Pennsylvania, and New England than in Texas and Oklahoma.

[10] Robert L. Williamson, "The Muzzle-Loading Rifle: Frontier Tool," in Harold M. Hollingsworth and Sandra L. Myres, editors, *Essays on the American West* (Austin and London, 1969), pp. 66–88.

does. Examine the cowboy in that context—and, whether in manifestations fictive or real, he is on record from time to time as having abused his technological superiority by hazing greenhorns, plugging gamblers, and ambushing Mexicans, Negroes, and Indians—and you discover that something is amiss. Shooting someone while subscribing to a code of chivalry, honor, courage, and loyalty does not square, unless the shooter has right, or at least right thinking, on his side. But purveyors of the cowboy myth have lately shown us both blood and ambiguity, and they have suggested, while raising the cowboy to even loftier heights, that his boots are muddy and his feet are clay. He may still be the good guy, but he is no longer necessarily right.[11]

Whether or not this turn of events bodes ill for the future of the cowboy myth is certainly debatable, but debates are not without profit. It may be well to suggest that what we are observing in American popular culture at present is an unraveling of the mythic fabric of the cowboy. A major thread in that fabric is what cynics call the "good vs. evil stereotype," but which might better be termed the gambit of ethical and moral evaluation. When that is absent, the focal point in fiction or film becomes carnage, feigned for the audience in loving and clinical detail.[12] The cowboy becomes as ambiguous and pragmatic as a Raymond Chandler or Ross Macdonald detective, and the presentation, regardless of medium, becomes an exercise in catharsis. We, too, are ambiguous and pragmatic, and, when the cowboy sinks to our level, we see no difference between him and us. His vehicle, be it Saturday afternoon movie or two chapters of a paperback novel taken before retiring, acquires all the animalistic characteristics of a professional wrestling match. We, like a thousand screaming fans, are surrogate victims of hideous outrage, and we rejoice in our vindication.

The cowboy as catharsis is less than satisfactory. We hardly need a larger dose of emotional purgative than that afforded by our spectator sports and the evening news. Catharsis is acceptable, of course. The very word reeks of the sort of sophistication to which we as a nation aspire. Myth is less acceptable, which perhaps explains why we spend as much time as we do trying to separate it from reality, so that we may better debunk it. Yet,

[11] All of this may have begun with Henry King's 1950 film *The Gunfighter*, which had little to do with cowboys. See Robert Warshow, *The Immediate Experience: Movies, Comics, Theatre & Other Aspects of Popular Culture* (Garden City, N.Y., 1962), pp. 135–54.

[12] The foremost cinematic clinician is, of course, Sam Peckinpah. Extreme violence is the order of the day in paperback fiction, and when American writers cannot produce enough of it, publishers import the work of authors who can. J. T. Edson, an Englishman who has never been to America, writes western novels "which average 12 principal killings" apiece, an acceptable number, his publisher suggests, because Edson does not describe "the physical details of a violent death." J. T. Edson, *The Floating Outfit* (New York, Toronto, and London, 1974), p. 167. See also Dereck Williamson, "Pocket Violence," *The New York Times Book Review*, March 10, 1974, pp. 23–24.

few realize the extent to which myth is ingrained in the national consciousness. It is simply not fashionable, except in its institutional forms. Popularly, it is something reserved for long-dead Greeks. But it is essential, which is to say that no people can do without it.[13]

The case for myth assumes that what people believe about their past is more important than what their past actually was—more important in regard to the formation of their attitudes, the determination of their responses, and their conception of self. The notion is not that myth can or should supplant history (an impossibility in a nation such as ours, which prides itself on its extensive record-keeping machinery), but rather that myth performs a vital function in human society, a function that must be understood. As a young country whose physical growth has been accompanied by rapid technological change, America has not developed, or had time to develop, a culture of genuine substance. In comparison to much of the rest of the world, America has only a small shelf of myth, and that is the preserve of a handful of scholars who deal swiftly and summarily with those they deem poachers, and who seem determined to restrict the utilitarian aspects of myth to those things which can provide periodical grist for academic mills. Myth in the hands of academicians is very often only a device for getting at reality, a decent enough undertaking for scholars, but one which serves to remove myth even farther from the people. When the scholar of myth makes public the results of his labors, he is very much like the biologist who returns a dissected frog to its pond. It may be a nice gesture, but it is futile, because something irretrievable has been lost in the course of the study. Myth thus rendered is useless to the people it must serve.[14]

Questions of sociology, psychology (as it is popularly understood), and (perhaps) terminology aside, what America needs is a renaissance of myth. The likeliest candidate for canonization in the event of such a re-birth is of course the cowboy. And what we would have, if the thing were properly done, would be a substantial item, a cowboy of heroic proportions.

[13] Anyone who discusses the cowboy in this context is certain to run afoul of the scholarly literature pertaining to myth. Nevertheless, one should consult Ernst Cassirer, *Language and Myth*, translated by Susanne K. Langer (New York, 1946) and the works of Joseph Campbell, including *The Masks of God* (4 vols., New York, 1959–1968) and *The Hero With a Thousand Faces* (revised edition, Princeton, N.J., 1968). The problem for the nonspecialist, as Mircea Eliade demonstrates in *Myth and Reality*, translated by Willard R. Trask (New York and Evanston, 1963), p. 2, is that " 'myth' means a true story' and, beyond that, a story that is a most precious possession because it is sacred, exemplary, significant." Even so, there seems to be little about myth upon which scholars will agree, and general usage is reflected by Richard Schickel's comment, made in a review of a television program about Abraham Lincoln, that a "nation needs its mythic heroes, and no nation needs them more than the U.S. at this moment." Richard Schickel, "Viewpoints," *Time*, September 9, 1974, p. 60.

[14] The means by which one may transform silk purses into sows' ears are demonstrated in Richard M. Dorson, *American Folklore & the Historian* (Chicago and London, 1971).

According to the lights of those who want everything laid out for them, he who urges an end must also suggest a means. But the construction of myth is in large measure a creative process, and it ill behooves anyone, be he sage, pundit, or impoverished scholar, to dictate the steps of creation. Nevertheless, it seems clear that, while the cowboy, his physical environment, and his historical context, provide the elements for the fabrication of a superb myth, the people who have worked with those elements have used them to poor advantage. They have not produced a cheap (in the sense of inexpensive) image, but they have produced a shoddy one. Were it not that these people—writers, promoters, producers, directors—have their collective fingers in the pie of America's national consciousness, they might simply be warned about the evils of poor workmanship, and that would be that; but as it is, they are helping to shape values, attitudes, and responses on a wide scale, and consequently they must accept greater responsibility for their efforts than they have in the past. If the cowboy is to be viewed as a commodity to be bought and sold, he will not be available for the making of myth, and his image will never be better than it already is.

In all, the cowboy hero appears to have gone by the boards. Realism and the rise of the "dirty Western" have left us only the rodeo cowboy, and he is no cowboy at all. Rather, he is a professional athlete, a performer, and he bears less relationship to a working cowboy than he does to a linebacker or a shortstop. Still, he looks to be a cowboy, if clothes indeed make the man, and he has to do with horses. And occasionally he is quite the hero, or so his exponents would have us believe. He bridges the century between the images of the cowboy-that-was and the cowboy-as-he-is-thought-to-be, and he is necessarily popular. Because he is a contemporary figure, he may be readily identified with the themes of alienation and isolation so common in mid-twentieth-century American thought. He offers a ready-made image as an outsider, a loner, a man who spurns society and who, if he is victimized at all, victimizes himself. To purveyors and consumers of popular culture, his neuroses are not as dramatic as the gunfighter-cowboy's, but they are more complex. In film and fiction, the rodeo cowboy's man-to-man confrontations are rare, but his battles to subdue Nature, whether disguised as bronc or brahma, and his struggles against Time are relentless. His world is a violent one, but he moves through it armed only with muscle and will. He offers a corrective to blood and gore and suggests heroic potential. He is no cowboy, but he is close to myth.[15]

[15] See Clifford P. Westermeier, *Man, Beast, Dust: The Story of Rodeo* (Denver, 1947); [Gerald C. Lubenow], "Rodeo: The Soul of the Frontier," *Newsweek*, October 2, 1972, p. 27; Jay Cocks, "Overreacher," *Time*, April 17, 1972, p. 91; and Arthur Knight, "The New Old West," *Saturday Review*, July 29, 1972, p. 70. Rodeo cowboys were the subject of two 1962

This, however, is digression. The questions at hand are, can the cowboy as hero be salvaged, and can his myth be made better in the process? The prognosis calls for major surgery, to be sure, but the only real problem involved in that will be to find some skillful folk to wield the scalpel. Despite J. Frank Dobie's worst fears that the "literature of the range," and thereby the fictive cowpoke, might never mature,[16] even the most pessimistic observer must conclude that the cowboy can be a good patient and recuperate quickly. Yet, metaphor is not method, and the means do require comment, even if it smacks of dictation.

Once there was a literary form known as the epic. Briefly, an epic was the work of a single author, and it began *in medias res*, carried a statement of epic purpose, contained descriptions of warfare, and employed the supernatural as a literary device. It offered a central character, a hero, and through him united a series of adventures or episodes which, taken together, contributed to an explanation of the formation of a race or nation. Those with which we are most familiar have to do with a journey, a quest of some sort, if you will, in which the hero's mettle, muscle, and mind are continually tested and tried by man, beast, and god alike. They have entertained and instructed a good many for a good while.

There is much in the cowboy experience that lends itself to epic treatment. The long drive comes immediately to mind. It is frequently the subject of cowboy fiction, but its potential as a literary vehicle has hardly been explored. Indeed, the long drive story has become a matter of convention, and stasis is its primary characteristic. The long drive story, as it is currently written, seems to contain certain fundamental parts, and if we wish to juxtapose what is with what could be, we had best consider them:

> 1. The drive begins. Date, place of origin, destination, and number of cattle are obligatory elements.[17]

television series, "Stoney Burke" and "The Wide Country." Representative rodeo novels include Hal Borland, *When Legends Die* (Philadelphia, 1963); William Crawford, *The Bronc Rider* (New York, 1965); and Herbert Harker, *Goldenrod* (New York, 1972). The 1974 documentary film *The Great American Cowboy*, a rodeo extravaganza, was billed in theater advertising as, "The exciting true story of a vanishing american [*sic*] and his special kind of freedom." For additional insights, see A. M. Gibson, "The National Cowboy Hall of Fame," *Agricultural History*, Vol. XXXIII (July, 1959), pp. 103–106, and James E. Serven, "National Cowboy Hall of Fame and Western Heritage Center," *Arizona Highways*, Vol. XLVI (October, 1970) pp. 36–37, 42–44.

[16] J. Frank Dobie, *Guide to Life and Literature of the Southwest* (revised edition, Dallas, 1952), p. 92.

[17] In Andy Adams, *The Log of a Cowboy: A Narrative of the Old Trail Days* (Boston, 1903), 3,100 cattle are being moved from the Rio Grande to northwestern Montana in 1882. In Emerson Hough, *North of 36* (New York, 1923), some 4,000 cattle move from a point near Austin, Texas, to Abilene, Kansas, in 1867. And so on.

2. Personalities are established—trail boss, *segundo*, cook, lead steer, cowhands, favorite horses, etc.[18]

3. Conflicts are developed—who dislikes whom and why.

4. Encounters in the wilderness—crises in all shapes and sizes, including but not limited to

    (a) stampedes,

    (b) death of a good old boy by (a) or

    (c) Indian attack,

    (d) drought, and

    (e) fire.

5. The surprise—one of the cowboys is a girl, the bad guy is really the good guy, or, the greatest surprise of all, nothing happens.[19]

6. The anti-climax, wherein the drive ends, as we all knew it would, and everyone (except the dead) is back where he started, a little the worse for wear.

There is a dreary sameness about long drive stories that may doubtless be attributed the admixture of melodrama and specificity of detail typical of most "western" writing. There are notable exceptions, of course. These include Robert Flynn's *North to Yesterday*,[20] a book that surely achieves the status of literature, but by deflating and debunking myth rather than by elaborating upon it. It has been suggested, with regard to the "western" genre, that people lampoon those things which they hold most dear, and if Flynn's novel and—leaving the long drive—exercises like Ishmael Reed's *Yellow Back Radio Broke-Down* are not sufficient evidence, then the popularity of such curious manifestations as the film *Blazing Saddles* certainly is.[21] These things may be simply isolated phenomena, revealing more about American life in the 1960's and 1970's than they do about national mythic constructs, but they mark a shift away from the prosaic. And if their direction is not what it should be, in terms of meaningful development of mythic forms, at least they stimulate comment. The stage they represent may be a necessary evil, a conclusion which assumes, perhaps incorrectly, that their function is to destroy clichés so that something of consequence may emerge. The question, at this point, is not whether something of consequence is possible; rather, one should ask, is it probable?

[18] Of Hough's *North of 36*, J. Frank Dobie said, "The best character in it is Old Alamo, lead steer." Dobie, *Guide to Life and Literature*, p. 107.

[19] Cowboy Reddie Bayne is really a girl in Zane Grey, *The Trail Driver* (New York, 1936), and so is Tommy Ryden in Mel Marshall, *Longhorns North* (New York, 1969), which suggests that in "western" fiction some things never change. Nothing happens in Adams, *The Log of a Cowboy*, or, oddly, in Benjamin Capps, *The Trail to Ogallala* (New York, 1964), a book that somehow manages to be interesting anyway.

[20] New York, 1967.

[21] See C. L. Sonnichsen, "The Wyatt Earp Syndrome," *The American West*, Vol. VII (May, 1970), pp. 26–28, 60–62. Reed's book was published in 1969 by Doubleday & Company, Inc., New York.

In sum, then, the cowboy as myth is in poor condition in American popular culture. His rescue, if it is to be effected at all, must come through the efforts of intelligent people acting intelligently. Exploitation is a constant with which we must live, one supposes, but it can perhaps be circumvented in the proper circumstances. We would do well, however, to consider the possibility that the cowboy image is already so debased through commercial exploitation that people who might otherwise deal maturely with it cannot, as Frank Waters once suggested to Frederick Manfred, "get into the mood."[22] And at bottom a "mood" may be exactly what the cowboy is in twentieth-century America. If it cannot be "gotten into" by responsible members of the creative community, then the nation stands to lose a substantial article in its cultural inventory.

[22] John R. Milton, editor, *Conversations with Frank Waters* (Chicago, 1971), p. 86.

About the Authors

CHARLES W. HARRIS, co-editor of this volume, is Assistant Professor of History in Southeastern Oklahoma State University in Durant, Oklahoma.

BUCK RAINEY, co-editor, is Professor and Chairman of Business Education at East Central Oklahoma State University at Ada, Oklahoma. He has published extensively on Western movie personalities and film history.

DON RUSSELL, honorary life member of the Western History Association and a member of the Civil War Round Table of Chicago is editor of the Chicago *Westerner's Brand Book*. He is the author of many books and articles on Western history.

PHILIP D. JORDAN, Emeritus Professor of History from the University of Minnesota, has written many books and articles in the course of a career that has focused particular attention on the history of medicine and of frontier law and order. He is a Fellow of the Royal Historical Society of England.

CLIFFORD P. WESTERMEIER is Professor of History in the University of Colorado and has written many books, articles, and essays on Western History.

LAWRENCE R. BORNE is Associate Professor of History at Northern Kentucky State College, and his article in this book was drawn from material to be included in a book he is writing on dude ranching.

GUY LOGSDON is Director of Libraries at the University of Tulsa. Folklore and country and folk music are his primary interests, and he has written extensively about these topics. A performer himself, Logsdon often sings and makes presentations on the music of the Southwest.

ARRELL M. GIBSON, George Lynn Cross Research Professor of History in the University of Oklahoma, is widely acclaimed for his scholarship in Oklahoma history. A well-known Western historian, also, Gibson is the author of many books and articles in his chosen field.

WILLIAM W. SAVAGE, JR. is Assistant Professor of History in the University of Oklahoma and the author or editor of several other books and many articles in the field of Western history.

Index

Abbott, Teddy Blue (E. C.):
6, 88, 89
Acord, Art: 33, 37, 49
Adams, Andy, 6, 8, 14, 60, 81,
134, 142, 155
Adams, Ramon: 2, 5, 6, 7, 91
Allen, Bob: 51
Allen, Jules Verne (The Sing-
ing Cowboy): 130
Allen, Rex: 53, 138
Anderson, G. M. (Broncho
Billy): 6, 13, 22–23, 25, 26,
28, 51
Arnspiger, Wills & Herman:
136
Arthur, Chester A.: 8
Atherton, Lewis: 86
Autry, Gene: 6, 13, 22, 24, 25,
28, 36, 40, 41, 44, 50, 51–53,
135, 136

Badger, Joseph E.: 63
Baker, Bob: 51, 53
Baker, Johnnie: 10
Baker, Johnny: 138
Ballew, Smith: 51, 53
Barnard, Parson: 148, 149, 150,
151–52
Barnes, Will C.: 130, 131, 132
Barry, Donald (Red): 50, 54
Beadle novels: 10, 11
Becker, Carl: 20
Bell, Rex: 18, 28, 38, 46, 49
Bengough, Clement: 112
Bergman, Jules: 156n.
Boulding, Kenneth: 98
Bowers, B. M. (Bertha): 14
Boyd, Bill (Cowboy Ram-
bler): 53
Boyd, William: 6, 24, 25, 37,
46, 50, 51
Branch, E. Douglas: 59–60, 90

Brand, Max: 14, 18
Bronson, Edgar Beecher: 96
Brown, Johnny Mack: 37, 47
Brown, Milton: 136
Buffalo Bill: see Cody
Buffalo Bill, Jr.: 49
Buntline, Ned: see Judson
Burns, Fred: 49
Burt, Struthers: 117

Calgary Stampede: 12
Cameron, Ewen: 7–8
Cameron, Rod: 51
Canutt, Yakima: 20, 34, 46, 47,
49
Carey, Harry: 16, 19, 20, 26,
28, 31, 32, 33, 34, 37, 38, 51
Carson, Kit: 17
Carson, Sunset: 49
Cassidy, Hopalong: 6, 13, 50
Catchings, Eugene: 61
Chandler, Lane: 49
Chapman, Arthur: 131
Cheetham, Everett: 135
Cherokee Nation: 144, 146
Cherokee Outlet: 144, 145, 146,
148
Cherokee Strip Cowpunchers
Association: 152
Cherokee Strip Livestock As-
sociation: 144
Cheyenne Arapaho Agency:
146
Cheyenne Frontier Days: 12
Chickasaw Nation: 145
Chisholm, Jesse: 140
Chisholm Trail: 8, 24, 61, 64,
139, 140, 150
Chittenden, William Lawrence:
128, 131
Choate, Julian Ernest, Jr., 6
Cisco Kid: 24, 53

Clark, Charles Badge: 128, 131
Clauser, Al: 135
Cobb, Edmund: 49
Coburn, Walt: 18
Cody, William F. (Buffalo
Bill): 8–9, 10, 11, 12, 13, 17,
19, 22, 46, 49
Cohen, David: 130
Coleman, Don: 49
Collins, Billie: 71–72
Colt (revolver): 64, 66, 69, 70,
71, 72, 73–74, 79, 80, 83, 141
Cooley, Spade: 137
Coolidge, Dane: 130
Cooper, Gary: 13
Corrigan, Ray: 47, 51
Crabbe, Buster: 38, 48–49, 54
Custer, Bob: 49

Dale, Dick: 101, 102
Davis, Art: 53
Dawson, Jim: 123
Deadwood Dick: 17
Dean, Eddie: 24, 53, 135
Desmond, William: 49
Dobie, J. Frank: 88, 98, 130,
161
Dodge City Cattle Trail: 140
Dorson, Richard M.: 6
Drago, Henry Sinclair: 96
Dude Ranchers' Association:
111
Duffield, George: 60, 142–43
Duncan, William: 26, 33, 49
Dwyer, Richard A.: 130
Dykstra, Robert R.: 96

Earp, Wyatt: 69, 82, 100
Eaton, Alden: 108–10, 115, 124
Eaton, Howard: 108–10, 115,
117, 122–23
Eitt, Mrs. G. Embey: 130

Elam, Jack: 100
Elliott, William (Wild Bill):
34, 38, 39, 51
Emrich, Duncan: 137
Essanay Film Manufacturing
Co.: 13, 22–23
Everson, William K.: 30–31,
38, 94

Fairbanks, William: 49
Farnum, Dustin: 26
Farnum, Franklyn: 35, 49
Farnum, William: 26, 35
Fenin, George N.: 30–31, 94
Field, Peter: 17
Fife, Alta S. & Austin E.: 127,
130
Finger, Charles J.: 129
Fisher, Big Nose Kate: 96, 100
Fishwick, Marshall W.: 6, 14
Fletcher, Curly: 131
Flynn, Robert: 162
Foote, Mary Hallock: 12
Foran, Dick: 53, 135
Ford, John: 20, 33, 34, 37, 42,
44
Fox, William: 41
Frantz, Joe B.: 6

Gardner, Gail: 119–21
Gibson, Hoot: 6, 13, 19, 20, 31,
33, 39, 41, 44–45, 46, 51, 55
Goodnight, Charles: 6
Goodnight-Loving Trail: 61
Gordon, Robert W.: 130
Graham-Tewksbury Feud: 15
Grant, Kirby: 53
Gregory, Jackson: 17
Grey, Zane: 6, 14, 15, 17, 18,
36, 38, 48, 134
Griffith, D. W.: 22, 25, 26, 31
Gulick, Bill: 14
Guthrie, Woody: 137

Hale, Monte: 53
Hall, Sam S. (Buckskin Sam):
11
Hall, Sharlot M.: 130
Hart, Neal: 49
Hart, William S.: 6, 13, 16, 26,
27, 28, 30, 31, 32, 33, 37, 38,
41, 44, 51
Hartung, Philip: 103
Haycox, Ernest: 14, 18
Hayden, Russell: 51
Heiser, Karl: 98–99
Henderson, Alice Corbin: 128
Henry, Stuart: 96
Hickok, Wild Bill: 69, 96

Holliday, Doc: 57, 96
Holmes, Pee Wee: 49
Holt, Jack: 26, 36, 37, 46, 51
Holt, Tim: 37, 46, 50
Hornblower, Wallaby: 98
Hough, Emerson: 8
Houston, Cisco: 137–38
Houston, George: 53
Howell, Billy: 113
Hoxie, Al: 49
Hoxie, Jack: 33, 39, 49
Humes, Fred: 49
Hunter, J. Marvin: 134
Hyndrix, James B.: 18

Ince, Thomas H.: 22, 25, 26, 28
Indian reservations: 144, 145
Indian Territory: 139–53
passim
Indian tribes: 142, 143, 144,
150
Ingraham, J. H.: 10
Ingraham, Prentiss: 10, 11, 63

Jackson, Harry: 137
Jarrett, Art: 53
Jones, Buck: 4, 16, 18, 19, 20,
25, 31, 34, 35, 36, 40, 46, 49,
51, 52, 55, 135
Jones, Ken D.: 20–21
Judson, Edward Zane Carroll
(Ned Buntline): 9, 10, 11, 17

Keene, Tom: 38
King, Charles: 12, 20, 54
King, John: 24, 53
Kinsey, Alfred C.: 95–96
Kintner, Robert E.: 99–100
Knibbs, Henry H.: 128
Knievel, Evel: 156n.
Kynes, Peter B.: 34

Ladies' Friend (gun): 67
LaFarge, Oliver: 113–14
L'Amour, Louis: 15, 17
Lane, Allan (Rocky): 51
Larkin, Margaret: 129, 130
LaRue, Lash: 24, 53
Lease, Rex: 19, 38, 49
LeDoux, Chris: 138
Lehman, Henry: 115
Levine, Nat: 51
Lewis, Alfred Henry: 14
Lindsay, Merl: 137
Lingenfelter, Richard E.: 130
Livingston, Robert: 51
Lockhart, Caroline: 123
Lomax, John A.: 127–28, 129,
131, 132, 137

Loomis, Noel M.: 14

McAuliffe, Leon: 137
McClure, Arthur F.: 20–21
McCoy, Joseph G.: 8, 87, 98,
133
McCoy, Tim: 13, 19, 20, 36,
37, 46–47, 51
MacDonald, Wallace: 49
MacDonald, William Colt: 17
McMurtry, Larry: 90, 97
Maloney, Leo: 19, 33, 49
Mann, E. C.: 17
Maynard, Ken: 4, 13, 16, 19,
22, 25, 31, 34, 35, 36, 37, 38,
41, 42–44, 45, 46, 49, 51, 135
Maynard, Kermit: 48, 49
Midnight Cowboy: 100–101,
104
Miller, Bill: 150
Miller, George W.: 145, 152
Mix, Paul: 40–41
Mix, Tom: 6, 13, 16, 19, 20, 24,
25, 26, 28, 29, 34, 35, 37,
40–42, 45, 46, 48, 49, 51, 135
Moore, Charles: 116–17, 123
Morrison, Pete: 18, 49
Mulford, Clarence E.: 6, 18

Nail, Joe: 145
National Cowboy Hall of
Fame and Western Heritage
Center: 153
Newill, James: 53

O'Brien, Dave: 51
O'Brien, George: 19, 20, 27,
37, 38, 40, 49, 51
O'Daniel, "Pappy": 136, 137
Ohrlin, Glenn: 134, 137
O'Malley, D. J.: 131
Omohundro, John Burwell,
Jr. (Texas Jack): 9–10, 11
Osborne, Bud: 49

Patton, Bill: 49
Paulding, John: 7
Peck, George W.: 58–59
Pendleton Round-Up: 12
Perlstrom, William: 58, 75
Perrin, Jack: 18, 38, 49, 51
Phillips, Foreman: 137
Pickens, Slim: 134
Pierce, Shanghai: 6
Pomroy, F. B.: 61
Porter, Edwin S.: 21–22
Porter, William Sidney (O.
Henry): 14
Potter, Edgar R.: 91

Pound, Louise: 130

Raine, William MacLeod: 14, 18
Randall, Dick: 106, 111, 114, 115, 117
Randall, Jack: 53
Reed, Ishmael: 162
Remington, Frederic: 12–13
Renaldo, Duncan: 24, 53
Reynolds, Burt: 99
Rhodes, Eugene Manlove: 5, 6, 14
Ridings, Sam: 142
Rinehart, Mary Roberts: 114
Ritter, Tex: 51, 53, 135–36, 138
Robb, J. D.: 130
Rocky Mountain National Park: 115
Rogers, Roy: 6, 13, 24, 30, 41, 52–53, 135
Rogers, Will: 6, 33
Rollins, Philip Ashton: 5
Roosevelt, Buddy: 18, 49
Roosevelt, Theodore: 12, 85, 109
Russell, Charles M.: 13, 56, 59, 65, 82, 105
Russell, Reb: 20, 30, 48, 51
Russell, William: 49

Sayers, Loretta: 19
Schaefer, Jack: 14
Schein, Harry: 94
Scott, Fred: 53

Scott, Randolph: 20, 26, 34, 38, 51
Shawnee Trail: 140
Shawver, Mary: 111, 113
Shirley, Glenn: 33
Short, Luke: 14, 17, 82
Siberts, Bruce: 86, 89
Silber, Irwin: 130
Siringo, Charles A.: 88, 89, 129
Smith, Helena Huntington: 88
Smith, Henry Nash: 11
Smith and Wesson (gun): 69, 71
Smythe, Pete: 121
Sonnichsen, C. L.: 90, 91
Sons of the Pioneers: 135, 137
Spoor, George K.: 13, 22
Starrett, Charles: 20, 46, 47, 51, 53
Steele, Bob: 19, 28, 37, 38, 39, 45–46, 49, 50, 54, 55
Stewart, Roy: 33, 37, 51
Sublette, Bill: 108

Taylor, William Levi (Buck): 10, 11–12
Thompson, Hank: 137, 138
Thomson, Fred: 31, 33, 34, 39, 45, 51
Thorp, N. Howard (Jack): 92, 127, 128, 129, 130, 131, 132, 134
Tuska, Jon: 33, 35
Tuttle, W. C.: 18
Twain, Mark: 99
Tyler, Tom: 20, 49

Unassigned Lands: 144, 145, 151

Van Buren, Abbey: 101
Vestal, Stanley: 96
Virginian, The: 6, 11, 13, 19, 56, 88

Wakely, Jimmy: 24, 53
Wales, Wally: 49
Walker, Tacetta: 119
Warhol, Andy: 102, 103
Wasserman, John: 102
Waters, Edward H.: 129
Wayne, John: 13, 20, 26, 38, 47–48, 51, 97, 100
Wells, Ted: 49
White, John I.: 130–31
Whitley, Ray: 53
Williams, David: 7
Williams, T. G.: 63
Williams, Tex: 135
Willing, Foy: 135
Wilson, Whip: 53
Wills, Bob: 135, 136, 137, 138
Wills, Johnnie Lee: 137
Winchester (rifle): 57, 64, 66, 70, 74, 83, 141, 149
Wister, Owen: 6, 11, 12–13, 14, 67, 81, 88
Wyman, Walker: 89

XIT ranch: 83

Yellowstone National Park: 115, 123

167